Dear Alex,

In gratitude for your commitment and dedication to EUSI

Yours truly,

Christian Leypoldt

Edmonton
22 Sep 18

Advanced Sciences and Technologies for Security Applications

The series Advanced Sciences and Technologies for Security Applications comprises interdisciplinary research covering the theory, foundations and domain-specific topics pertaining to security. Publications within the series are peer-reviewed monographs and edited works in the areas of:

- biological and chemical threat recognition and detection (e.g., biosensors, aerosols, forensics)
- crisis and disaster management
- terrorism
- cyber security and secure information systems (e.g., encryption, optical and photonic systems)
- traditional and non-traditional security
- energy, food and resource security
- economic security and securitization (including associated infrastructures)
- transnational crime
- human security and health security
- social, political and psychological aspects of security
- recognition and identification (e.g., optical imaging, biometrics, authentication and verification)
- smart surveillance systems
- applications of theoretical frameworks and methodologies (e.g., grounded theory, complexity, network sciences, modelling and simulation)

Together, the high-quality contributions to this series provide a cross-disciplinary overview of forefront research endeavours aiming to make the world a safer place.

More information about this series at http://www.springer.com/series/5540

Christian Leuprecht · Joel J. Sokolsky
Thomas Hughes

Editors

North American Strategic Defense in the 21st Century:

Security and Sovereignty in an Uncertain World

 Springer

Editors
Christian Leuprecht
Department of Political Science
Royal Military College of Canada
Kingston, ON
Canada

and

Flinders University of South Australia
Bedford Park, SA
Australia

Joel J. Sokolsky
Department of Political Science
Royal Military College of Canada
Kingston, ON
Canada

Thomas Hughes
Department of Political Studies
Queen's University
Kingston, ON
Canada

ISSN 1613-5113   ISSN 2363-9466   (electronic)
Advanced Sciences and Technologies for Security Applications
ISBN 978-3-319-90977-6   ISBN 978-3-319-90978-3   (eBook)
https://doi.org/10.1007/978-3-319-90978-3

Library of Congress Control Number: 2018941222

This Springer imprint is published by the registered company Springer International Publishing AG part of Springer Nature
The registered company address is: Gewerbestrasse 11, 6330 Cham, Switzerland

This volume is dedicated to Christian's daughter Heidi, a long-time loyal follower of NORAD's Santa Tracker.

And

To the combination of Brum and Geordie, which has made Thomas's contribution possible.

And

To Joel's grandsons, Pierce and Drew, on whose behalf it is always a delight to "have the watch."

Foreword

It is both interesting and concerning to note that the most recent book on North American Strategic Defence was published prior to the end of the Cold War. Given the breadth of changes in the security environment, especially in the technological and political dimensions, this volume is, therefore, not just highly welcome but long overdue. It will serve well to inform cogent debate on an important topic at a critical juncture for the North American Aerospace Defense Command (NORAD). The defence relationship between Canada and the US is notable for its endurance, flexibility, and longevity, and stands as a model for international cooperation. As a former command team at NORAD, we have had the privilege to experience first-hand the professionalism and dedication that American and Canadian personnel bring to this unique command, and of providing leadership for an organization that now celebrates 60 successful years.

Lingering doubts about NORAD's relevance after the end of the Cold War were promptly discarded after 9/11, an attack that emphasized the importance of NORAD in the era of both transnational terrorism and the rising aspirations of traditional adversaries. The defence relationship between our two countries remains vital. A rapidly changing security environment has recently brought North American regional security into acute focus. We must confront the hard reality of a broad and growing array of threats that will test our resolve and capabilities across the entire defence and security spectrum. Although there are differences in the way these threats affect each country, how they are perceived, which incidents and consequences need to be managed and how, both the countries remain aware that this binational security and defence relationship is one of the most successful in history. Ultimately, NORAD is at the tip of the spear in protecting the continent and everything its people hold dear. NORAD represents an indispensable deterrent to our adversaries and plays a key role in preserving our two nations' latitude for foreign-policy decision-making: by containing potentially threatening adversaries, we ensure that democratically elected political executives and legislatures can realize the will of the people without fear of foreign retribution.

Given the scope and depth of the agreement, a scope and depth that reaches broadly and deeply into the domestic security fabric of both the US and Canada, it is somewhat surprising that NORAD has received so little scholarly attention. On the one hand, this benign neglect can be seen as a reflection of the extent to which NORAD's success is taken for granted; while on the other, it means that North American strategic defence rarely receives the political attention it warrants in our respective capitals, attention it needs to ensure that it will continue to perform so well, not only relative to current threats but also to the challenges that loom on the horizon.

NORAD has proven its value alongside the two respective sovereign combatant commands: United States Northern Command (USNORTHCOM) and Canada's Joint Operations Command (CJOC). As these commands have developed, NORAD's agility has made it indispensable. As the global security environment continues to evolve, NORAD and its role will likely continue to evolve and adapt across domains: air, space, maritime, and now cyber. No organization shapes North America's strategic defence in the same way that NORAD does.

This volume is notable for the broad and detailed character of its contributions from many of the most respected scholars in the field whose insights make for compelling reading for decision- and policy-makers, military practitioners, civil servants, researchers, and students looking for an informed understanding of the future of North American strategic defence. The volume will also appeal to anyone with an interest in international relations, regional security, and strategic and defence studies in the context of the broader global trends that are shaping our times.

In surveying a host of issues that are pertinent to the US and Canada, the contributions broach a wide range of subjects, from Mexico's regional security to tensions relating to the sovereignty–security trade-off in North America. The volume rekindles our collective appreciation of the pivotal role of North American strategic defence in the West's overall security posture, while offering granularity on the defence issues and challenges confronting North America from a strategic, regional, and domestic perspective.

The confidence we have in the steadfastness of the U.S.-Canada security relationship, represented well by NORAD, transcends episodic political and economic differences that might otherwise threaten to sour a strategically critical relationship. That relationship, and its possible futures, are superbly described and analyzed in the pages that follow. We are pleased to be able to endorse this superb and timely collection and delighted to commend it to anyone interested in the world's most important and unique binational command.

NORAD: We have the watch.

Colorado Springs

Ottawa

Gen (Ret'd) Charles H. Jacoby, Jr.
Commander, NORAD (2011–2014)
Commander of USNORTHCOM (2011–2014)
Gen (Ret'd) Thomas J. Lawson
Chief of the Defence Staff, Canada (2012–2015)
Deputy Commander, NORAD (2011–2012)

Contents

Introduction: We Have the Watch

Christian Leuprecht[1,2](✉), Joel J. Sokolsky[1], Thomas Hughes[3], and Kathryn M. Fisher[4]

[1] Royal Military College of Canada, Kingston, ON K7K 7B4, Canada
christian.leuprecht@rmc.ca
[2] Flinders University of South Australia, Adelaide, Australia
[3] Queen's University, Kingston, Canada
[4] National Defense University, Washington D.C, WA, USA

Abstract. Over the years, there have only been a handful of books on North American continental security. In this volume U.S., Canadian, and Mexican scholars broach key issues, challenges, and uncertainties that confront the strategic defense of North America in the 21st century and weigh possible trajectories for the future in light of developments that are anticipated to shape the global security environment. The cases, contexts, and analyses in this volume jettison monolithic conceptions of 'security' and 'strategic defense' in favor of a robust and dynamic engagement with issues facing North American continental security: from defense procurement challenges and Canada's ongoing involvement with NORAD, to the effect of the perceptions and reality of U.S. policy and international partners. The volume is split into four parts: North American strategic defense from global, U.S., and Canadian perspectives, and an assessment of the nature, structure, and future of North American strategic defense and NORAD's role.

The defense[1] dimensions of North American security have been largely absent in the vast literature on the international strategic environment for some time. While NORAD and specific aspects of Canada-U.S. security relations have been the subject of study (mainly by Canadian scholars or those with an interest in Canada) and while Mexican scholars have concentrated on their country's relations with the U.S., there have only been a handful of books on the broader topic of North American strategic defense that places it in the essential context of global relations and U.S. defense policy.[2] The relative paucity of works on this wider topic over the years signals the extent to which the subject has received short shrift. That is a problem. Never has the future of the strategic defense of North America been more uncertain. Hitherto, U.S.-Canada

---

[1] The opinions and conclusions expressed in this volume are those of the contributors and do not necessarily represent the views of the National Defense University, the U.S. Department of Defense, or any other U.S. government entity, nor those of the Royal Military College of Canada, the Department of National Defence or any other Canadian government entity.

[2] Examples of these works would include: B. Bruce-Biggs, *The Shield of Faith: A chronicle of strategic defense from zeppelins to star wars* (New York: Simon and Schuster,1988); S. Guerrier, W. Thompson, Eds. *Perspectives on Strategic Defense* (Boulder, Colorado: Westview, 1987); Stephen J. Cimbala, Ed., *Strategic Air Defense* (Lanham, MD: Rowman & Littlefield 1989); and Joseph T. Jockel, *Security to the North: Canada-U.S. Defense Relations in the 1990 s* (East Lansing, MI: Michigan State University Press, 1991).

© Springer International Publishing AG, part of Springer Nature 2018
C. Leuprecht et al. (eds.), *North American Strategic Defense in the 21st Century:*,
Advanced Sciences and Technologies for Security Applications,
https://doi.org/10.1007/978-3-319-90978-3_1

defense and security relations have not generally captured the imagination of the broader strategic studies scholarly community. However, recent trends highlight the need for analysis that deepens our understanding of North American strategic defense. The general aim of this volume is to contribute to a more informed discussion. Its particular objective is to gauge different futures for North American strategic defense over the short and long term with a special focus on the bi-national (U.S.-Canada) North American Aerospace Defense Command and NORAD's associated American and Canadian combatant commands—U.S. Northern Command (USNORTHCOM) and Canadian Joint Operational Command (CJOC). USNORTHCOM's prime mission is to manage the role of the U.S. armed forces in the strategic defense of the U.S. and, secondarily, to provide military aid to civilian authorities for homeland security as needed and requested. Yet, this book deals with neither national and continental homeland security writ large, nor security cooperation between the U.S. and Canada beyond the military. The 'strategic defense of North America' is understood strictly as the role of the armed forces in deterring, containing, and defending against external threats. In this light, this volume broaches key issues, challenges, and uncertainties that confront the strategic defense of North America, and weighs possible future trajectories in light of the anticipated developments that will be shaping the global security landscape.

May 12, 2018, marks the 60th anniversary of the U.S. and Canada signing their first formal NORAD agreement. This bi-national organization is "charged with the missions of aerospace warning and aerospace control for North America" [1], a role that was augmented by a maritime warning mission in 2006. NORAD's enduring relevance is a function of the "on-going adaptation of NORAD's mission and capabilities to meet the challenges posed by ever-changing threats and testifies to the strength of the NORAD Agreement and the close cooperation between Canada and the United States" [2]. Long relegated to near obscurity on the security agendas of the U.S. and most other international actors, for the first time in modern history, the North American homeland, and by extension the strategic importance of the immediate approaches to North America, is no longer secure by mere dint of its geopolitical location. Recent years have seen an acute proliferation of threats to North America: advances in North Korean missile and nuclear capabilities [3], Russian and Chinese missile technology, along with a proliferation of cyber threat vectors originating with these and other state and non-state actors. While the threat environment continues to evolve rapidly, the attention North American strategic defense has received is negligible; that is having a fundamental impact on what it means to be 'secure' and adopt a 'strategic defense' posture that is responsive to the emerging security landscape.

According to NORAD/USNORTHCOM's most recent posture statement, "USNORTHCOM and NORAD operate in a strategic environment that is as ambiguous and dangerous as any in our recent history. Threats to the U.S. and Canada are increasingly global, transregional, all-domain, and multi-functional in nature." [4] The 2017 U.S. National Security Strategy (USNSS) identifies as its first pillar the protection "of the American People, the Homeland, and the American Way of Life." It goes on to say: "Canada and the United States share a unique strategic and defense partnership" [5]. The U.S. National Defense Strategy prioritizes "defending the homeland" and attention to regional alliances and partnerships in the "Western

Hemisphere" and missile defense [6]. Those vectors all converge on NORAD. Similarly, Canada's Defence Policy *Strong, Secure, Engaged* puts a "renewed defence partnership in NORAD and with the United States" [7, p. 3] at the crux of a secure North America. In a changing security environment, continental defense is ultimately the armed services' top priority.

The recent release of these strategic documents and NORAD's 60th anniversary makes this is a propitious juncture to shed some light on 'strategic defense', and what it means for North America. Strategy, defense and security offer a way to grasp how political, military, economic, environmental, and societal sectors intersect more broadly [8]. What these concepts mean is hardly self-evident yet they shape the contours of contemporary security discourse and practice: from military posture statements and official policies, to political objectives and research agendas. The range of cases, contexts, and analyses in this volume challenges monolithic conceptions of 'security' and 'strategic defense'. The very idea of 'North American security' is framed and operationalized by particular security practices. Although continental defense conventionally refers to the U.S.-Canadian relationship [9], the question of Mexico's role continues to loom large. On the one hand, the changing security environment has reinvigorated a more encompassing regional approach to continental security. On the other hand, Canada is intent on safeguarding its privileged relationship with the U.S. [10–12].

The actors, processes, and issues that shape North American continental defense are necessarily wedded to competing perceptions of hemispheric, international, and/or global security and defense. Populist narratives such as "America First" or "Canada is back" compete with the complexity of global interdependence.[3] How strategic defense is prioritized vis-à-vis economic and commercial interests affects issues such as sovereignty, national identity, and domestic politics [9]. Competing takes on the contemporary global international order influence different conceptions about NORAD's futures. Canada, for instance, is reluctant to make NORAD a twin to USNORTHCOM as an all-services, all-domain, command, even as it has encouraged greater cooperation between USNORTHCOM and CJOC. Such uncertainty about North American strategic defense is compounded by new Inter-Continental Ballistic Missiles (ICBMs) and hypersonic missiles, cruise missiles, cyber threats, conventional great power challenges, changing air/aerospace threats, a shifting Arctic landscape (both politically and ecologically), and debates on border security as it relates to migration, trafficking, and trade.[4]

Nearing the end of the second decade of the 21st century, the strategic defense of North America has assumed greater importance than at any time since 1945. Three different organizations are tasked with national and international roles and missions in securing North America: NORAD, USNORTHCOM, and CJOC. NORAD is a

---

[3] These phrases come from the Trump and prior Harper administrations, but such inward looking priorities in contrast to ideals of liberal internationalism are not exclusive to the U.S. or Canada and can be observed across a range of political spaces, such as the UK with Britain First.

[4] These issues are not, by definition, exclusive to North America but play a particular role in how the key state actors of Mexico, the U.S., and Canada (as well as the Bahamas in this context) construct their respective domestic agendas and approach their bi/tri-regional partnerships.

functional arrangement, in particular in the context of U.S. combatant commands and CJOC. It is also a bi-national command and not a military alliance, although that may well change. And what role for Mexico in North American security? A decade has passed since the 2007 Mérida Initiative; will a future trilateral command replace the bilateral system that is currently in place? How will Canada and Mexico adapt to changing security relations, such as 'offshore balancing'?

NORAD's future will be marked by continuity and change as older threats evolve and new ones arise, both warranting greater attention to strategic defense. The world's closest bilateral defense relationship has now endured some eighty years, since the "Kingston Dispensation" of 1938 and the Ogdensburg Declaration of 1940.[5] Yet much has changed since, with respect to deterrence in general and 'mutually assured destruction' in particular. By way of example, the evolution of ICBMs deflated the strategic value of Canadian territory in the strategic defense of North America. What role for the northern and southern flanks in hemispheric defense, notably the Arctic and the North on the one hand, and Mexico and the Caribbean on the other? What threats are 'existential' to the continent, and how have these been evolving? On the occasion of NORAD's 60th anniversary the chapters in this volume lay the groundwork for a reinvigorated conversation on the future(s) of strategic defense and North American security in the 21st century.

1 Overview

The first section sets the subject in the broader global context of the relationships of the U.S. and Canada with Mexico, Russia, and China. The chapters highlight the way in which perception and misperception influence behavior in the international arena. The strategic defense of North America is driven as much by endogenous factors as by exogenous ones, foremost among them preconceptions and beliefs of non-North American actors with which the region interacts.

In "Putin's Security Policy and its Implications for NORAD", Mark N. Katz explains that the Russian government under Vladimir Putin believes that the U.S. and NATO are colluding to limit or reduce Russia's power. In Putin's view, this represents the most significant threat that Russia is confronting, protests of innocence from Western policy-makers notwithstanding. While Putin and the West may differ on the greatest threats Russia faces, perception nevertheless clouds the current and probable near-future Russian approach to international relations, and will thus continue to shape North American security for the foreseeable future. This is made particularly acute by

---

[5] Speaking in Kingston, Ontario in 1938, President Franklin Roosevelt declared that the U.S. would not stand idly by if Canada were ever threatened. In response, Canadian Prime Minister W. L. Mackenzie King said that Canada's obligation as a "good and friendly neighbour" was to see to it that enemy forces did not attack the U.S. by land, sea or air by way of Canada. The essence of the bilateral security relationship—its close, friendly and cooperative nature notwithstanding—is that Canada cannot become a security liability for the U.S. After Western Europe fell to the Nazis in the Spring of 1940, the two governments cooperated to secure North America. Following a meeting that August in Ogdensburg, New York, Roosevelt and King issued a declaration of mutual defense and established the Permanent Joint Board on Defense (PJBD).

the Russian use of a hybrid strategy short of war that is designed to exploit and undermine the democratic underpinnings of Western societies, such as free and fair elections, freedom of expression, individual rights, and the rule of law. This presents a considerable challenge for NATO. While a backlash against Russian interference may unite NATO members, it may also exacerbate existing fissures among allies, undermine coherence, and splinter the alliance into a series of bilateral relationships.

To break this negative spiral and reassure Russia is not straightforward, as Nina Rathbun and Brian Rathbun demonstrate in their chapter, "Misplaced Prudence", which explores the concept of restraint and signal interpretation. Behavior that one side characterizes as non-provocative defense, such as the deployment of missile defense systems, may be seen by another as asserting military dominance. Breaking a spiral of conflict by demonstrating overt restraint has audience costs for politicians in terms of criticism from the electorate on whom they rely for their power and legitimacy. These two chapters also reinforce that the threat of nuclear war did not disappear with the end of the Cold War. Russia is modernizing its nuclear arsenal, North Korea is developing nuclear weapons despite international sanctions, and Iran's nuclear ambitions are cause for consternation in some quarters of the international community. How the implementation of the 2015 Joint Comprehensive Plan of Action plays out remains to be seen. In this light, Katz and Rathbun and Rathbun conclude that missile defense is but one component of an effective approach to North American strategic defense.

Mexico's geo-strategic importance to continental defense is not up for debate. However, the idea that Mexico should be an equal partner in a trilateral approach to North American regional security is controversial. Abelardo Rodríguez Sumano reminds us that Canada and the U.S. cooperate far more closely with one another on security than with Mexico. Mexico's role in continental defense should thus be seen from a global instead of a regional perspective. Assessing U.S.-Mexico security relations through the lens of Regional Security Complex Theory, "Challenges and Contradictions" shows how responses to local threats that intersect with global hazards are hampered by mutual mistrust. Both Mexico and Canada look to balance their sovereignty and U.S. hegemony, and some branches of Mexican policy-making institutions still perceive the U.S. as a historic enemy. Foreshadowing the chapter by Bessma Momani and Morgan MacInnes which assesses 'Jacksonian' U.S. foreign policy, Rodríguez suggests that the political rhetoric that has accompanied the election of Donald Trump perpetuates this suspicion. How Mexico shapes the future of North American strategic defense is heavily influenced by domestic politics and developments in the ongoing cycles of cooperation and conflict that characterize U.S.-Mexico relations.

The second section focuses on the U.S. role in the future of North American strategic defense. While the U.S. remains the pre-eminent global power, rapid changes in the global security environment are generating new challenges. Nevertheless, the privileged position it occupies means that U.S. decisions will reverberate with its immediate neighbors to the north and south, and the international system. Together, the three chapters in this section gauge the domestic and geopolitical pressures that the U.S. faces in maintaining its current role in the global system.

The concept of U.S. 'Primacy', the challenges arising from sustaining this position, and the tension between the foreign policy establishment and domestic politics are at the core of "Hoping Primacy Stays Cheap", in which Harvey Sapolsky suggests that U.S. engagement in the international system, which had previously been founded on an arm's-length approach, became more involved following the Second World War. The end of the Cold War did not, however, result in the U.S. retrenching to its pre-Second World War position. It has instead maintained a considerable overseas military presence, relying heavily on its technological capacity and air power dominance. The tempering of the U.S.'s technological edge due to the globalization of technology, combined with the proliferation of nuclear weapons, and the extraordinary financial cost of Primacy makes this position increasingly untenable. Yet, ceding Primacy runs counter to the interests of the U.S. foreign policy establishment. As such, should these interests remain, it seems difficult to foresee a U.S. political position in which Primacy is no longer the cornerstone of its strategic defense posture.

In "NATO and NORAD in the Sino-Russo-American Configuration of Power", Alexander Moens puts the discussion of U.S. Primacy in the context of the triangular relationship among Russia, China, and the U.S. This balance is in a state of flux given Russia's increased military strength and belligerence, and China's growing economic, military, and technical capability. These changes affect multilateral institutions and potentially undermine the centrality of commonly held liberal values as the glue that holds them together. The role of NATO is no longer confined to defense and deterrence. Crisis management in particular now figures prominently and some states seemingly act under NATO's banner without the overt buy-in of all members. This transformed role, however, puts the organization in tension with Russian strategic goals. In addition, China's approach to foreign policy differs from U.S. and Western European models, and the country's growing influence in Asia in particular stretches U.S. resources in offering an effective counterbalance. At the heart of these changes, however, are values that NATO and the U.S. have previously espoused. The reconfiguration of a unipolar environment requires states to reconsider the structure of their alliances. In the current environment, a 'strategically appropriate' decision may be for states to forego connections with the U.S. and the West, a position that may mean moving away from the promotion of liberal democracy. Furthermore, and for Canada in particular, any weakening of NATO could have significant repercussions for Arctic sovereignty and security.

The analysis of the U.S. approach to strategic defense is muddied by the dislocation of policy engendered by the election of Donald Trump. "NORAD in an Age of Trump's Jacksonianism", by Bessma Momani and Morgan MacInnes, explores the resurgence of Jacksonian foreign policy in the U.S. The durability of Trump's foreign policy remains to be seen, as does the creation of a coherent pattern of rhetoric and behavior but, as Momani and MacInnes indicate, this uncertainty is not confined to defense policy; it marks a questioning of the security and stability of a liberal world order. Rounding out Moens's discussion of adherence to liberal democratic values and Sapolsky's assessment of the cost of Primacy, Momani and MacInnes consider the way in which international actions by a U.S. administration steeped in a Jacksonian-style foreign policy can destabilize multilateral institutions that it had previously supported. As the U.S. quantifies the threats it faces, it engages only in activities that result in their direct mitigation. That may bolster NORAD as it protects the continental homeland against tangible dangers. However, pressure may mount on Canada to make a greater financial contribution to an institution that is not designed to mitigate risks that Canada may see as more urgent, such as home-grown terrorism or climate change [13].

The third section of this volume deals with the Canadian experience of North American strategic defense. Continuity and change is an overarching theme. In "New Wineskin, Old Wine" and "Canada's New Defence Policy and the Security of North America", both Kim Richard Nossal and Allen Sens highlight continuity in the Canadian approach to strategic defense, which has prioritized North American security alongside Canadian security, as part and parcel of international engagement. The latest evolution of this theme is Canada's 2017 *Strong, Secure, Engaged* defense policy statement, which, according to Nossal, merely re-packages old ideas. As with previous Canadian defense policies, the objective is to distinguish the incumbent government from its predecessor, rather than a comprehensive strategic outlook that is truly reflective of the security context and Canada's approach to this threat environment.

Strong, Secure, Engaged, does, however, highlight two areas of particular significance that point to an evolving strategic landscape. The first of these is the emphasis on defense spending. The enhanced discussion of personnel in *Strong, Secure, Engaged* aside, the most obvious departure from previous Canadian defense policies is the overt costing of reinvestment in the military. The ultimate rationale for this is unclear, but the inclusion coincides with a U.S. administration that had railed against inadequate defense spending amongst allies. In a remarkable legislative sleight-of-hand, *Strong, Secure, Engaged* has these costs borne largely by future governments. In so doing, one of the fundamental political impediments to Canada advancing its strategic defense is made clear, as Sens encapsulates the choices that Canadian governments face as they attempt to engage in international affairs with a military that is under-funded and over-stretched for the spectrum of tasks governments want them to perform. This is exacerbated by the tension inherent in working alongside the U.S. and leaning on its resources to enhance Canadian security, and maintaining Canadian sovereignty and independence as a global actor.

Even with the increased spending that is outlined in *Strong, Secure, Engaged*, Nossal deems the reinvestment insufficient to provide adequate resources to the Canadian Armed Forces in the "short to medium term" [p. 106]. In combination with Sens's discussion of the diversity of threats facing North America in the post-Cold War environment, it highlights the need for a truly comprehensive approach to North American security, beyond that envisioned in *Strong, Secure, Engaged*. Although, or perhaps because, Canada and the U.S. have had a broadly common defense and security identity, with the exception of NORAD, the security relationships between the two countries have historically developed through what Sens characterizes as "incremental adaptations based on catalytic events or evolving circumstances", [p. 119] rather than holistic strategic planning. The new and likely future threat environment requires the engagement of a broader array of government agencies and, potentially, a review of the institutional architecture of Canada-U.S. cooperation. That is premised on acknowledging security needs and a favorable political climate. In such a climate, the creation of a permanent North American security advisory council beyond the PJBD could become a real possibility.

Uncertainty about the evolution of this future environment is further reason to consider the shape of defense cooperation. As Anessa Kimball examines in "Future uncertainty, strategic defense, and North American defense cooperation", this raises significant questions about NORAD's role, and whether the arrangement could, or should, be changed to ensure that it can be effective in the anticipated future threat environment. Kimball assesses the potential future of NORAD through the lens of rational institutionalism, stressing the trap of viewing the respective U.S. and Canadian involvement in North American strategic defense in the context of relative gains. The ongoing existence of NORAD "signals an indivisible close strategic link" [p. 132]. Nevertheless, the security environment in which NORAD was created has transformed and in meeting these threats, adaptation is critical. The non-treaty status of NORAD provides flexibility to meet the new challenges that face North American security. The creation of a replacement structure rather than adapting the existing arrangement is likely to necessitate a formal agreement between the parties involved, a process that would almost certainly be lengthy and beset with the problems arising from "domestic partisan politics and deterrence diplomacy" [p. 135]. Although its form is subject to change it seems, therefore, that NORAD is here to stay.

The final section of the volume looks at the potential evolution of the strategic defense of North America and its impact on NORAD and Canada-U.S. relations. The tension between sovereignty and coordinated security frameworks figures prominently, notably in light of historical relationships and the current socio-political context.

NORAD's evolution could follow different trajectories, including that it remains relatively unchanged and continues to perform its existing function. In "NORAD's Future", Joseph Jockel examines the implications of some of these pathways, with the potential for a greater role in missile- and/or enhanced maritime-defense. The Canadian political position has, historically, been averse to developing a missile defense network.[6] However, as Jockel notes, technologically the U.S. does not require Canadian support for a missile defense system that covers the U.S. mainland. Such a system would also provide a protective shield for Canada. The Canadian government may thus be drawn into a balancing act, offering an asymmetric contribution to maintain a role in all facets of the defense of Canada and the U.S., without relinquishing its stance on missile defense.

A further challenge to sovereignty and control of military assets arises in the potential expansion of maritime activities under NORAD's command. Aside from the control of military assets, a tension arises from the possibility that Canadian vessels may be used to pre-empt what U.S. commanders believe to be an impending ship- or submarine-launched attack. Such an action, which blurs the line between offensive and defensive operations, would be antithetical to the position Canada has taken historically. This concept is explored in greater detail by Andrea Charron and James Fergusson in "Beyond Modernization", which juxtaposes the discussion about 'counter-offense' activities in the maritime domain with an analogous conversation about the air domain. Their work suggests, however, that while NORAD may be at the center of North American defense cooperation, not all aspects of defense have to form part of a

---

[6] Ballistic missile defense (BMD) is a role that is currently led and performed by USNORTHCOM.

single unified command, which opens the prospect of further multilateral security frameworks to deal with threats such as that arising from the cyber domain.

At the same time, NORAD's original function remains front and center: air defense. Echoing Sapolsky's discussion of the importance of technological dominance in maintaining 'Primacy', Richard Shimooka examines the nexus of "NORAD, Tactical Fighter Modernization, and the F-35." The politicization of and conflict over the procurement of the F-35 Joint Strike Fighter (JSF) illustrates the challenges that Canada faces in remaining relevant to North American strategic defense. Criticism of cost overruns notwithstanding, the U.S. perception that the aircraft is needed has not changed, and the commitment to bringing it into service has been unwavering. Neither applies in Canada, where military procurement often gets mired in bureaucracies ill-experienced in projects of such magnitude and complexity, and usurped by electoral politics that trades on public opinion ignorant of security and defense. Canada's wavering on procuring a new tactical fighter reinforces the challenges and pitfalls of major defense procurement projects, which calls into question Canada's role in North American defense. If Canada fails to live up to its commitment to aerial capability, in the context of an evolving technological threat environment, it may well engender hard questions about the future of the arrangement.

The final chapter turns our gaze North, to an area that is critical to North American strategic defense yet has long suffered from benign neglect: the Arctic. As Rob Huebert demonstrates, this geographical region is fast becoming the crucible in which many of the complex and challenging geopolitical issues raised in previous chapters are coming to the fore. In resuming the 'long polar watch' of the early Cold War years, North American policy makers are increasingly preoccupied with the North. Capability development and a more aggressive posture by Russia, in particular cruise missile and ICBM technology, has caused the value of NORAD to appreciate in both the aerospace and maritime domains. Growing Chinese interest in the region adds a layer of complexity to the relationship between the pre-eminent global powers, and the specter of North Korean nuclear-tipped ICBMs drives home the placement of missile defense systems along their Arctic trajectory and the controversy over Canada partnering with the U.S. in operating and maintaining such systems. Reprising to a theme from the first section of this volume, how the development of Arctic-focused military technology by North American states is perceived by international actors is also bound to shape the future of strategic defense in the region.

North American strategic defense is a complex and wide-ranging subject that has taken on new meaning and urgency: developments in the North Korean nuclear and missile programs have catapulted it to the top of strategic priorities. President Trump, in his 2018 State of the Union address, stressed the need to "modernize and rebuild" the U.S. nuclear arsenal: while "someday in the future" nuclear weapons may be eliminated, "we are not there yet" [14]. Although not necessarily directed solely at North Korea, the comments reflect the escalating threat of a conflict going nuclear. The development of nuclear weapons by a regime in North Korea that adheres to a social and political play-book different from its Western peers is perhaps the most troubling example.

The threat of nuclear weapons striking North America is hardly new, nor is the development of nuclear weapons by states with which North America has a rocky relationship. North Korea, however, is unique. The 2018 U.S. Nuclear Posture Review describes it as the "most significant" component of the challenges facing "nuclear non-proliferation today" [15, p. 8]. Its weapons threaten mainland North America and destabilize a delicate geo-political equilibrium. The web of alliances in the region, and the growing influence of China and its military capability, combine to create a strategic context in which North America must tread carefully if it is to avoid alienating allies, antagonizing a peer (or near-peer) 'competitor', or triggering a pre-emptive (or retaliatory) nuclear strike by a North Korean regime that perceives an existential threat. North Korea's ongoing development of nuclear weapons also appears to have contributed to the Trump administration's nuclear weapons policy. The 2018 Nuclear Posture Review suggests that uncertainties about the threat environment, to which the North Korean situation contributes, necessitate an increase in the number and variety of weapons in the U.S. nuclear arsenal [15, p. xi]. Such a change in stated U.S. policy seems likely to influence the way in which the U.S. is perceived, and thus alters the parameters within which efforts to enhance North American strategic defense will occur.

Military options in striking North Korean targets to destroy nuclear launch capability or force regime change are not the only actions to bolster the strategic defense of North America [10, p. i]. Arguably the most consequential alternative with direct political implications for the Canada-U.S. defense relationship is the potential deployment of BMD systems. A BMD system capable of intercepting ICBMs would likely be land-based and thus raises questions about the placement and operation of such a system, a subject that is taken up by several contributors to this volume. Should the further development of a BMD system come up for discussion, Canada and NORAD will be part of the conversation, and Canadian policy-makers will be forced to consider the balance of sovereignty and security that is integral to BMD in North America, and confront the possibility of the U.S. developing the system without Canadian involvement. The implications of investing in 'defensive' weapons systems has long been part of the theories of international relations, and a BMD system, even if installed with North Korea in mind, may have broader consequences for North America's relations with China and Russia in particular. The diplomatic repercussions of the deployment of a Terminal High Altitude Area Defense (THAAD) battery in South Korea [3, p. 48] as well as the negative rhetoric that followed the proposed deployment of a similar system in Europe, may well have ramifications if a broad and mature North American BMD system, effective against ICBMs, was developed and implemented.

The BMD program and the potential for a strike on the North American continent aside, heightened tensions with North Korea have repercussions for North American strategic defense. The threat to U.S. allies in the region is acute, and the reputational damage to the U.S. if they were not to provide support for these partners would be severe. Similarly, if support is not provided to allies in Asia, the balance of power in the region seems likely to tip away from North America, limiting the ability of the U.S. to wield its current level of influence [15, p. 3]. This altered geopolitical dynamic would shape North American strategic defense for generations.

Similarly, although primarily directed at NATO's Eastern flank, Russia is seeking to restore is global reach. The reported development of the 'Avangard' hypersonic missile, and the 'SARMAT' superheavy thermonuclear armed ICBM whose multiple independently targeted reentry vehicles (MIRVs) are purportedly invulnerable to interception, add a new dimension to its strategic relationship with the U.S. [16]. Recent years have seen a marked increase in Russian air activity near North America as Moscow reminds Washington that it retains the capacity to strike directly at the U.S. homeland. As in the past, any confrontation between the U.S. and Russia anywhere in the world that carries the risk of escalation registers in North America. In this sense, the strategic defense of the continent may increasingly be a matter of going 'back to the future.'

2 Conclusion

Recent security postures put forward by the U.S. and Canada, alongside continued shifts in the threat environment and the 60th anniversary of NORAD, underscore the need for an invigorating assessment of the future of North American strategic defense in the 21st century. There is no singular or self-evident meaning of 'strategic defense'; its meaning depends on one's position and priorities in and around security, thereby shaping questions and tensions over the past, present, and future(s) of North American strategic defense. Are current continental defense arrangements between Canada and the U.S. adequate to confront current, looming and future threats? Is it time to consider alternative or more integrated defense arrangements, such as a single North American Defense Command? What role for Mexico in a potential trilateral combined and joint defense arrangement for North America?[7] Canada covets its privileged ties with the U. S., and its existing position would be jeopardized were it to be reduced to one of two junior partners in North American strategic defense—as would be the case if Mexico were to be drawn more closely into the defense relationship. Overtures about elevating Mexico's contribution to North American defense notwithstanding, Canada is likely to be reluctant, especially as it concerns NORAD.

There is a wide variety of literature on security and strategy, and U.S. grand strategy and defense policy, as well as North American regional security cooperation and the U.S. security perimeter [17],[8] including work on the intersection of identities,

---

[7] For discussions on different aspects of the trilateral relationship with Mexico see the work of Simon Dalby and Geoffrey Hale in particular.

[8] Scholarship on North American defense includes Andrea Charron, James Fergusson, Rob Huebert, Joseph Jockel, Ellie Malone, Sara McGuire, Joel Sokolsky, Alan Stephenson, Matthew Trudgen, Dana Tucker, and Paul Aseltine, "NORAD in Perpetuity? Challenges and Opportunities for Canada," University of Manitoba, 31 March 2014; Andrea Charron, James Fergusson, Nicolas Allarie, Anastasia Narkovich, Joseph Jockel, Joel Sokolsky, Alan Stephenson, Matthew Trudgen, "'LEFT of BANG': NORAD's Maritime Warning Mission and North American Domain Awareness," University of Manitoba, 8 October, 2015; David G. Haglund and Joseph T. Jockel, "The Non-Vanishing Border: Change and Continuity in Canadian-American Relations," in *Canada: Images of a Post/National Society*, edited by Gunilla Florby, Mark Shackleton & Katri Suhonen (New York: P.I.E, Peter Lang, 2009), pp. 55–69; R.D. Hooker Jr., Ed. *Charting a Course: Strategic Choices for a New Administration* (Washington, D.C.: National Defense University Press, December 2016); Joseph T. Jockel, *Canada in NORAD 1957-2007: A History* (Montreal: McGill-Queen's

interests and institutions, and evolving transnational threats such as terrorism, migration, drug cartels and natural disasters through the lens of Regional Security Complex Theory (RSCT) in North America [18]. From the Mexican perspective, the major issues confronting North American security are transnational organized crime tied to hemispheric dynamics of production, market and drug consumption on the one hand, and illicit guns and money laundering from the U.S. that is propelling insecurity and violence in Mexico and Central America [19]. The uncertain future of NAFTA may also prove problematic: the future of North American strategic defense cooperation may not be directly affected by the content of a renegotiated pact, but an acrimonious end to NAFTA would, at a minimum, make it difficult for the governments of Canada and Mexico to maintain public support for a significant enhancement of NORAD and continental defense cooperation in general [20].

Strategic defense in the 21st century confronts a "new threat environment" in which North American sovereignty and security will be challenged as never before. This increasingly demanding setting encompasses a "new Russian strategic doctrine" alongside shifts in the way NORAD's command is organized and Russian bravado about new ballistic missiles, as well as 'Kalibr' submarine-based cruise missiles and underwater drones, that, if actually deployed, will greatly complicate NORAD's essential aerospace warning mission and raise the question of "whether NORAD should evolve into a binational air-maritime defence command" [21, p. 1]. Much existing work focuses on particular aspects of North American defense and security relations, such as new strategic threats, BMD, issues related to NORAD's aerospace and maritime warning missions, border security, USNORTHCOM's assistance to civil authorities, the Arctic, and cybersecurity. This makes this book's holistic and continental perspective on North American strategic defense all the more relevant and timely.

References

1. NORAD History. http://www.norad.mil/About-NORAD/NORAD-History/. Accessed 24 Jan 2018
2. NORAD Agreement. http://www.norad.mil/About-NORAD/NORAD-Agreement/. Accessed 24 Jan 2018

University Press, 2011); Patti Biellig, "NORAD: A Model to Address Gaps in US-Mexico Security Coordination" (School of Advanced Military Studies U.S. Army Command and General Staff College Fort Leavenworth, Kansas, USA, 2016); Imtiaz Hussain, Satya R. Pattnayak, and Anil Hira, *North American Homeland Security: Back to Bilateralism?* (Westport, CT: Praeger Security International, 2008); David G. Haglund and Joel J. Sokolsky, Eds., *The U.S.-Canada Security Relationship: The Politics, Strategy and Technology of Defense* (Boulder, CO.: Westview, 1989); Stephen J. Cimbala, Ed., *The Technology, Strategy and Politics of SDI* (Boulder, CO.: Westview, 1987); Joseph T. Jockel and Joel J. Sokolsky, Eds., *Fifty Years of Canada-U.S. Defense Cooperation: The Road From Ogdensburg* (Lewiston, NY: Mellen Press, 1992).

3. McInnis K, Feickert A, Manyin ME, Hildreth SA, Nikitin MBD, Chanlett-Avery E (2017) The North Korean nuclear challenge: military options and issues for congress. Congressional Research Service 7-5700. R44994. (November 6)
4. Robinson LJ (2017) Statement of General Lori J. Robinson, U.S. Air Force Commander, U. S. Northern Command and North American Aerospace Defense Command, Before the Senate Armed Services Committee. http://www.northcom.mil/Portals/28/NC%202017%20Posture%20Statement%20Final.pdf?ver=2017-04-06-110952-160. Accessed 20 Jan 2018 (April 6)
5. United States National Security Strategy (USNSS) (2017) https://www.whitehouse.gov/wp-content/uploads/2017/12/NSS-Final-12-18-2017-0905.pdf. Accessed 23 Jan 2018
6. United States Department of Defense (2018) Summary of the 2018 National Defense Strategy of the United States of America
7. Canada, Minister of National Defence (2017) Strong, Secure, Engaged: Canada's Defence Policy
8. Buzan Barry, Waever Ole, de Wilde Jaap (1998) Security: a new framework for analysis. Lynn Rienner Publishers, Boulder, Colorado
9. Jockel JT, Sokolsky J (2011) Special but not especially important: Canada-U.S. Defense Relations through the Doran lenses. In Anderson G, Sands C (eds) Forgotten partnership redux: Canada-U.S. relations in the 21st century. Cambria Press, New York, pp 149–168
10. Haglund D (2010) *Pensando lo imposible*: Why mexico should be the next new member of the North Atlantic treaty organization. Lat Am Policy 1(2):264–283
11. Thompson J (2014) Making North America: trade security and integration. University of Toronto Press, Toronto
12. Lagassé P, Sokolsky J (2005/2006) Suspenders and a belt: perimeter and border security in U.S.-Canada relations. Can Foreign Policy 12, 15–29
13. Leuprecht C, Sokolsky J (2015) Defence policy, 'Walmart Style': Canadian lessons in 'not-so-grand' strategy. Armed Forces Soc 41(3):541–562
14. Trump DJ (2018) President Donald J. Trump's State of the Union Address. https://www.whitehouse.gov/briefings-statements/president-donald-j-trumps-state-union-address/. Accessed 3 Feb 2018. (January 30)
15. Office of the U.S. Secretary of Defense (2018) Nuclear posture review.
16. National Post Staff (2018) Introducing 'Avangard' and 'Sarmat': Putin shows off new hypersonic, nuclear missiles. Natl Post. http://nationalpost.com/news/world/introducing-the-avangard-hypersonic-missile-a-look-inside-putins-new-high-tech-arsenal. (March 1)
17. Kilroy R, Rodíguex Sumano A, Hataley T (2010) Toward a new trilateral strategic security relationship: United States, Canada and Mexico. J Strateg Secur. http://dx.doi.org/10.5038/1944-0472.3.1.5
18. Kilroy R, Rodíguex Sumano A, Hataley T (2012) North American regional security framework: a trilateral framework? Lynne Rienner Publishers, Colorado
19. Rodíguex Sumano A (Coordinador) (2012) Agendas Comunes y Diferencias en la seguridad de América del Norte. (¿De dónde venimos?, ¿dónde estamos?, Y ¿a dónde queremos ir? *Presentación del Almirante Francisco Saynez Mendoza y Prólogo de Marco Antonio Cortés Guardado*. Universidad de Guadalajara, Centro de Estudios Superiores Navales de la Armada, México (November)

20. Kilroy R, Rodíguex Sumano A, Hataley T (2017) Security inequalities in North America: reassessing regional security complex theory and the role of identity politics. J Secur Stud. https://doi.org/10.5038/1944-0472.10.4.1613
21. Charron A, Fergusson J (2017) Beyond NORAD and modernization to North American defence evolution. Policy paper, Centre for Defence and Security Studies University of Manitoba (May)

The Global Perspective

Putin's Security Policy and Its Implications for NORAD

Mark N. Katz[✉]

Schar School of Policy and Government, George Mason University,
Fairfax, VA, USA
mkatz@gmu.edu

Abstract. Especially since the beginning of his third term as Russia's president in 2012, Vladimir Putin has pursued an increasingly hostile policy toward America and the West. In addition to overseeing Russian military interventions in Georgia, Ukraine, and Syria, Putin has overseen an enormous buildup in Russian nuclear and conventional forces. In addition, Putin has supported nationalist politicians and parties in the West that question or even oppose NATO and the EU in order to undermine Western cohesion. Putin's support for these nationalist forces may be less aimed at seeing them come to (or remain in) power than to disrupt and even discredit Western democracy. Further, Putin is pursuing these aims with a hybrid strategy short of war that relies on disinformation aimed at exploiting existing tensions (including ethnic and racial) within the West. Putin's hostility pose a serious challenge to America and the West, not least because the disinformation campaign in particular takes advantage of the freedom of expression that Western societies value so highly, and hence are loathe to curtail. This chapter discusses the nature of the challenge that Putin's Russia poses, and its implications for America and Canada in particular.

1 Putin's Hostility Toward America and the West

Russian President Vladimir Putin has made clear on numerous occasions that he regards America and the West as the primary threat that Russia faces. This conviction appears to be based on several strands of thinking prevalent within the Kremlin, the Russian security and foreign policy elites, and Russian society generally. One is deep resentment that the Cold War ended with the loss of Soviet influence in Eastern Europe and elsewhere, the collapse of the Soviet Union itself, and a series of American foreign policy actions thereafter viewed by Moscow as taking advantage of Russia's "temporary weakness" (as many Russians insist on describing it). These included: the expansion of NATO; American and European military action against Russia's ally, Serbia, vis-à-vis Bosnia-Herzegovina and Kosovo; recognition of Kosovo's declaration of independence from Serbia without Belgrade's consent; American efforts to limit Russia's relations with Iran; U.S. withdrawal from the Anti-Ballistic Missile Treaty soon after Putin had expressed support for the U.S. after 9/11; the U.S.-led intervention in Iraq without UN Security Council (and hence Russian) approval; American support for "color revolutions" in former Soviet republics Georgia (2003) and Ukraine (2004) in particular; American support for the "Arab Spring" opposition to governments allied to Russia in

© Springer International Publishing AG, part of Springer Nature 2018
C. Leuprecht et al. (eds.), *North American Strategic Defense in the 21st Century:*,
Advanced Sciences and Technologies for Security Applications,
https://doi.org/10.1007/978-3-319-90978-3_2

both Libya and Syria; and American support for another color revolution in Ukraine in 2014 as well as negative reaction to Russia's annexation of Crimea and support for secessionists in eastern Ukraine [1]. America, of course, is not alone in incurring Russian resentment; European governments, and the expansion of the European Union, have also been seen by Moscow as directed against Russian interests [2].

Underlying this resentment is the predominant Russian notion, which Putin definitely shares, of how international relations—especially relations between great powers —"should" work going back to Soviet and even Tsarist days. Moscow sees the great powers as the primary actors in international relations, and that they are capable of making agreements among themselves demarcating "spheres of influence" for each that the others respect [3]. Examples of this kind of great power agreement include the 1939 Nazi-Soviet Pact (which Putin himself has praised) and the 1945 Yalta agreement concerning the post-World War II international order [4]. Many Russians came to believe that the end of the Cold War would lead to an international order co-managed equally by Washington and Moscow [5]. In 2008, then President Medvedev asserted Russia's "privileged interests" in countries where Russia has "traditionally had friendly cordial relations" [6]. The U.S. rejection of this approach has been seen in Moscow both in the past and now not as reflective of American concern about whether the countries Moscow claims to lie within its sphere of influence want this, but of an American desire both to deprive Moscow of any sphere of influence and include even former Soviet republics in America's instead [7].

In addition to this pessimistic view of American intentions, a highly optimistic view of Russia's ability to "rise like the phoenix" after suffering setbacks or even defeats is pervasive within Russia. Russian history itself is seen as the proof for the validity of this belief. Russia, after all, was able to reassert itself as a great power after suffering numerous catastrophes, including centuries of Mongol rule, the 17th century "Time of Troubles" between the downfall of one tsarist dynasty and the rise of another, Napoleon's invasion, the collapse of the Russian Empire in World War I, the Nazi invasion in World War II, and the collapse of the Soviet Union and the 1990s-era "Time of Troubles" under the weak leadership of Boris Yeltsin. An integral part of this view is the belief that because Russia overcame previous setbacks and became stronger than before, it can and will do so again. Russia's re-emergence as a great power under Putin, then, is seen as yet another instance of this occurring. Russia's previous revivals after setbacks also involved the recapture of much (if not all) of the territory lost by Russia during them. Putin's annexation of Crimea in 2014 fit within this narrative, and was very popular with the Russian public [8].

But in addition to the prevalence within Russia of the strong belief that Russia can and will rise again after whatever setbacks it suffers is a belief that another catastrophic setback can occur in the future. Conflating his own interests with those of Russia as a whole, Putin appears to take seriously the possibility that America could support a successful "color revolution" in Russia that would overthrow his regime and replace it with a "democratic" regime that would be subservient to the U.S. [9]. In other words, even though Russia always overcomes all setbacks and rises like the Phoenix afterward, Putin would prefer not to experience such a setback even if Russia would survive but his regime would not.

While firmly believing that America and the West (or powerful forces within them) seek to overthrow him via democratic color revolution, Putin also sees America, other Western governments, and Western institutions such as NATO and the EU as being weak and vulnerable [10]. There is something of a contradiction in holding these two beliefs simultaneously. If America and the West are powerful enough to overthrow Putin via color revolution, then they must not be all that weak. But if they are indeed weak, then they are hardly strong enough to bring about Putin's overthrow. Notwithstanding the inconsistency between these two beliefs, holding them both simultaneously would lead to the conclusion that Russia must act to further weaken the West before the West, which is still strong enough to threaten Russia, can actually do so [11]. And indeed, Putin has acted to undermine America and the West through promoting right-wing parties and politicians who question or even oppose both NATO and the EU.

Finally, compared to the other external challenges Russia faces, Putin sees America and the West as a greater threat than either Sunni Muslims or China. For whatever threat Sunni Muslims or China pose to Russia and its interests, they do not pose the threat of undermining Putin's regime through promoting democratic revolution like Putin (whether accurately or not) sees America and the West as doing. For all these reasons, then, America has been the dominant focus of Moscow's military strategy under Putin, just as it was during the Cold War.

One notable aspect of Putin's military strategy has been his re-emphasis on the Russian nuclear arsenal. Allowed to deteriorate during the 1990s in particular, this has been modernized and updated by Putin. Russian commentary has discussed how at a time when Russia no longer appears to have many other advantages compared to other nations, its being one of the two leading nuclear weapons powers (along with the U.S.) is an advantage that Russia should capitalize on. Precisely how Russia can do this, however, is unclear. Actually employing nuclear weapons would undoubtedly have very high, unpredictable costs. Of course, if Moscow really did fear an attack from the West (or anywhere else), then modernizing the Russian nuclear force could be meant to deter this. Putin's nuclear modernization program, though, may also be intended to intimidate NATO into not "provoking" Russia over an issue that is of more importance to Moscow than to the West. Even if Putin has no intention of ever launching any sort of nuclear attack, he may calculate that he benefits if his adversaries cannot be certain that he will not, or what would trigger him to do so [12].

In addition, Putin has undertaken the modernization and upgrade of Russia's conventional forces as well [13]. These had fallen into a parlous state during the 1990s. Even though successful, the Russian war against Georgia in 2008 revealed numerous deficiencies that Putin has energetically worked to overcome since then [14]. An important obstacle that Moscow faces in maintaining large-scale conventional forces, though, is the smaller cohort of young, ethnically-reliable (i.e., Russian) males available as a result of Russia's demographic decline. Decreased revenue resulting from the prolonged low petroleum price environment has also constrained the financial resources available for modernizing Russian conventional (as well as nuclear) forces [15, 193].

Thus, despite what modernization they have undergone, it does not appear that Russia's conventional forces are intended to fight a major land war in Europe. Indeed, this is something Putin wants to avoid, as Russian forces would quickly run into serious problems in fighting against NATO ones over a prolonged period of time. Putin has instead opted for an aggressive military strategy just short of war that involves provocative Russian actions designed to probe how NATO responds. This has involved Russian military aircraft flying near or even within the airspace of many European countries as well as Japan without permission or warning. Russian warplanes have also flown perilously close to American naval vessels and military aircraft [16].

Under Putin, Russia has also built up an impressive cyber-warfare capability [17]. Indeed, it appears to have actually utilized it on occasion—such as against Estonia when that country's government moved a Soviet war memorial (which was something many Russians were offended by) [18]. One of the advantages of launching cyber-attacks is that a state doing so can do it in a way that allows it to plausibly deny responsibility—which Russia has done—and thus making retaliation against it difficult.

With constraints on his ability to strengthen Russia, Putin has sought to compensate through undertaking actions that weaken the West, including through support for politicians and parties that are pro-Russian as well as anti-NATO and anti-EU [19]. Putin, it must be emphasized, did not create the economic grievances, xenophobia, and nationalism that have led to the rise of these forces, but he has certainly sought to exploit them—as he did most noticeably, the U.S. intelligence community has concluded, during the 2016 American presidential elections by taking actions designed to discredit Hillary Clinton [20]. The aim of this Russian strategy seems clear: if America and the West are Russia's principal adversary, then Russia is better off if they are weak and divided.

Thus, while Putin has not been willing (at least so far) to intervene militarily in any NATO country, he has demonstrated a willingness to intervene politically in them—including the U.S. itself—through efforts aimed at affecting the outcomes of their elections. While perhaps not a purely military strategy, then, Moscow's broader politico-military strategy may be more focused on weakening the West than on initiating additional Russian military interventions.

2 Putin's Strategy: How Durable?

How durable is Putin's military strategy? The answer to this question may depend largely on how durable Putin's rule is. While it must obviously come to an end at some point, in March 2018 he won his fourth term as president. The Russian constitution says that he cannot run for a third consecutive term in 2024 (in 2008–12, there was a gap between Putin's first two terms and his second two when his loyal lieutenant, Dmitry Medvedev, served as president though Putin clearly remained in charge). Putin, though, clearly has the power to either change the constitution or to rule through one of his close associates like he did after his first two consecutive terms as president ended in 2008. Putin, then, might well rule until 2030, or even later.

This being the case, the immediate question about the durability of his military strategy hinges on the question of whether there is any reason why he would alter it. Since he has been steadily implementing this strategy that identifies America and the West as Russia's primary opponents, and since he probably sees it as having been highly successful up to now, there is little reason to think that he is going to change his mind—unless something happens that induces him to do so.

One possibility for this is a dramatic improvement in Russian relations with America and the West. There was actually some anticipation after the election of Donald Trump as president of the U.S. in 2016 that Russian-American relations would at least improve somewhat, but even this limited expectation now appears unwarranted given continued Russian-American differences over sanctions, Crimea, Ukraine, and NATO. And despite Trump's own relatively friendly tone toward Russia, several of his top appointees as well as many Senate and House Republicans have taken a much tougher approach toward it. In President Trump's first phone conversation with Putin, Trump reportedly spurned Putin's offer to extend the New START agreement, declaring that it was a "bad deal" for America [21]. Putin's displeasure over this may go a long way to explaining why Russian media coverage of Trump went from being warm and friendly to being cold and distant in mid-February 2017 [22]. Putin's expectations were clearly disappointed.

It is worth considering what his initial expectations of Trump might have been. As noted earlier, the preferred ordering of international relations for Putin, as it was for his predecessors, is a world in which the great powers recognize one another's respective spheres of influence. But whatever hopes Putin may have initially had that Trump, "the deal maker," would go along with this approach have not been met. In fact, the publicity in America about Trump and his presidential campaign having had close ties to Russia that have not yet been disclosed makes it difficult for Trump to cooperate closely with Putin without furthering suspicion about this. Indeed, Republican concern in Congress about Russia had grown to such an extent that a bill imposing additional U. S. sanctions on Russia (as well as on Iran and North Korea) that limited President Trump's ability to lift them was passed by overwhelming majorities in both the House and the Senate. Despite his opposition to it, Trump signed the bill (since a veto would have been easily overridden) [23].

While Putin would prefer a great power acceptance of each other's spheres of influence approach to world order, this requires that other great power leaders—especially of the U.S.—share it. Identifying the circumstances under which an American president would do this are beyond the scope of this chapter, but the fact that Trump, who at first seemed amenable to this great power bargain approach, turned away from it suggests that this is unlikely.

Another reason why Putin might change his mind about prioritizing America and the West as Russia's principal adversaries is that he decides that the strategy has succeeded to the point where it is no longer necessary. This might occur as the result of the election of pro-Russian and/or anti-NATO/EU parties and leaders in enough Western countries that Western governments focus more on their own internal politics or differences with one another than on Russia. If those differences are severe enough, some Western governments may even turn to Russia for support against other Western ones. But while Putin may indeed be seeking to weaken the West through supporting the election of nationalist parties and politicians as well as promoting differences within it, whether the Western alliance actually does weaken depends more on the strength of divisive forces inside the West rather than Russian efforts to promote them. Indeed, these Russian efforts may actually serve to discredit Moscow in the West, as negative public reaction in many Western countries (including the U.S.) about signs of Russian attempts to influence elections in them have shown [24].

Putin might also change his mind about prioritizing America and the West as Russia's principal adversaries if he decides that an even greater threat to Russia, and his rule over it, has emerged. If, for example, something happens that leads Putin to view China and/or the Sunni Muslim world as more threatening, then Putin may well seek Western support against what he will portray as (and which may actually be) a common threat. And in this case, a strong and united West will be of far greater value to Russia than a weak and divided one.

It does not seem likely at present, though, that Putin will change his mind about the military strategy he is now pursuing. The Russian leadership that comes after him, of course, may take quite a different view than he does. This would be especially true if the Putin regime was replaced by a democratic one. But much like the Franco-American relationship, the relationship between a democratic Russia on the one hand and America and other Western governments on the other might be somewhat contentious instead. But a democratic Russian government would presumably not share Putin's fear of being overthrown in a Western-backed "color revolution" (especially if this post-Putin government resulted from such a revolution, whether supported by the West or not). A democratic Russian government would be far more likely to share Western concerns about threats to both emanating from the Muslim world and from China.

But while the emergence of a democratic Russia might offer the best prospect for Moscow altering Putin's current focus on America and the West as being the main threat to Russia, the prospects for democracy replacing Putin do not appear to be at all good. Far more likely is that Putin will be succeeded, ousted, or otherwise replaced by someone inside his regime. In such a scenario, a continuation of Putin's strategy of focusing on America and the West as being the main threat to Russia by another authoritarian leader who also fears democratization is a strong possibility. But this is not the only possibility, or perhaps even the most likely one.

In looking back at Russia's leaders over the past century, what is noteworthy is that each one has changed significant aspects of the foreign and/or domestic policies of the one he replaced. Some dramatically revised even their own foreign policies. Changing circumstances drove some of these changes, but so did personal preference as well as a desire to distinguish oneself from previous leaders, whose policies new leaders have often criticized, as when Khrushchev denounced Stalin; Brezhnev denounced Khrushchev; Gorbachev denounced Brezhnev; Yeltsin denounced Gorbachev; and Putin criticized Yeltsin. The fact that Medvedev did not criticize Putin after replacing him as president was an indicator that he had not replaced him in power [25].

It would not be surprising if, after Putin is no longer Russia's ruler, even a successor he himself chose became critical of him and altered significant aspects of Putin's policies. This could occur if the state of Russia's economy continued to stagnate or even deteriorate under Putin, and his successor decided that improved relations with the West was a necessity not just for appeasing the Russian public, but also Russian elites more concerned about their own well-being than whether Moscow is more influential than the West in places such as Syria or eastern Ukraine. In other words, there may not only be the opportunity for a new leader to change Putin's defense policy, but there may be compelling domestic political reasons for him to do so—especially if there is an increased Russian threat perception on the part of Putin's successor about China and/or the Muslim challenge (both from within and without).

Yet while it is quite possible that even Putin's own hand-picked successor might well alter Putin's defense policy, Putin could remain in power (as was noted earlier) for many years, and that he seems unlikely to alter his belief that America and the West are the main threats that he faces—and which events like the surprise demonstrations across Russia that broke out in late March 2017 are only likely to confirm his views on [26]. With Putin's defense policy identifying America and the West as Russia's primary opponents likely to remain durable so long as Putin remains in power (and perhaps longer still), the question that arises is: what is the adequacy of Putin's defense strategy for satisfying Russia's principal geopolitical aims?

The answer to this question depends on an assessment of whether Putin has accurately identified and prioritized the threats facing Russia as well as whether he has fashioned a strategy to deal with them effectively. If indeed America and the West are not only a threat to Russia, but more of one than either China or the Sunni jihadists, then Putin's military strategy is not only sensible, but successful. But are America and the West really a threat to Russia? They hardly seem likely to invade Russia, as this could lead to a nuclear conflagration as catastrophic for them as for Russia. Putin, of course, does not seem to fear a Western invasion, but its promotion of a democratic color revolution against him instead. But is the West really trying to democratize Russia? There was a period after the end of the Cold War when many in the West thought that Russia was on the road to democratization, and Western governments sought to encourage this process. But they really did not do much of anything to stop Putin from reversing whatever progress toward democracy Russia had made and reviving authoritarianism there. Putin's belief that the color revolutions in former Soviet republics, the Arab Spring, and the demonstrations against him inside Russia in 2011-12 were all instigated by the West underestimated popular support for them in each country that these upheavals took place in. The fact that widespread demonstrations against Putin broke out in Russia in March 2017 over two months after Donald Trump—who is definitely not trying to promote a color revolution against Putin—took office indicates that America and the West are not the main instigators of these types of anti-authoritarian protests.

Putin's strategy, then, may well have succeeded in undermining (or perhaps more accurately, encouraging trends within the West that undermine) the strength and cohesion of the Western alliance. But if Putin has overestimated the extent to which America and the West actually pose a threat to Russia, then his efforts to neutralize that threat have been completely unnecessary. It is, of course, possible that Putin does not really see the West as a threat, but merely says so to justify the pursuit of an aggressive and offensive effort to undermine it. But whether Putin's prioritization of America and the West is defensively or offensively motivated, his success in weakening the West does nothing to enhance Russian capacity for dealing with other external threats from China and the Sunni jihadists. In fact, Putin's success in weakening the West will lessen Western capacity to aid Russia if it faces growing threats from either. And, of course, a weakened West will be one less able (not to mention less willing) to provide the investment and trade Putin needs to bolster the Russian economy and placate both the Russian population and the elite whose support he especially depends on. The prioritization of America and the West in Putin's strategy, then, is a huge bet that China and the Sunni jihadists will either not become a serious threat to Russia, or that Moscow can manage them (along with maintaining internal stability inside Russia) without the aid of the West. Of course, if Putin's efforts to weaken the West do not succeed, then perhaps these other threats either will not grow stronger than they are, or the West will overlook Putin's efforts against it if it deems China and/or the Sunni jihadists as common threats to both the West and Russia.

But whatever the inadequacy of Putin's strategy as well as the risks that it exposes Russia to, Putin himself appears to be quite satisfied with it. He seems likely to pursue it so long as he is in power, and he may long be in power. Whatever successes or failures Putin's strategy vis-à-vis America and the West may have, Russia's relations with the West are likely to remain contentious so long as it is pursued. Irrespective of whatever additional geopolitical gains for Russia Putin can make (indeed, especially if he does make them) in Ukraine, Belarus, or elsewhere, the more likely that Western sanctions on Russia will remain or even increase. Hostile Russian actions vis-à-vis the Baltic states risks the possibility of a larger conflict between Russia and NATO—or NATO being seen as irrelevant if it does not act to defend the Baltics. Either way, Russian economic interaction with the West is likely to decline further—and so will the Russian economy. What Putin does not seem capable of accomplishing is making geopolitical gains for Russia at Western expense and at the same time garnering Western willingness to going back to doing business as usual (or preferably, increasing its economic interaction) with Russia. Further, whatever success Putin has in promoting nationalist, anti-EU/NATO, and pro-Russian politicians and parties in the West actually come to power does not mean that they will be willing or able to do Putin's bidding once they are in power. Further, Putin's success in expanding Russia's geopolitical reach and weakening the West may eventually result in his successors facing the choice between expending scarce resources to defend Putin's territorial gains which do little to enhance Russia's actual security, or end up withdrawing from them in order to reduce costs as well as improve relations with a West with which it needs good relations economically and perhaps even militarily against a rising Chinese and/or Sunni jihadist threat.

But even if Putin's strategy ultimately proves harmful to Russian interests, America and the West will have to devote considerable energy and resources to countering or at least containing it for as long as Putin pursues it, or face internal disarray if they do not do so. And America and the West having to respond to Putin's strategy targeting them only distracts from their ability to respond to a rising Chinese and/or Sunni jihadist threat as well. It certainly will not promote cooperation between Russia and the West against what may be common threats.

3   Implications

Russia does not just pose a nuclear and conventional military challenge to the Western allies, but also a political one affecting their domestic politics via a sophisticated information campaign. America and its allies, then, must clearly learn to respond to the multifaceted nature of this Russian challenge. Space here does not allow for a detailed discussion of what needs to be done by the Western alliance in general and NORAD in particular. Something, though, can be said about the implications of the Russian challenge for NORAD under two scenarios: an optimistic one in which the Russian challenge is successfully contained (if not ended), and a pessimistic one in which the Russian challenge grows stronger if only because the Western response to it grows weaker.

There is a strong case to be made for the optimistic scenario that the West will successfully contain Russia. Not only have most NATO governments become increasingly aware of the Russian challenge and have taken steps to beef up their defenses, but there has been a backlash in Western public opinion about Russian interference in their elections. In 2017, for example, Emmanuel Macron won the French presidential elections and not the candidate favored by Moscow, while Angela Merkel and her allies won the largest portion of the German national elections. The perception that Moscow is supporting a particular candidate or party may now be more of a liability than previously when Western public opinion was not so focused on Russian activity. Under this scenario, NATO remains united and even reinvigorated. The participation of some members, such as Turkey, may diminish or even end, but this is something that NATO has encountered previously, as with France and Greece during the Cold War. Under this scenario, NORAD may play an important role through continuing to broaden its scope from a focus on North American aerospace defense to North American defense more generally.

It is under the pessimistic scenario, though, that the importance of NORAD may become greater still. For if the cohesion of the multilateral NATO alliance frays as a result of several members significantly reducing their cooperation with or even withdrawing from it, those countries that continue to value defense cooperation with the U.S. are likely to pursue this through informal or even formal bilateral relationships, as occurs outside Europe (i.e., with Japan and South Korea). NORAD already is a bilateral Canadian-American defense pact whose importance up to now has been subsumed in both countries' common membership in NATO. In other words, the more that NATO loses cohesion and functionality, the more important NORAD and the Canadian-American bilateral defense relationship will become not just for North American defense, but also as partners for those European nations continuing to seek defense cooperation with the U.S. and Canada.

The emergence of this more pessimistic scenario, it must be emphasized, may be encouraged by Russia, but cannot develop without serious fissures within and between Western states being sufficiently strong in them for Moscow to exploit. Hopefully this can be avoided. But if not, then Canadian-American defense cooperation may become more important than ever.

References

1. Stent AE (2014) The limits of partnership: U.S.-Russian relations in the 21st century. Princeton University Press, Princeton
2. Chaban N, Elgström O, Gulyaeva O (2017) Russian images of the European Union: before and after Maidan. Foreign Policy Anal 13(2):480–499

3. Hill F (2015) This is what Putin really wants. National Interest, 24 Feb 2015. http://nationalinterest.org/feature/what-putin-really-wants-12311. Accessed 19 Jan 2018
4. Birnbaum M (2015) A day after marking Nazi defeat, Putin praises a Soviet-era pact with Hitler. Washington Post, 11 May 2015. https://www.washingtonpost.com/news/worldviews/wp/2015/05/11/a-day-after-marking-nazi-defeat-putin-praises-a-soviet-era-pact-with-hitler. Accessed 19 Jan 2018
5. Suslov D (2016) The Russian perception of the post–Cold War era and relations with the West. Harriman Institute lecture, Columbia University, New York. 9 Nov 2016. https://www.sant.ox.ac.uk/sites/default/files/university-consortium/files/suslov_harriman_lecture_on_post-cold_war_era.pdf. Accessed 19 Jan 2018
6. Economist (2016) Medvedev on Russia's interests. 1 Sept 2008
7. Liik K (2015) How to talk with Russia. European council on Foreign relations, 18 Dec 2015. http://www.ecfr.eu/article/commentary_how_to_talk_to_russia5055. Accessed 19 Jan 2018
8. Katz MN (2015) Will Putin lead Russia to glory or disaster? Moscow Times, 21 June 2015. https://themoscowtimes.com/articles/will-putin-lead-russia-to-glory-or-disaster-op-ed-47552. Accessed 19 Jan 2018
9. Korsunskaya D (2014) Putin says Russia must prevent 'color revolution.' Reuters, 20 Nov 2014. http://www.reuters.com/article/us-russia-putin-security-idUSKCN0J41J620141120. Accessed 19 Jan 2018
10. Judah B (2014) Why Russia no longer fears the West. Politico Magazine, 2 March 2014. http://www.politico.com/magazine/story/2014/03/russia-vladimir-putin-the-west-104134. Accessed 19 Jan 2018
11. Katz MN (2015) Inside the confused mind of Vladimir Putin. Moscow Times, 1 April 2015. https://themoscowtimes.com/articles/inside-the-confused-mind-of-vladimir-putin-45355. Accessed 19 Jan 2018
12. Cimbala SJ, McDermott RN (2016) Putin and the nuclear dimension to Russian strategy. J Slav Mil Stud 29(4):535–553
13. Sokov N (2017) Russia's new conventional capability: implications for Eurasia and beyond. PONARS Eurasia Policy Memo, no. 472, April 2017. http://www.ponarseurasia.org/sites/default/files/policy-memos-pdf/Pepm472_Sokov_May2017.pdf. Accessed 19 Jan 2018
14. Cohen A, Hamilton RE (2011) The Russian military and the Georgia war: lessons and implications. Strategic Studies Institute, Carlisle. http://ssi.armywarcollege.edu/pdffiles/pub1069.pdf. Accessed 19 Jan 2018
15. International Institute for Strategic Studies (2017) The military balance 2017. Routledge, London
16. Grygiel JJ, Mitchell AW (2016) The unquiet frontier: rising rivals, vulnerable allies, and the crisis of American power. Princeton University Press, Princeton
17. Thomas T (2014) Russia's information warfare strategy: can the nation cope in future conflicts? J Slav Mil Stud 27(1):101–130
18. McGuinness D (2017). How a cyber attack transformed Estonia. BBC News, 27 April 2017. http://www.bbc.com/news/39655415. Accessed 19 Jan 2018
19. Wesslau F (2016). Putin's friends in Europe. European council on Foreign relations, 19 Oct 2016. http://www.ecfr.eu/article/commentary_putins_friends_in_europe7153. Accessed 19 Jan 2018
20. Office of the Director of National Intelligence and National Intelligence Council (2017) Assessing Russian activities and intentions in recent U.S. elections, Intelligence Community Assessment, ICA 2017-01D, 6 Jan 2017. https://www.dni.gov/files/documents/ICA_2017_01.pdf. Accessed 19 Jan 2018

21. Landay J, Rohde D (2017) Exclusive: in call with Putin, Trump denounced Obama-era nuclear arms treaty—sources. Reuters, 9 Feb 2017. http://www.reuters.com/article/us-usa-trump-putin-idUSKBN15O2A5. Accessed 19 Jan 2018
22. Rosenberg S (2017) Russian media no longer dazzled by Trump. BBC News, 17 Feb 2017. http://www.bbc.com/news/world-europe-39004987. Accessed 19 Jan 2018
23. Collins K, Herb J, Diaz, D (2017) Trump signs bill approving new sanctions against Russia. CNN, 3 Aug 2017. http://edition.cnn.com/2017/08/02/politics/donald-trump-russia-sanctions-bill/index.html. Accessed 19 Jan 2018
24. Weber Y (2017) Russia looks out for own interests in Europe's elections but risks long-term blowback. Russia Matters, 19 April 2017. https://www.russiamatters.org/analysis/russia-looks-out-own-interests-europes-elections-risks-long-term-blowback. Accessed 19 Jan 2018
25. Katz MN (2014) Imagining the post-Putin era. LobeLog, 17 July 2014. https://lobelog.com/russia-imagining-the-post-putin-era. Accessed 19 Jan 2018
26. Meyer H, Kravchenko S, Andrianova A (2017) Putin takes tough stance on protests, warns of Arab spring chaos. Bloomberg Politics, 30 March 2017. https://www.bloomberg.com/politics/articles/2017-03-30/putin-takes-tough-stance-on-protests-warns-of-arab-spring-chaos. Accessed 19 Jan 2018

Misplaced Prudence: The Role of Restraint in the Nuclear Threat Environment for North American Strategic Defense

Nina Srinivasan Rathbun[✉] and Brian C. Rathbun

School of International Relations, University of Southern California, Los Angeles, CA, USA
{nrathbun,brathbun}@usc.edu

Abstract. International relations theory provides analytic lenses for evaluating the dynamics of today's dangerous and unstable nuclear threat environment. Both realist and constructivist theories recognize the importance of restraint in these environments. Realists focus on the security dilemma, understanding that the pursuit of security can mistakenly incite fears of aggression on the part of others. Constructivists focus on normative, rather than strategic, restraint. Psychological insights deepen concerns about the wisdom of bellicose policies, given the potential to create spirals of conflict based on emotional and vitriolic reactions and the possibilities of misinterpreting signals. When psychological dynamics are added, restraint becomes more imperative, even as it becomes more difficult to achieve. These insights undermine strategies based on apparent 'prudence', requiring practitioners to consider not just interpretations of signals from adversaries but also how their own signals may be misinterpreted. We evaluate the threat posed by Iran and North Korea to North American strategic defense. Restraint remains one of the most difficult decisions for policy makers, one for which practitioners are often heavily criticized, yet key for North American defense. By relying more heavily on the special interlacing institutions providing North American strategic defense—U.S. Northern Command (USNORTHCOM), bi-national North American Aerospace Defense Command (NORAD) and Canadian Joint Operations Command (CJOC)—policymakers acquire more perspectives to help overcome misperception, reinforce reassurance, and better safeguard North America.

1 Restraint in International Relations Theory

The nuclear threat environment presents one of the most significant threats to a stable international security environment. International relations (IR) theory provides analytic lenses for evaluating the dynamics of this threat environment. We will first review the concept of restraint in IR theory from the viewpoint of two dominant and often conflicting IR theories: realism and constructivism. These international theories interpret the international environment extremely differently and, therefore, typically prescribe different policy responses. However, in the current situation, realism and constructivism come to the same conclusions: restraint is key to stabilizing this threat environment. This strengthens the prescriptive power of the analysis. Second,

C. Leuprecht et al. (eds.), *North American Strategic Defense in the 21st Century:*,
Advanced Sciences and Technologies for Security Applications,
https://doi.org/10.1007/978-3-319-90978-3_3

psychological dynamics make it difficult for practitioners to see signals of restraint. Objective perception of signals is taken for granted in both realism and constructivism. When psychological dynamics are added to realism and constructivism, restraint becomes even more imperative, even as it becomes more difficult to achieve. This additional obstacle to restraint suggests particular strategies and requires practitioners to engage in more care in interpreting signals from others as well as understanding how their own signals may be misinterpreted. Third, we apply this analysis to the strategic defense of North America, particularly addressing the differentiated threat environment in the Persian Gulf and the Korean peninsula. Together, USNORTHCOM, the bi-national, Canada-U.S. North American Aerospace Defense Command (NORAD) and the Canadian Joint Operations Command (CJOC) form this strategic defense. Working together, these institutions can potentially overcome misperception and develop policies based on rational considerations to avoid the dangers highlighted by this analysis. Refraining from action is the rational course of action under current circumstances. Yet, it remains one of the most difficult decisions for 'prudent' policy-makers, and one for which practitioners are often heavily criticized. Institutionalized cooperative frameworks, as currently exist in North America, may assist with this effort.

Restraint—the conscious and deliberate non-exercise of power, force and violence—has been a central theme in realist scholarship as well as other IR traditions [1–4]. Under realism, coercion and force are not necessarily the most cost-effective way of reaching one's goals or the best strategy in the long-run. Too much bellicosity in foreign affairs can undermine one's interests, even if they are defined in an exclusively egoistic fashion. Realists focus on strategic restraint in foreign policy—that is, restraint based on egoistic considerations and an anticipation of the reaction of others. This means a balancing of the short-term against the long term as well as a willingness to separate the necessary from the purely desirable. Other IR traditions theorize about the role of restraint in foreign affairs in normative and/or generalized ways [5]. Realist restraint, in contrast, will always be situational, with each problem judged on its own merits rather than through the formulation of universal principles or solutions [6]. Realists would caution against the application of any type of generalized restraint. Sovereignty, being a vital interest of any state, should not be compromised across domains or over a long period of time.

Constructivists argue that states are sometimes restrained by normative obligations that place limitations on the exercise of pure state egoism. Whether it be moral injunctions against the use of particular weapons [7, 8] or the willingness to redefine alliance goals in light of allies' input [9], constructivists think of restraint in a non-instrumental manner, rather than in an egoistic and instrumental way based on a rational calculation of costs and benefits. Constructivist restraint is driven by social norms, in this case, the norm of working through multilateral institutions and considering the impact of foreign policies on the legitimacy of the nuclear nonproliferation regime [10, 11]. For legitimacy to be achieved, fairness and equality/voice are key. Following legitimate processes has an important impact on the reactions of other states. This normally includes using established multilateral institutions, such as the United Nations Security Council or the International Atomic Energy Agency (IAEA), or following the negotiated process of a multilateral nuclear deal in Iran.

Realism and constructivism often prescribe the same policies in practice but for very different reasons. While realism recommends "not to advance by destroying the obstacles in one's way, but to retreat before them, to circumvent them, to maneuver around them, to soften and dissolve them slowly by means of persuasion, negotiation and pressure" [3, p. 546], constructivism values Habermas' "communicative action" or the process of argumentation, deliberation and persuasion based on "reasoned consensus" [12]. Where realism sees a self-serving calculation behind following rules and standards, constructivism sees these processes as having their own impact on states' conceptions of interests and the threat environment. Risse believes that self-interested strategic argumentation will be transparent and therefore less successful than persuasion for neutral participants engaged in "truth-seeking argumentation" [12, p. 18]. Nevertheless, both traditions prescribe persuasion and the non-use of force. Trachtenberg argues that a world governed by Realpolitik principles is one in which force is rarely used due to "judgments about how power might be intelligently used—and, above all, for judgments about when its use is to be avoided" [13, p. 167]. Thus, two quintessentially different theories prescribe policies with similar effect for different reasons.

Restraint in foreign and military policy can have at least three distinctive and interrelated advantages, summed up nicely by Onea: "Restraint proponents nearly always portray expansive national interests as self-defeating due to counterbalancing, imperial overstretch, and resentment" [5, p. 113]. First, restraint lessens security dilemma dynamics, thereby avoiding unnecessary conflicts and tensions. In IR, the pursuit of security by any state is often indistinguishable to outsiders from the pursuit of aggrandizement because military power is utilized towards both ends [14, 15]. The security dilemma is often described as a "tragic" situation given that the structural nature of the dilemma makes it difficult to resolve. Nevertheless, restraint, perhaps through cooperation with others, offers the ability to send signals of reassurance to other states [16]. Realist scholars stress that leaders should "look at the political scene from the point of view of other nations" [3, p. 553]. Similarly, constructivists in the Habermasian tradition emphasize the "ability to empathize, that is, to see things through the eyes of one's interaction partner" [12, p. 11]. Without this ability (strategic or communal), one might falsely inflate the threat posed by others or clumsily convince the other incorrectly of having malign intentions.

Since power can be used for offense as well as defense, a state can have too much if it induces fear on the part of the other side and balancing to restore an equilibrium, generating spiral dynamics that lead to mutually detrimental outcomes even among status quo states [14, 17, 18]. In the nuclear realm, ballistic missile defense (BMD) and its predecessor anti-ballistic missile systems (ABM) have long been understood to be potentially destabilizing since they detract from mutual deterrence or mutually assured destruction [19, 20]. When combined with offensive use of force to prevent nuclear proliferation, the dynamic is only more dangerous. U.S. use of force in Iraq on the basis of weapons of mass destruction has an impact on the judgements of other states. Mearsheimer and Walt clearly warn about the implications of US use of force: "War may not be necessary to deny Iraq nuclear weapons, but it is likely to spur proliferation elsewhere... Iran and North Korea will be even more committed to having a nuclear deterrent after watching the American military conquer Iraq. Countries like Japan, South Korea and Saudi Arabia will then think about following suit" [4, p. 15].

Second, bellicose foreign and military policies often engender emotional and vitriolic reactions on the part of targets, creating the possibility for spirals of conflict. They serve to rally others around the flag, creating headaches and risks that might otherwise have been avoided. It is best, if possible, to avoid hatred and anger on the part of others. Cycles of acrimony and indignation are also possible [21]. Realists are particularly concerned about stoking nationalism in other countries. This means remaining attentive to identity politics.

Third, restraint helps statesmen avoid the problem of defining interests in such an expansive manner as to exceed one's own power to defend them. "Restraint requires that great powers use military force sparingly and only in defence of their physical security from direct attack or from a major revision of the balance of power" [5, p. 113]. Realists caution states to "promote the national interest with moderation and leave the door open for compromise in the form of a negotiated settlement" [3, p. 534].

These three reasons to exercise restraint are interrelated, of course. By exercising too much power in foreign affairs given a lack of security dilemma sensibility, one can attract both fear and hatred on the part of others, which makes it harder to defend one's interest with the power available. Security dilemma sensibility entails attentiveness to other reactions on the part of states, such as national indignation and anger. One of the reasons that a state bites off more than it can chew is by underestimating the resistance of others or the fear that its own actions might generate. Not all leaders act strategically according to the structural constraints of the situation. This turns us to the next important factor in restraint: signaling and its interpretation.

2 Signaling and Interpretation

Both realists and constructivists assume that signals of restrain are easily received and interpreted. Yet, psychology insights question this rationalist assumption that all individuals respond objectively to new information and update their understanding of the other based on this new information. Canonical models of costly signaling in IR tend to assume costly signals speak for themselves: the costliness of a signal is understood to be a function of the signal, not the recipient's perception. Integrating the study of costly signaling in IR with research on motivated skepticism, biased assimilation and asymmetric updating from the study of political psychology, individuals' tendencies to embrace information consistent with their overarching belief systems (and dismiss information inconsistent with it) becomes clear, with important implications for how costly signals are interpreted.

Unlike their rationalist counterparts, psychologically-informed theories of foreign policy behavior have long problematized objective perception and information-processing by state leaders [18, 22, 23]. One of the most consistent findings in the psychological literature in IR as well as the cognitivist tradition more broadly is that individuals engage in belief assimilation and belief perseverance. Rather than continually adjusting their beliefs in light of objective evidence, they pick and choose the information that matches their prior attitudes and then explain away anomalies [22, 24–26]. There are likely important individual differences in the perception of signals as a result.

Studies of political behavior have consistently demonstrated in recent years that preexisting attitudes condition our ability and willingness to update our beliefs in light of disconfirming information—which is germane for the study of costly signaling, since we only send signals of reassurance when there is an established negative image of the other. Studies in American politics, meant to highlight the problem of ideological polarization, have shown that we are 'motivated skeptics', dismissing evidence that doesn't align with our preexisting beliefs. In as much as we change our beliefs it is generally in the direction of strengthening them, not reevaluating them. The implication for costly signaling is that to know whether a signal is credible enough, we have to know something about the preexisting beliefs of the perceiver and that those most likely to change their beliefs are the ones who already want to do so. Emotions help form beliefs, since we use 'feelings' as evidence of our beliefs [27]. This is particularly true for evaluating intent, necessary for reacting to material capability. Holmes argues that fear induces potentially irrational 'prudent' actions even when rational belief contradicts them, making it nearly impossible for practitioners to follow security dilemma sensibility even when they understand the mechanism [28].

Psychological research shows that restraint is difficult because the way we think often makes conflict spirals more dangerous. Signals of reassurance are more likely to be misinterpreted, particularly in conflict situations where states have strong negative attitudes to the other. Conflict spirals are more likely to start and to become more dangerous due misinterpretation of others' signals and obliviousness to the likely reactions to one's own signals. But, they are also due to misplaced prudence, reacting to fear and capabilities even though security dilemma sensibility rationally proscribes such behavior [28]. When these psychological insights are added to the theoretical logic of restraint, threat environments present greater challenges, particularly to those with strong negative attitudes of competitor states.

3 The Nuclear Threat Environment

The most serious current threats to North America in the nuclear environment are from the Korean peninsula and, to a lesser degree, the Persian Gulf. The nuclear threat environment is embedded in the larger security environment and continually impacted by national security policies of the main parties and the perceptions of these signals by other actors. The UN Security Council and the IAEA not only provided key fora for concerted international pressure through increasing sanctions and inspections, but also the main parties for defending the nuclear nonproliferation regime and the norm of nonproliferation of nuclear weapons. The recent outcomes of international negotiations create very different situations in Iran and North Korea. In both instances, international cooperation has unified and strengthened, creating the possibility for diplomatic breakthrough. However, the Joint Comprehensive Plan of Action (JCPOA) negotiated between Iran and the U.S., United Kingdom, France, Germany, the European Union, China and Russia created a multilateral framework for signaling restraint by all parties, while the failure of the six-party talks in the Korean Peninsula has allowed North Korea to continue to advance its nuclear capability and undermined restraint in the other parties, the U.S., South Korea, Japan, Russia and China. In both situations, missile tests and larger security concerns, particularly of state sponsorship of terrorism and regional balance of power, present additional obstacles for stability within the nuclear environment. Similarly, in both situations, the ratcheting up of bellicosity and rhetoric on the part of both sides increase the danger of conflict spirals leading to risky actions and encourage overreach in the definitions of national interest, decreasing the unity of the international community's response and increasing the threat to North America. And, finally, in both situations, the nuclear nonproliferation regime and the regional multilateral efforts to maintain its norms are under threat. While the changing threat environment presents challenges to North American strategic defense, the lessons from the JCPOA and the possibility for the layered institutions for North American defense provide a logical path forward for addressing the most serious destabilizing threats.

4 Lessons from Iran and the Joint Comprehensive Plan of Action

Iran presented a major threat to the stability of the Middle East region and the nuclear nonproliferation regime through its nearly two decade old clandestine nuclear program, discovered in 2002. This was only one of several serious threats to North America strategic defense, including Iran's ballistic missile developments and its sponsorship of terrorist organizations. Only nuclear negotiations proved amenable to compromise. Though the negotiations lasted over a decade and involved many different parties, Iran signaled its willingness to compromise through the early suspension of its nuclear program during the EU-3 talks in 2004–2005 and the continued engagement with the IAEA inspections (including implementing the Additional Protocol measures since 2005) even after the IAEA Board reported Iran to the UN Security Council in 2006. Continual efforts in confidence building measures and engagement by numerous parties, combined with strengthened international sanctions, set the conditions for the diplomatic breakthrough in 2015 on the JCPOA [29]. The agreement was limited to the nuclear realm and did not address ballistic missile technology or state sponsored terrorism. Nevertheless, the agreement indicated restraint on the part of all the parties in the increasingly tense regional dynamics and set the stage for reintegrating Iran into the international community. It also further strengthened the legitimacy of the nuclear nonproliferation regime by compromising on enrichment while reducing the threat of nuclear weapons development for over a decade.

The JCPOA strengthened the nuclear nonproliferation regime by strengthening the IAEA and UN Security Council enforcement roles. First, this agreement authorizes the IAEA to verify nuclear weaponization work that does not involve nuclear materials for the first time. Iran commits to never engage in neutron initiator development and multi-point explosive detonation as well as to allow the IAEA to verify this [30]. Second, the snap-back procedure in the event of a U.S. charge that Iran is in significant non-performance of its commitments automatically restores the UN Security Council sanctions unless a new Security Council resolution is adopted that maintains the

suspension of sanctions (which the U.S. could, of course, veto). Both these developments create precedents for cooperation and compromise on the difficult balancing of
the competing aims of the nuclear nonproliferation regime: preventing nuclear weapons
proliferation and promoting nuclear energy and peaceful uses.

This positive development in the nuclear threat environment created by the JCPOA
is continually challenged by differences in perceptions of the Iran threat. Iran's signals
and the JCPOA have been perceived very differently in the U.S. by Republicans and
Democrats, as well as by other countries. We turn to the role of cognitive processes in
decision-making to explain the impact of the different perceptions of signals and
varying levels of appreciation of the role of restraint. It is this difference of perception
that can be mitigated to a degree by the international institutions and multiple parties to
the agreement. In other research on both mass and elite U.S. perceptions of signals in
the case of Iran, we have found that both groups contain substantial variation in
responses to costly signals as a function of prior dispositions. Existing research shows
that elites and masses both rely on foreign policy dispositions to form beliefs about
foreign policy issues but that for elites these are more closely tied to their underlying
political ideology, with liberals endorsing cooperative internationalism more than
conservatives [31]. While on average respondents change their views of Iran in
response to costly signals on their part, others do not: in particular, cooperative
internationalists, a foreign policy orientation that stresses concern for others abroad,
with whom one should work toward common goals, and international institutions and
multilateralism as a means through which to achieve mutual gains [32–36], and liberals
will seek out and embrace corrective information that bolsters their beliefs, a confir-
mation bias, while others will largely ignore such signals, a disconfirmation bias.[1] In
other words, it is precisely those who are motivated to find evidence of a costly signal
who act as classic signaling models would expect, while those are motivated not to
update their beliefs do not respond to the treatments to the same degree, and sometimes
not at all.

Rathbun has also found in other research that political ideology mediates the effect
of core values on foreign policy dispositions, particularly for those who know a lot
about politics, suggesting a potentially tight fit between ideology and dispositions
among elites, tighter than for the mass public [31]. Through discriminant analysis of all
statements, press releases, hearings and speeches on the Iran deal from all members of
the U.S. Senate from July 14, 2015—the day the deal was announced—to September
19, 2015, two days after the final vote, we found strong evidence for the same variation
in perception of costly signals on the elite level as we found at the mass level. First,

---

[1] Joshua Kertzer, Brian C. Rathbun and Nina Srinivasan Rathbun, "The Price of Peace: A Behavioral
Approach to Costly Signaling in International Relations," Working Paper (2017). In the run-up to the
2015 Joint Comprehensive Plan of Action (JCPOA) seeking to limit the Iranian nuclear program, we
asked an online sample of nearly 2000 American adults questions about potential outcomes of
negotiations between the U.S. and Iran. Manipulating the signals of reassurance that Iran might send
to the U.S. along two dimensions—being willing to limit uranium enrichment to various degrees as
well as to allow inspection with different degrees of intrusiveness—we look to see whether such
signals, represented in the form of hypothetical negotiating positions, change estimates of Iran's
trustworthiness, the threat it poses, and support for a nuclear deal in which economic sanctions are
lifted.

more conservative Senators were significantly more likely to focus their comments on the threat posed by Iran. The representative responses portray the deal as rewarding Iranian bad behavior, highlighting Iran's links to international terrorist organizations. Second, more liberal Senators, who tend to be higher in cooperative internationalism, were significantly more likely to focus their comments on the nuts and bolts of the deal itself. This analysis clearly demonstrates the dispositional lens through which Senators and elites in the United State perceive Iran's signal and the productiveness of the JCPOA. Republicans do not update their threat perception of Iran based on the JCPOA.[2] This is true for the current Republican administration as well with President Trump calling it "the worst deal ever" and "disastrous". While President Trump reluctantly certified Iran's compliance with the JCPOA for the first two required reporting periods, he refused to do so for the October 2017 reporting period despite the IAEA's certification of Iranian compliance through over 400 inspection and the advice from both the Secretary of Defense and the Secretary of State, punting the issue back to Congress to decide whether or not to reinstate U.S. sanctions against Iran. The administration claims that Iran has not complied with the "spirit" of the deal, citing language from the preamble, Iran's missile program and its support of Hezbollah. Indeed, it is supported by Republicans on the Hill in this perception of the deal [37]. Nevertheless, experts and the other parties to the JCPOA make clear that these additional issues were never part of the agreement and that Iran has resolved ambiguous provisions to the satisfaction of the Joint Commission set up to implement compliance with the agreement [38, 39]. As long as the U.S. does not violate the agreement by re-imposing sanctions unilaterally, the EU3, Russia and China have made clear their intention to salvage the agreement, arguing that Iran has clearly moved away from its nuclear program since the JCPOA took effect.

Both realists and constructivists analyses view these actions as destabilizing and question their usefulness for promoting North American strategic defense. Security dilemma sensitivity would entail recognizing the likely impact of the Trump administration's decertification on Iran's decisions and domestic politics. Realists already emphasize the impact of rescinding the JCPOA on uniting currently divided Iranian public behind the current regime [40]. Restraint in defining one's national interest would require dividing the nuclear concerns from other regional security concerns. Increasing the nuclear threat environment in the Middle East will not ameliorate the threats posed by state-sponsored terrorism or missile development. Re-imposing U.S. sanctions will not induce change on the part of Iran, but only weaken the ability of the U.S. to work with others to increase pressure on Iran on the remaining issues and make Iran (and others like North Korea) less likely to negotiate a compromise within the nuclear arena [40]. The U.S. has never been able to induce change in Iran unilaterally. Without support from European allies, Russia and China, the nuclear threat environment becomes more dangerous.

---

[2] Senate vote September 10, 2015 cannot overcome filibuster to have vote on disapproval of the Iran deal (58 voted for cloture against 42). House passed two resolutions Sept 10 and 11: the first HR 411 claiming that Pres Obama had not submitted all the elements of the plan as required by the Iran Nuclear Review Act; the second HR 3460 to prevent the U.S. from lifting the sanctions. The third HR 3461 failed to approve the Iran deal 162-269.

These concerns are only expanded through a constructivist lens. As Rathbun demonstrated, the legitimacy of the nuclear regime is under strain due to the differential treatment of nuclear and non-nuclear weapon states and particularly by the expansion of the differential treatment to enrichment technology, which was explicitly included in peaceful nuclear technology during the negotiations of the NPT [10]. In addition, as states pursue nuclear weapons within and outside of the nuclear nonproliferation regime, the norm deteriorates and further weakens the legitimacy of the regime. Holding Iran to different standards than others also weakens the regime, particularly following a successful multilateral diplomatic agreement. Without the underlying legitimacy of the nonproliferation regime and the NPT in particular, it is increasingly difficulty to achieve progress in nuclear nonproliferation. When combined with the strong realist concerns of overreaching and creation of conflict spirals, the logic of North American restraint is clear.

5 North Korea and the Failure of the Six Party Talks

The threat situation is North Korea is more dangerous to North American defense than Iran and may also be influenced by efforts to undermine the JCPOA deal. North Korea has continually presented a nuclear security threat as well as created concerns on its ballistic missile development and state sponsorship of terrorists. However, many assess that this threat has risen in 2017 to a direct security threat to North America, even as most believe North Korea's goals to be for deterrence [41]. Significant diplomatic engagement in the 1990s, combined with the Sunshine Policy between the two Koreas, allowed for stability, though it was unsuccessful in reducing the threat in the long-term. Renewed engagement during the six-party talks (2003–2009) was less successful in achieving stability, though the increasingly strong international cooperation in opposition to North Korea's increasingly belligerent behavior provides potential opportunities in the future. The most dangerous nuclear threat environment developed in the current period characterized by an absence of significant diplomatic engagement and increasingly belligerent rhetoric and behavior by both North Korea and the U.S., which not only threatens miscalculations and conflict spirals but also threatens the unity of the international community response to North Korea. The Iranian agreement provides a useful framework for considering future progress. While restraint has been less successful in achieving diplomatic breakthrough to date, it is still key to North American strategic defense according to both constructivist and realist lenses. More heavy reliance on the innovative layered institutions' defense of North America by NORAD, USNORTHCOM and CJOC can help prevent misperception and temper nationalist responses.

The comparison between the earlier U.S.-North Korean and JCPOA is particularly helpful for demonstrating the benefits of restraint. International agreement over the North Korean derogation from its nuclear nonproliferation obligations, joined with diplomatic engagement and restraint by the main parties, allowed for stability within the region for nearly a decade. Based on the North and South Korea agreement in 1992 to the Joint Declaration of the Denuclearization of the Korean Peninsula, forbidding either state from possessing uranium-enrichment and plutonium-separation facilities, together with the Agreed Framework between the U.S. and North Korea whereby North Korea froze and promised to dismantle its graphite-moderated reactor and related programs under IAEA inspectors in exchange for energy assistance and eventually assistance with two light-water reactors and heavy fuel from the U.S. While both were never fully observed nor implemented, they provided a key normative agreement for the international community to rally around. Similar to the situation in Iran, the nuclear agreement was easier to reach than a ballistic missile agreement. The U.S. and North Korea unsuccessful negotiations on halting North Korea's missile proliferation continued to bedevil the implementation of the Agreed Framework. North Korea progress in its nuclear weapons program was limited during this period according to the State Department and the CIA.

The situation deteriorated following President Bush's refusal to certify North Korean compliance and subsequent declaration of North Korean violation of the Agreed Framework in 2002. Since the agreement was bilateral without the strong snap-back sanctions, the international response was slower and more limited. North Korea expelled the IAEA inspectors, withdrew from the NPT, and restarted its nuclear program. The IAEA Board of Governors condemned North Korea's actions and referred North Korea to the UN Security Council, which expressed its concern of the situation [42].

Both realist and constructivist lenses prescribed restraint, combined with stronger international cooperation, which resulted in the six-party talks. Negotiations through the six-party talks, including the U.S., China, Russia, Japan, North Korea and South Korea, began in 2003 and continued until 2009, with periods of stalemate and crisis. The Agreed Framework had created a blue-print for future international negotiations, which had more potential if they included more interested parties. As today, the situation in the Korean peninsula was not conducive to military response according to realist analysis due to the immediate costs of any military action on both U.S. and South Korean troops and civilian populations, as well as possible expansion of the conflict regionally. North Korea continued to expand its nuclear weapons program without IAEA monitoring. Nevertheless, increasing international pressure encouraged parties to pursue restraint and a tentative agreement was reached through the six-party talks in September 2005. North Korea committed "to abandoning all nuclear weapons and existing nuclear programs," and returning to the NPT and IAEA safeguards, while the U.S. affirmed its peaceful intentions to North Korea and promised to coordinate the implemention of agreed-upon obligations and rewards [42, p. 15]. North Korea reaffirmed its right to peaceful uses of nuclear energy and the parties agreed to discuss the provision of light-water reactors to North Korea, though disagreements continued to block final agreement.

Similar to the situation in Iran, the North Korea signals were perceived differently. Nevertheless, the international community continued to strengthen and unify through multiple UN Security Council resolutions, which continually brought North Korea back to the negotiating table though always following more belligerent actions and more dangerous nuclear threat environments. After many false starts, a breakthrough in 2007 developed the action plan delineating the first steps for implementing the 2005 joint statement.[3] Following significant progress implementing the agreement, the six-party talks ended in stalemate due to disagreements on verification at the end of 2008, and disagreements between the U.S. and China and Russia regarding the steps necessary for energy assistance.

Following a familiar path, North Korea continued to respond in a spiraling manner to sanctions by the international community. This conflict spiral is precisely what realist scholars aim to avoid through restraint. The deterioration of the relations between North and South Korea has only exacerbated this situation. The conservative South Korean Presidents Lee Myung-bak (2008–2013) and Park Geun-hye (2013–2017) interpreted North Korean actions in an even more negative light, questioning the 1990s Sunshine Policy of engagement with North Korea and favoring pressure on the nuclear issue. Following tit-for-tat interactions, North Korea declared South Korea's participation in the U.S. Proliferation Security Initiative (in reaction to nuclear tests) an act of war and voided the 1953 Armistice Agreement, setting the stage for military spirals. North Korea also responded with increased bellicose actions, including the unveiling of a uranium enrichment plant and its own light-water reactor and firing artillery rounds at South Korea. The U.S. and South Korea engaged in large-scale joint military exercises.

Reassurance signals are particularly difficult to perceive following dramatic increases in tit-for-tat spiraling responses. The international community's role in assisting is crucial. While North Korea and China indicated interest in restarting the six-party talks, the U.S. and South Korea refused without North Korean indications of a commitment to denuclearization of the peninsula prior to multilateral talks. North Korea rejected any preconditions, yet it reaffirmed its willingness to consider a moratorium on the production and testing of nuclear weapon and missile during renewed six-party talks to restart dialog in 2011. Even following Kim Jong Il's death at the end of 2011, progress appeared to continue into 2012, though the agreement again fell apart following North Korea's ballistic missile development.

While the pattern appears similar with North Korea provocations leading to substantially more international cooperation and strengthened sanctions, the change in leadership in North Korea has worsened the situation, as Kim Jun Un appears significantly more dedicated to missile and nuclear weapon development than his father. To date, the international sanctions have not succeeded in returning North Korea to the negotiating table and the Obama administration's "strategic patience" has not led to renewed diplomatic success. Indeed, some criticize the Obama administration for holding too tightly to preconditions for multilateral talks [43, 44]. Yet, the precondition of a denuclearized Korean peninsula is required by the norms of the nonproliferation regime. Expansion of states with nuclear weapons undermines the norm and makes it more difficult to restrain other states from following the precedent [11, 45]. Here realists and constructivists part ways. Yet, it appears that an opportunity was missed to

---

[3] North Korea agreed to shut down its nuclear facilities at Yongbyon, provide a complete declaration of all nuclear programs, disable all existing nuclear facilities and allow IAEA inspections in exchange for 100,000 tons of heavy fuel and normalization of relations. In particular, the U.S. promised to remove North Korea from its list of state sponsors of terrorism and application of the Trading with the Enemy Act and unfreeze North Korean funds held in Banco Deltz Asia.

agree on a negotiated compromise before the massive investment of Kim Jun Un in both the missile and nuclear programs. The nuclear and missile technology advancements of the last several years make international negotiation more difficult, even in the face of unanimous UN Security Council resolutions expanding the scope of sanctions and financial asset freezes, renewed Chinese concern and U.S. and South Korean stronger military ties. North Korea's response worsened the threat environment by continuing expanding missile tests. South Korean and the U.S. announced the installation of Terminal Altitude Area Defense battery (THAAD) to defend against North Korean ballistic missiles. North Korea continued its nuclear tests in September 2016, with its fifth and largest test, and the on-going barrage of various types of missile tests.

The current situation presents significant challenges for the international community and the U.S. 2017 has seen the worst deterioration of the security situation in the Korean peninsula. Tit-for-tat responses continue the escalation of the threat environment following the move away from restraint by the Trump administration, the installation of the THAAD missile defense system and North Korea's ICBM test. Renewed international cooperation, including multiple unanimous UNSC resolutions, has failed to halt North Korea's increasing rapid progress on missile and nuclear weapon development. The rhetoric on both sides increased in bellicosity in August and September 2017. Yet, North Korea tested its first likely successful thermonuclear weapon in September 2017. The U.S. and South Korea have responded with strengthened military exercises, accelerated deployment of the THAAD system following significant disagreements between the U.S. and South Korea, and increasingly destructive missile warheads in South Korea [46]. Analysts expect that North Korea will achieve nuclear-tipped ICBM capability with the ability to reach North America in 2018 [41].

Diplomacy, though difficult following successive failures and more provocative actions by North Korea, increasingly appears to be the best policy choice. The U.S. and South Korea no longer agree on a policy of non-engagement and pressure, following the election of liberal President Moon Jae-in [47]. This change provides more evidence for our research that the liberal side of the political spectrum is more likely to respond to North Korean signals more readily than the conservative side. A strong U.S.-South Korean alliance is key for any stabilization of the situation on the Korean peninsula, thus instigating change in the U.S. position. The recent reintroduction of North and South Korean talks over the Olympics and confidence building measures and military to military connections, severed in 2016, prevents dangerous miscommunications and miscalculations and allow for the beginning de-escalation of the situation. The international community must participate to encourage North Korean change. Both China and Russia have pushed for security assurances and a halting of South Korean-U.S. military exercises in return for North Korean freeze of nuclear and missile tests. The Iran Deal demonstrated the potential for effective sanctions to bring parties to the negotiation table, but only if there is strong international cooperation. Temporary halts to military exercises and renewed contact and confidence building measures could strengthen international cooperation. While this may not lead to success in the near term, it would follow realist prescriptions of de-escalation and crisis management in situations where no successful military option exists. Refraining from reaction may be one of the most difficult choices to make, particularly in highly publicized conflict. Nevertheless, it is the pragmatic choice given the strategic situation and the normative importance of multilateral action.

6   North American Defense

The nuclear threat environment is dangerous and unstable, creating risk for North America. The dangers of conflict spirals and overreach are significant. In such situations, both realists and constructivists prescribe restraint. But, restraint is hard. Stepping away from a tit-for-tat situation is not a natural human reaction, and signals of reassurance are often missed. Pressures to do something, even if there are no good policy options, propel decision-makers. The key takeaway for policy-makers is that they must be as aware as possible about the psychological dynamics of themselves *and* their adversary. Our analysis calls for an objectivity about subjectivity. Practitioners must be honest with themselves about how they are responding to others *and* how others actually see them, an often painful process that Jervis has long reminded us is a difficult task and empirically rare. We normally assume that if a party interested in cooperation sends a costly signal of reassurance, given the obvious intent behind the policy concession, we can make a judgment about the cooperativeness of the recipient based on its response. If it reciprocates, the adversary has underlying cooperative intentions; if it does not, it is belligerent. Yet, this is likely premature given the difficulty in reaching restraint and the likelihood of misperception in conflict situations.

Psychological research has demonstrated that adversaries tend to underreact to reassurance signals, not overreact, as our research supports. Adversaries rarely interpret reassurance signals as lack of resolve, since they fail to credit those signals [25]. Signals of reassurance are often perceived as wily moves to trick one (as can be seen with perceptions of the Iran deal), rather than as signaling a weakness. Humans use emotions to interpret capabilities [27]. Emotional beliefs about the danger posed by material capaibilities are difficult to change. At the same time, our research shows that in the aggregate, opinion does shift in the direction of updating to incorporate the new information. This indicates that multiple, perhaps unreciprocated, costly signals of reassurance might be necessary to convince motivated skeptics. Coordinated signals from multiple actors, for example those protecting North America, may assist. We believe that even skeptics are capable of updating, albeit at a slower pace. Successful reassurance requires a series of larger costly signals, in addition to a process of small, confidence-building measures and, most importantly, requires a more forgiving strategy than tit-for-tat. The JCPOA deal was difficult to achieve and should not be thrown away due to outside concerns or even low level possible compliance issues. The crisis on the Korean peninsula would look very different had the Agreed Framework not been abandoned due to tit-for-tat strategies. Of course, signals of reassurance entail risk, though they are significantly less likely to be perceived as weakness or irresolve than we think. Yet, even when restraint and reassurance fails, it does not mean that it was the wrong policy choice. We must also continually keep in mind the risk entailed in the policy alternatives.

Policies to increase military capabilities can reduce security through the security dilemma dynamic. Prudence entails risk too. Developing military capabilities to destroy a first strike with some degree of certainty involve new BMD technologies. One's adversary perceives those actions as increasing its insecurity by reducing the deterrent value of its weapons. Those very actions to increase our (our adversary's) security are perceived as an increasing threat by our adversary (us). Nuclear deterrence, though involving more restraint than pre-emption, can develop into conflict spirals through escalating tit-for-tat security strategies. Yet, existing U.S. nuclear capabilities should already provide deterrence in both these nuclear threat environments. When pre-emption and prevention fail, as in the case of North Korea, a restrained deterrence combined with diplomacy remains a stable policy choice, particularly when knowledge of psychological dynamics are incorporated. Restraint in the North Korean case requires restraining military responses and curbing actions that imply a U.S. willingness to use nuclear weapons against North Korea, restraining South Korea from pursuing an independent nuclear capability, and reducing the chances for low level military conflicts escalating [45]. To the degree that the THAAD system provides a potential protection from a North Korean nuclear attack, it enhances security. However, to the degree that it creates stress on the U.S.-China relationship–the key relationship for international cooperation—and is perceived by North Korea as increasing the U.S. threat or permitting preemption, it reduces security. The same is true for North American BMD. It can provide more room for restraint by reducing the perceived threat posed by rising nuclear powers. However, should it be perceived as threatening the fundamental second strike capability of Russia, and to a lesser degree China, the unintended consequences of undermining mutually assured destruction may make international cooperation to restrain nuclear proliferation only more elusive. This suggests that substantial increases in BMD resources and technological development are unnecessary and potentially dangerous—in direct opposition to many BMD analyses [48].

The threat environment creates many dangers for North America. History has shown that humans engage in conflict spirals that lead to less security for all. Yet, it is hard to follow the security dilemma prescriptions due to emotions and misperceptions. The layered institutional framework for North American strategic defense provides a potential advantage to avoiding the misperceptions rife in international relations. By more overtly relying on the multiple interlacing institutions charged with protecting North America—USNORTHCOM, NORAD and CJOC—policy makers can benefit from multiple interpretations of signals, as well as coordinate reassurance and restraint signals, potentially weakening the security dilemma dynamic.

References

1. Waltz K (1998) The origins of war in neorealist theory. J Interdiscip Hist 18(4):615–628
2. Gholz E, Press D, Sapolsky H (1997) Come home, america: the strategy of restraint in the face of temptation. Int Secur 21(4):5–48
3. Morgenthau H (1948) Politics among nations: the struggle for power and peace. Knopf, New York

4. Mearsheimer J, Walt W (2003) Keeping saddam hussein in a box. New York Times, 2 Feb 2003
5. Onea T (2017) Immoderate greatness: is great power restraint a practical grand strategy? Eur J Int Secur 2(1):111–132
6. Carr EH (1964) The twenty years' crisis. Macmillan, London
7. Price R (1997) The chemical weapons taboo. Cornell University Press, Ithaca, NY
8. Tannenwald N (1999) The nuclear taboo: the united states and the normative basis of nuclear non-use. Int Org 53(3):433–468
9. Risse-Kappen T (1995) Cooperation among nations. Princeton University Press, Princeton
10. Rathbun NS (2014) Glass half full? evaluating the impact of new U.S. policy on the legitimacy of the nuclear nonproliferation regime. In: Fields J (ed), State behavior and nuclear nonproliferation regime. University of Georgia, Atlanta, pp 40–83
11. Rathbun NS (2006) The role of legitimacy in strengthening the nuclear nonproliferation regime. Nonproliferation Rev 13(2):227–252
12. Risse T (2000) 'Let's argue!': communicative action in world politics. Int Org 54(1):1–39
13. Trachtenberg M (2003) The question of realism. Secur Stud 13(1):156–194
14. Jervis R (1978) Cooperation under the security dilemma. World Polit 30(2):167–214
15. Herz JJ (1950) Idealist internationalism and the security dilemma. World Polit 2(2):157–180
16. Glaser C (2010) Rational theory of international politics: the logic of competition and cooperation. Princeton University Press, Princeton
17. Glaser C (1994) Realists as optimists: cooperation as self-help. Int Secur 19(3):53–60
18. Jervis R (1976) Perception and misperception in international politics. Princeton University Press, Princeton
19. Schelling T (1985) What went wrong with arms control? Foreign Aff 64(2):219–233
20. Schelling T (1966) Arms and influence. Yale University Press, New Haven
21. Meinecke F (1957) Machiavellianism: the doctrine of raison d'etat and its place in modern history. Yale University Press, New Haven
22. Jervis R, Lebow RN, Stein JG (1989) Psychology and deterrence. John Hopkins University Press, Baltimore
23. Breslauer GW, Tetlock PE (eds) (1991) Learning in U.S. and soviet foreign policy. Westview Press, Boulder, CO
24. Tetlock PE (1998) Social psychology and world politics. Handb Soc Psychol 4:868–914
25. Mercer J (1996) Reputation and international politics. Cornell University Press, Cornell
26. Yarhi-Milo K (2014) Knowing the adversary: leaders, intelligence, and assessment of intentions in international relations. Princeton University Press, Princeton
27. Mercer J (2010) Emotional beliefs. Int Org 64(1):1–31
28. Holmes M (2015) Believing this and alieving that: theorizing affect and intuitions in international politics. Int Stud Quart 59(4):706–720
29. Davenport K (2017) Timeline of nuclear diplomacy with Iran. Arms Control Association Fact Sheets (Sep)
30. Fitzpatrick M (2015) Iran: a good deal. Survival 57(5):47–52
31. Rathbun BC, Kertzer JD, Reifler J, Goren P, Scotto TJ (2016) Taking foreign policy personally: personal values and foreign policy attitudes. Int Stud Quart 60(1):124–137
32. Chittick WO, Billingsley KR, Travis R (1995) A three-dimensional model of american foreign policy beliefs. Int Stud Quart 39(3):313–331
33. Nincic M, Ramos JM (2010) Ideological structure and foreign policy preferences. J Polit Ideol 15(2):119–141
34. Rathbun BC (2007) Hierarchy and community at home and abroad: evidence of a common structure of domestic and foreign policy beliefs in american elites. J Conflict Resolut 51 (3):379–407

35. Holsti OR, Rosenau JN (1988) The domestic and foreign policy beliefs of american leaders. J Conflict Resolut 32(2):248–294

36. Holsti OR, Rosenau JN (1990) The structure of foreign policy attitudes among american leaders. J Polit 52(1):94–125

37. Royce E (2017) Opening statement of the honorable ed royce (R-CA), chairman house foreign affairs committee hearing: 'confronting the full range of iranian threats.' Testimony before U.S. House of Representatives Committee on Foreign Affairs, 11 Oct 2017. https:// foreignaffairs.house.gov/hearing/hearing-confronting-full-range-iranian-threats/

38. Sullivan J (2017) Statement by jake sullivan to house foreign affairs committee hearing: 'confronting the full range of iranian threats.' Testimony before U.S. House of Representatives Committee on Foreign Affairs, 11 Oct 2017. https://foreignaffairs.house.gov/hearing/ hearing-confronting-full-range-iranian-threats/

39. Blanc J, Acton J (2017) The trump administration and the Iran nuclear deal: analysis of noncompliance claims, Carnegie Endowment for International Peace, 12 Oct 2017. http:// carnegieendowment.org/2017/10/12/trump-administration-and-iran-nuclear-deal-analysis-of-noncompliance-claims-pub-73214

40. Sadiadpour K (2017) Why donald trump's new Iran policy is united Tehran while dividing the world. Carnegie Endowment for Peace, 27 Oct 2017

41. McInnis KJ, Feickert A, Manyi ME, Hildreth SA, Nikitin MD, Chanlett-Avery E (2017) The north korean nuclear challenge: military options and issues for congress. Congressional Research Service Report R44994

42. Davenport K (2017) Chronology of U.S.-North Korean nuclear and missile diplomacy. Arms Control Association Fact Sheet, pp 1–36, Sep 2017

43. Kimball D, Davenport K (2017) Recalibrating U.S. policy towards North Korea. Arms Control Associate Issue Brief, 9(1)

44. Thielmann G (2016) North Korea's nuclear threat: how to stop its slow but steady advance. Arms Control Association Threat Assessment Brief, 19 Feb 2016

45. Jackson V (2017) Deterring a nuclear-armed adversary in a contested regional order: the 'trilemma' of U.S.-North Korean relations. Asia Policy 23:97–103

46. Lee S, Swantroem N, Forss A (2017) Containing crisis on the korean peninsula. Institute for security & development policy policy brief no. 201, pp 1–3

47. Choi K (2017) Prospects for U.S.-ROK alliance: returning to the old days or marching to the future? Asia Policy 24:19–25

48. Karako T, Williams I, Rumbaugh W (2017) Missile defense 2020: next steps for defending the homeland. The Center for Strategic and International Studies

Challenges and Contradictions: Mexico and the US in North American Security Cooperation

Abelardo Rodríguez Sumano[(⊠)]

Universidad Iberoamericana, AC, México, México
abelardo.rodriguez@ibero.mx

Abstract. Mexico approaches the future of the strategic defence of North America with an historical legacy and contemporary concerns markedly different than those of the US and Canada. Throughout much of its history the US–Mexico relationship has moved cyclically between divergence and convergence based on asymmetric interdependence of power and a distinctive notion of threats. Nevertheless, there is a deep, albeit not entirely uniform, perception in Mexico that the US is an external threat to Mexico's national security. Recent statements and policies emanating from Washington have re-kindled these sentiments. The historical legacy of Mexico's involvement with the US in particular is essential in understanding how Mexico deals with what it nevertheless acknowledges as the need for increased collaboration on defence and security, bilaterally and trilaterally, with its two regional neighbours. The approach that it takes to this collaboration, in an uncertain global environment, must remain consistent with its national and regional interests, ensuring a clear respect for Mexico's sovereignty and role in the world. In explaining how Mexico approaches these difficult North American security challenges, this chapter draws upon the conceptual lens of Regional Security Complex Theory. It examines the difficulties that Mexico experiences in contributing to regional security. The chapter analyses the role of US hegemony, the strategic relationship between Canada, Mexico, and the US, and the asymmetric and historical differences in political culture and institutions among these North American neighbors.

1 Introduction

Mexico approaches the future of the strategic defence of North America with an historical legacy and contemporary concerns markedly different than those of the US and Canada. Throughout much of its history the US–Mexico relationship has moved cyclically between divergence and convergence based on asymmetric interdependence of power and a distinctive notion of threats. Nevertheless, there is a deep, albeit not entirely uniform, perception in Mexico that the US is an external threat to Mexico's national security, and at least partly responsible for its internal problems of drugs, violence and crime. Recent statements and policies emanating from Washington have re-kindled these sentiments. With the notable exception of some concern and criticism regarding Canadian mining companies threatening natural resources and the health of those close to the operations, Canada has not figured significantly, favourably or unfavourably, in Mexico's foreign or domestic security policy problems. The historical legacy of Mexico's involvement with the US in particular is essential in understanding how Mexico deals with what it nevertheless acknowledges as the need for increased collaboration on defence and security, bilaterally and trilaterally, with its two regional neighbours. The approach that it takes to this collaboration, in an uncertain global environment, must remain consistent with its national and regional interests, ensuring a clear respect for Mexico's sovereignty, culture and role in the world.

In explaining how Mexico approaches these difficult North American security challenges, this chapter draws upon the conceptual lens of Regional Security Complex Theory. It examines the difficulties —internal and external— that Mexico experiences in contributing to regional security. The chapter analyses the role of US hegemony, the strategic relationship between Canada, Mexico, and the US, and the asymmetric and historical differences in political culture and institutions among these North American neighbors.

In international relations the Regional Security Complex Theory is one of the best epistemic frameworks for explaining the depth and autonomy of the regional dynamics of states, and linking local issues with global dynamics [1]. The theory allows for the specification of differences and roles in countries that comprise a region, the relevance of the contents and epicenters of their sovereign identity, their historical formation, the size of the country, territory, population, and natural resources. In doing so, Regional Security Complex Theory delineates actors in world politics into five levels: super-powers, great powers, regional powers, the state, and the local, as well as highlighting the way in which they interact in the international system. In addition, the theory demonstrates how the relationship between regions and superpowers can define the evolution of an entire international system, as well as the immediate locale.

Regional Security Complex Theory also represents an evolution from the state level analysis that prevailed during the Cold War. This approach was challenged by *Security: A New Framework for Analysis*, which divided the concept of security into five sectors: political, economic, military, societal, and environmental, and outlines the core drivers of state security:

> Security interdependence is markedly more intense among states inside such complexes than with states outside them. Security complexes are about the relative intensity of interstate security relations that lead to distinctive regional patterns shaped by both the distribution of power and historical relations of amity and enmity. A security complex is defined as a set of states whose major security perceptions and concerns are so interlinked that their national security problems cannot reasonably be analyzed or resolved apart from one another. The formative dynamics and structure of a security complex are generated by the states within that complex—by their security perceptions of, and interactions with, each other. [1, p. 8]

Kilroy, Rodríguez and Hataley applied this theory to relations among Canada, Mexico, and the US [2]. The explanatory power of the Regional Security Complex Theory allows us to understand that, despite differences in size and institutional development, the countries of North America need to cooperate in regional security as the cost of not doing so would be so great that it would erode the national security of each state. From a Mexican perspective, this was not easy as the historical practice and theory of the concept of national security involves distrust of the US, not interdependence, despite the North American Free Trade Agreement (NAFTA) and the Security and Prosperity Partnership of North America. Although the regional approach is practiced in Mexico, there is no consensus on it among national security policy makers and it does not appear in National Security Law (2005).

2 From the Regional Complex to the US Security Perimeter

In the wake of the terrorist attacks of September 11th, 2001, there was discussion, mainly originating in the US, about a new North American security perimeter in the context of wider discussions of the trilateral Security and Prosperity Partnership (SPP) [3]. In effect, the concept of a US security perimeter was born out of a revision to the Pentagon Unified Command Plan that created US Northern Command (USNORTHCOM), whose Area of Responsibility (AOR) included the continental US, Mexico, parts of the northern Caribbean, and Canada [4]. As a unilateral US move, the establishment of USNORTHCOM prompted some misgivings regarding implications for sovereignty on the part of Canada and Mexico, yet both countries have developed ah-hoc cooperative arrangements with the new American command.

At a 2011 conference on *Common Agendas and Differences in the Security of North America* held at the Mexican Navy's Center for Superior Naval Studies in Mexico City [5], the consensus among the diplomatic representatives of the three countries was that, collectively, the North America southern border was in Central America and the Caribbean. While the representatives of Canada pointed out the strategic relationship it has shared with the US since 1958, the armed forces of Washington and Ottawa also pointed out the common interests they have with Mexico by sharing a continent, terrestrial and maritime borders, as well as a free trade agreement [6]. This was not understood very well in Mexico, partly because of the structural differences between the Navy Secretariat—which is more liberal and international—and the National Defense Secretariat—which is more introverted and conservative. The Mexican armed forces therefore arrived divided to the trilateral meeting in Mexico City in 2011. The National Defense Secretariat, consistent with its doctrine that the US is the "historical enemy," even sought to ensure that Mexico would not hold this meeting. However, the Navy Secretariat managed to convince the Office of the President to make the trilateral seminar happen, demonstrating that the role of Mexico in North American security had not been defined, even within the country itself.

However, during the government of President Enrique Peña Nieto (2012–2018) the armed forces have sought to build a consensus between the Navy Secretariat and the National Defense Secretariat in order to specify the relationship between the US and Mexican national security [7]. Nevertheless, Mexico currently lacks a comprehensive doctrine on national and regional security that regulates the role of the armed forces in foreign defense and internal security beyond this administration.

3 The US, Hegemony and the Weight of History

From its founding up until the early years of the 20th century, the main security concerns of the US were quite narrow, limited primarily to the "safety of its northern and southern borders and the preservation of the Union" [8], notwithstanding the country's claims to universalism and its impulse towards territorial expansion [9, p. 144].

The new Republic first broke with Great Britain; second, it consolidated a political system with its own identity; third, it established temporary strategic alliances with France and Spain; fourth, it unsuccessfully tried to annex British Canada in 1776 and in 1812. However, after a war with Mexico, it annexed Texas, Arizona, New Mexico, and California and this expansionist project also endowed the US with support and legitimacy from its society.

The purchase of Louisiana (1804) and Florida (1819) were followed by the Monroe Doctrine (1823), which gave US security a hemispheric perspective that promoted the independence of new states within the region while opposing the future expansion of European territorial claims and influence. This approach was applied to Germany and Japan in World War II, to the Soviet Union during the Cold War, and is evident with regard to Chinese influence today. After the Spanish-American War (1898), the US established its presence as a major world power. It also improved its strategic relationship with Great Britain creating an informal Anglo-American entente.

4 Ottawa, Washington, and Mexico

Canada reacted to the creation and expansionist tendencies of the United States with a counter-revolutionary and pro-British movement. Subsequently, it secured its historical and cultural roots with the construction of a parliamentary-type political system, supported by the British Crown, to configure the Prime Minister's authority and decisions on security and foreign policy [10, p. 103]. Through this approach Canada has managed to define an identity that is based on both its British and French roots. That definition of identity has allowed it to specify interests and build its own institutions with a strong social base of backing and support for its sovereignty.

Early threats to that sovereignty from the United States abated by the beginning of the 20th century as US expansionist designs gave way to benign indifference toward Canada and a slow but steady atmosphere of cordial co-existence. This was aided by a growing Anglo-American entente and alliance in the two world Wars. In the post-1945 era Canada, with strong executive leadership and broad public support, entered close collective defense arrangements with the United States through the binational (US–Canada) North American Aerospace Defense Command (NORAD) and the multinational, transatlantic North Atlantic Treaty Organization (NATO). In stark contrast Mexico did not enter into this type of formal institutional strategic cooperation with the US.

The US–Canada defense relationship is based in part on two democratic civil-military traditions [11]. In the case of Canada and the US, the civil authorities are very strong and enjoy wide renown within society. In Mexico, it is currently unthinkable that a civilian could direct the National Defense Secretariat or the Navy Secretariat. However, since 1946 the president, who is also the Commander in Chief of the armed forces, has been civilian. However, in Mexico there is also a balance of power between the armed forces and the civilian presidents as part of the unwritten rules of the balance of power within the Mexican government; this balance of power forms part of an authoritarian system. In the administration of President Enrique Peña Nieto:

> The National Defense Secretariat plays an essential role within the context of the federation's external defense, in order to preserve the integrity, independence, and sovereignty of the nation; as well as to contribute to the internal security of the country in order to maintain the constitutional order and strengthen democratic institutions. [12]

Historically, in Mexico, the main concern is with internal security and neither the Sectorial Program of National Defense nor the National Security Law define a strategic, operational, or tactical link with the US [13, p. 1–2]. However, within the framework of the National Security Program that regulates all civil and military structures in the country, the strategic importance of the region is recognized:

> In this context, North America is the region with which Mexico has made the greatest efforts of institutional cooperation and intelligence information exchange in the last two decades. Our country has established a series of bilateral cooperation mechanisms with the United States of multidimensional scope, among which the following stand out: (1) the 21st Century Border Initiative, (2) the Mexico—US Border Health Commission, (3) the Border 2020 program, (4) the Joint Working Committee on Auto Transport, (5) the Working Group on Cooperation in the Administration of Emergencies in the Case of Natural Disasters and Accidents, and (6) the Binational Bridges and Border Crossings group, among others. At the trilateral level, Mexico also sustains, along with the United States and Canada, the North American Plan for Avian and Pandemic Influenza, and the set of cooperation and consultation mechanisms provided for in the North American Free Trade Agreement. [14]

Despite tensions in the political field, the military-to-military relationship between Mexico and the US has deepened over the last year. If the political leadership of Mexico began to stress greater nationalism, however, this would impact the position of the armed forces, given their need to respond to their Commander in Chief.

5   Mexico and the Exposed Memories of the Past

Unlike Canada in 1776 and 1812, Mexico did lose territory to the US. After the separation of Texas in 1836 and its annexation to the United States in 1845, the recognition of Texan independence by Washington led to a war with Mexico the following year. This was devastating for Mexico, since it lost about 55% of its territory in the 1848 Treaty of Guadalupe Hidalgo and about 80,000 Mexican citizens were left on the US side of the new border. The impact of Mexico on the US went far beyond territorial extension, as this sowed the seeds for the growth of a Hispanic population and border culture in the US.

While American annexation of Mexican territory ended in 1853 [15, p. 76], political and economic interventions did not stop until 1928, when Mexico found political and economic stability.[1] When the Mexican Revolution (1910–1928) broke out and the stability and political control of the Porfirian dictatorship (1876–1911) was broken, the US made numerous attempts to intervene in Mexican politics, ultimately resulting in foreign and domestic policies that inculcated a strong sense of Mexican nationalism.

In 1943, the Mexican Doctrine of War was born, which, notwithstanding a limited participation by Mexican forces in the Pacific war, argued for national security and national defense against the US [16]. It establishes that Mexico will never seek war with its neighbor, except in exceptional situations and when territorial independence and national sovereignty are at stake. Thus, in terms of foreign and domestic policy, national security, and defense, as well as in education and culture, the basis has been nationalism and the "historical enemy" the US. That policy legitimized an authoritarian government until the massacre of students in 1968, which resulted in a change towards democratization. However, it was not until the end of the Cold War, when President Carlos Salinas de Gortari pushed for integration with the US, that nationalism was revived on the left and within the armed forces.

Since 1994, when NAFTA was introduced, opinion in Mexico on the relationship that the country should seek with the US has been divided. First, the most technocratic and liberal sector, accepted integration with the US and Canada as part of a kind of manifest destiny. Second, the nationalist left and military sectors, did not abandon their distrust and resentment of the US. A third group based in academia and the intelligentsia shared some of the views of the technocratic liberals and the nationalist left and the military, but which believes that it is always better to engage in dialogue and cooperate for regional security than to break with the world. For each group, the arrival of Donald Trump to the White House is a clear reminder that Mexican domestic and foreign policy interests can be undermined by US policy.[2]

6 The Anarchy of the International System and the Challenge of Proximity: Threats Travel More Easily Over Short Distances Than Over Long Ones

The US was required to develop special relations with Mexico and Canada during World War I, World War II, the Cold War, the post-Cold War, and the post-September 11th era for the sake of its national interests. In each case, the threat originated from outside North America, but Washington realized that neglecting the neighborhood could threaten security at home. In the first case, Germany sought to counter US support for Britain by promising Berlin's support for the recovery of Mexico's lost territories [17]. In World War II, Washington built two special relationships, one with Ottawa and one with Mexico City, in order to secure the US homeland. In the Cold

---

[1] There are other versions arguing that the CIA intervened in Mexico during the Cold War. See, for example, Morley, J. (2008) *Our Man in Mexico: Winston Scott and the Hidden History of the CIA.* USA: University of Kansas.

[2] This is a real factor, taken seriously by the Mexican Armed Forces.

War, Canada and the US built a common defense system in order to deter the Soviet Union. And Mexico's presidents were very close to Washington in the fight against the guerrillas, students and any dissident movement that could be understood as post-communist, despite their nationalist rhetoric [18]. From the end of the Cold War until the arrival of Donald Trump, Mexico, the US, and Canada saw a convergence of interests, regardless of their differences and, especially in the case of US–Mexican relations, the problems of drug trafficking and illegal migration.

Because of geographic proximity, challenges to national, binational, and regional security can arise over short distances and within limited time frames. That is one of the keys to the explanatory power of the Regional Security Complex Theory: threats travel more quickly through countries that share geography.

The regional complex also identifies threats that come from other regions or continents. Complexity arises when local threats combine with global hazards that seek to harm one or more members of the regional complex. When there is convergence among member countries, agreements can be made to combat them. However, when there is divergence and differing perception of threats, conflict arises, not least because criteria that help securitize common threats in the regional security complex are lacking. In spite of this, and in the context of hostile rhetoric towards Mexico in the US, NORAD, USNORTHCOM, and the Mexican Air Force have coordinated the interception of aircraft that traffic illicit products across the common border between the two countries.

There are, however, doubts that this trilateral cooperation could advance beyond the fight against organized crime. Nevertheless, it is not impossible that the detection of early threats regarding terrorism, natural disasters, and the trafficking of guns, radioactive materials, and weapons of mass destruction may be sponsored by the Navy Secretariat and perhaps later by the National Defense Secretariat.

7 Amity or Enmity Among Neighbors

With NAFTA, the SPP, and the North American Leadership Summits, it was thought that differences and mistrust among the political elites of Canada, the US, and Mexico could be overcome. Notwithstanding these efforts to deepen social and commercial interdependence, in reality, distrust between the three countries has never fully disappeared. Canada does not forget 1812 and Mexico 1846–47. Implicitly, the current security systems of Canada and Mexico are built on the respective states' perceptions of history, despite their deep economic and commercial interdependence with the US. Moreover, there are two bilateral relationships in North America that are expressed in diametrically different ways. On the one hand, the Canada-US relationship is one of privileged interaction. On the other, the Mexico-US relationship is based on the context of conflict and cooperation. There is also a deep distrust of Mexico in some sectors of Canada, with the position being maintained that the special relationship between Canada and the US should be privileged instead of following the road towards trilateralism, despite economic interdependence (NAFTA) and the transnational nature of many threats [19].

Canada's hesitancy about trilateralism can be at least partly understood in the light of the structural lags in economic and social development, corruption and impunity that make Mexico a somewhat less than attractive partner nation for helping to build a stable neighborhood in North America. Canada cannot heal Mexico's problems, nor all of the disagreements between Mexico and the US. Nor should it try. But perhaps a more active role on Canada's part in fostering greater continental defense cooperation, one which draws upon Ottawa's long and largely successful expertise in managing security relations with the U.S., notwithstanding problems in other policy areas, can be of value. Such an effort might well foster a more professional, cordial and functional, if not always entirely amicable, trilateralism that can effectively address current and future challenges to North American strategic defense.

8   Homeland Defense and Homeland Security

Although former Secretary of State Rex Tillerson and former Secretary of Homeland Security John Kelly—now the White House Chief of Staff—have sought more con-ciliatory rhetoric with Mexico, the reality is that the campaign and inauguration of President Trump have positioned the country as an adversary. Likewise, in the context of risks to US national security and homeland security, there is a perception of threats from the Caribbean and Central America that use Mexico as a springboard to enter the US. Its homeland security policy focuses on the border and covers the level of inci-dence in Mexico and its southern border. It also puts pressure on exit controls and the expulsion of populations from the Caribbean, the Andes, and Central America for the sake of regional security.

In spite of these growing political tensions, military cooperation is closer than ever, not least because the militaries of both countries demonstrate a level of commitment to regional security. This is evident not least in the US Northern and Southern Com-mands' sponsorship of the Central American Security Conference 2017 at Cozumel, Quintana Roo, which was hosted by Navy Secretary Vidal Francisco Soberón and National Defense Secretary General Salvador Cienfuegos Zepeda [20].

Nevertheless, the White House is pushing for greater controls to deal with what it sees as major threats to American national security. The problem is that the trend in the current political era towards divergence presents difficulties in ensuring the exchange of information and intelligence with Mexico, the Caribbean, Central America, and the Andes due to the growing distrust in Mexico and the rest of the region. For example, while Mexico has been prepared to cooperate with the US in addressing issues such as organized crime, its government finds it unacceptable that Washington does not fully consider its responsibility for the criminal activities that have proliferated, at least in part, because of the failure of the US to curb gun sales and illicit money flows along the US–Mexican border. Most recently, the Trump administration is viewed as a threat to Mexico's national security, despite the fact of the current US–Mexico collaboration in military to military affairs.

9 Conclusion

Key within Regional Security Complex Theory is the role of the hegemon. In this case, the hegemon is the US. Current political trends have reopened past wounds for Mexico. However, as the neighbor of the superpower, it must find a way to live with Washington. Compared to Canada, Mexico has a major disadvantage in its relationship with the US: linguistic, cultural, and political differences that are ancestral and foundational. Although Canada also differs from the US on these axes, the differences are far less extreme. Most importantly, in profound contrast to Mexico, Canada approaches security relations in North America as a solid member of, and frequently active participant in, the broader American-led Western, liberal-democratic formal and informal collective defense system. Indeed, for Ottawa, North American security is in many ways the logical, if avoidable, regional manifestation of its global outlook. Adjusting to, cooperating with, and taking advantage of American hegemony is a skill Canadians have learned to master. Adding security relations with Mexico to this diplomatic repertoire has required something of an adjustment.

Nevertheless, geographic proximity, economic interdependence, and the movement of goods and persons require the region's three countries to constantly rethink their cooperation and security mechanisms. In the midst of these transformations, the armed forces of North America have improved communication and sought a common agenda, despite their differences. Notably, Mexico's armed forces have continued their dialogue, collaboration, and coordination with NORAD and the Northern Command. The Navy Secretariat has been the most active in this transformation, followed, with deep reservations, by the National Defense Secretariat.

The maintenance of the coordination and dialogue around defense is, to a large extent, dependent on stability and consistency in other areas of the social and political spectrum. In particular, if the White House is to build a positive relationship with Mexico, it must remain conscious of the importance of national sovereignty for Mexico in general, and its armed forces in particular. In effect, respect for national sovereignty is the key to cooperation between the two states. This is made even more acute by the current trend toward nationalism that is prevalent in Mexican society, and the consequent need for Mexican politicians to respond to demands for an energetic response to US policy that is seen to be against Mexican interests.

Although the lasting effect of President Trump's policies remains to be seen, in the context of the current US administration the perception among Mexicans that the US is a reliable partner is diminishing. Despite this, Mexico continues to cooperate with the US, but this distrust will become increasingly destabilizing if it is not addressed. As appears to be the case with Canada, any breakup of NAFTA seems likely to have spill-over effects on defense and security relationships. Should the US pull out of the deal, it is difficult to envisage Mexico engaging in North American regional defense without, at the very least, major reservations. This explains why Mexico's military doctrines are still based on its historical experiences, and this past includes disruptive conflict with the US.

Mexico's challenge is to work jointly with the United States and Canada to respond to a diverse array of security threats, even in the context of deep differences between the societies and political elites that military-to-military dialogue cannot totally overcome. Unless Mexico feels that it is able to trust the US, the fissures between the two states will become a North American vulnerability, reducing the ability of all three of North America's constituent states to maintain a robust and effective strategic defense.

References

1. Buzan B, Waever O, De Wilde J (1997) Security: a new framework for analysis. Lynne Rienner Publishers Inc, Boulder, Colorado
2. Kilroy R, Rodríguez Sumano A, Hataley T (2012) North American regional security: a trilateral framework?. Lynne Rienner Publishers Inc, Boulder, Colorado
3. Kilroy R (2007) Perimeter defense and regional security cooperation in North America: United States, Canada, and Mexico. Homel Secur Aff J. https://www.hsaj.org/articles/138. Accessed 8 Feb 2018
4. Department of Defense (2002) Special briefing on the unified command plan. http://www.defenselink.mil/transcripts/2002/t04172002_t0417sd.html. Accessed 8 Feb 2018
5. Rodríguez Sumano A (2012) Agendas Comunes y Diferencias en la seguridad de América del Norte, ¿de dónde venimos?, ¿dónde estamos? y "¿a dóndequeremosir? Centro de EstudiosSuperiores Navales de la Armada de México, Universidad de Guadalajara, Mexico
6. Lieutenant General Walter Semianiw, Commander, Canada Command (2012) Cooperación militar de Canadá enAmérica del Norte. In: Rodríguez Sumano A (ed) Agendas Comunes y Diferencias en la seguridad de América del Norte, ¿de dónde venimos?, ¿dónde estamos? y "¿a dónde queremos ir? Centro de Estudios Superiores Navales de la Armada de México, Universidad de Guadalajara, Mexico, pp 288
7. Gobierno de la República (2014) Plan nacional de desarrollo 2013–2018 programa sectorial de defensanacional 2013–2018. http://www.hacienda.gob.mx/LASHCP/pnd/07ps_defensa_nacional.pdf. Accessed 8 Feb 2018
8. Moy E (1992) National security in American History. In: Graham A, Treverton G (eds) Rethinking america's security: beyond the cold war to new world order. W. W. Norton, New York, pp 94–95
9. Milkis S, Nelson M (2003) The American Presidency: Origins and development, 1776–2002. CQPress, Washington, DC
10. Malcolmson P, Myers R (2003) The Canadian regime: an introduction to parliamentary government in Canada. 3rd edn. Broadview Press, Canada
11. Leuprecht C (2012) Complejidades al generar un equilibrio de seguridad trilateral en América Norte: acercamientos de las culturas en las relaciones civiles-militares. In: Rodríguez Sumano A (ed) Agendas comunes y diferencias en la seguridad de américa del norte, ¿de dónde venimos?, ¿dónde estamos? y "¿a dónde queremos ir? Centro de Estudios Superiores Navales de la Armada de México, Universidad de Guadalajara, Mexico, pp 334
12. SEGOB (2013) Programa Sectorial de la Defensa Nacional, 2013–2018. http://dof.gob.mx/nota_detalle.php?codigo=5326566&fecha=13/12/2013. Accessed 8 Feb 2018
13. Ley de Seguridad Nacional (2005) http://www.cddhcu.gob.mx/LeyesBiblio/pdf/LSegNac.pdf. Accessed 14 Oct 2009
14. SEGOB (2013) Programa Para la Seguridad Nacional, 2014–2018. https://www.gob.mx/presidencia/articulos/programa-para-la-seguridad-nacional-2014-2018. Accessed 8 Feb 2018
15. Vázquez J, Meyer L (1989) México frente a estados unidos (Un ensayo histórico 1776–1988). Fondo de Cultura Económica, Mexico

16. Alamillo L (1943) Doctrina mexicana de guerra. Mexico, Talleres de Costa. https://web. archive.org/web/20090723163555/http://mx.geocities.com/cencoalt/110901/doctrina.htm. Accessed 4 Feb 2018
17. National Archives (2016) The zimmermann telegram. https://www.archives.gov/education/ lessons/zimmermann. Accessed 10 Feb 2018
18. Aguayo S (1998) Myths and (Mis) perceptions: changing U.S. elite visions of Mexico. Lynne Rienner Publishers, Inc, Boulder, Colorado
19. Sokolsky J, Lagassé P (2005/2006) Suspenders and a belt: perimeter and border security in Canada-US relations. Can Foreign Policy 12(3):15–29
20. Rodríguez Sumano A (2018) Reconceptualizando la seguridaden México en la era Trump: elementosdomésticos e internacionales del poder. In: Rodríguez Sumano A (ed) Granos de Arena Evolución y ruptura del pensamiento en los estudios de seguridad nacional en México: de la democraciaagonizante a Donald Trump. Universidad Iberoamericana, Mexico City, pp 301–348 Forthcoming

Author Biography

Abelardo Rodríguez Sumano Professor at the Universidad Iberoamericana, Mexico City. Ph.D. in International Studies and Comparative Politics from the University of Miami.

United States Defense Policy

Hoping Primacy Stays Cheap: America's Grand Strategy

Harvey M. Sapolsky[✉]

Massachusetts Institute of Technology, Cambridge, MA 02142, USA
sapolsky@mit.edu

Abstract. The United States is a deeply divided society on many political topics, but not on its foreign policy. There is a consensus view among the leaders of both main political parties supported by most former and current officials, senior military, and the public that the United States should remain the world's most powerful nation and its continuing security depends upon the United States being the sole manager of global security. This stance, often labelled Primacy, stems from the lessons America's leaders drew from the Second World War, was seemingly confirmed in the peaceful end to the Cold War, and has continued essentially unchallenged into the 21st Century because it has been cheap to maintain despite expectations to the contrary.

1 Introduction

The United States is a deeply divided society on many political topics, but not on its foreign policy. There is a consensus view among the leaders of both main political parties supported by most former and current officials, senior military, and the public that the United States should remain the world's most powerful nation and its continuing security depends upon the United States being the sole manager of global security. This stance, often labelled Primacy, stems from the lessons America's leaders drew from the Second World War, was seemingly confirmed in the peaceful end to the Cold War, and has continued essentially unchallenged into the 21st Century.

Primacy means global engagement and a big defense budget.[1] Nearly three decades after the collapse of the Soviet Union, the United States still maintains hundreds of military bases overseas, a global command structure, an ability to strike anywhere, and ships on patrol in every ocean. We spend more on defense than during the peak of the Cold War (Fig. 1) [1], and more than the next eight nations, including China, Russia and our major allies, combined [2].

There are questions about the continuing value of the strategy and disagreement on its specific applications, but rule it does. President George W. Bush wanted to stop nation building, the not always successful effort to help weak nations acquire the economic and political institutions necessary for their long-term survival. President Barack Obama wanted to withdraw American forces from Iraq and Afghanistan to

---

[1] For a definition of Primacy as a grand national strategy for the United States and alternative strategies see Brown, Michael E., Cote Jr., Owen R., Lynn-Jones, Sean M., Miller, Steven E. (Eds.) (2000). *America's Strategic Choices, Revised Edition*. Cambridge MA: MIT Press.

© Springer International Publishing AG, part of Springer Nature 2018
C. Leuprecht et al. (eds.), *North American Strategic Defense in the 21st Century:*,
Advanced Sciences and Technologies for Security Applications,
https://doi.org/10.1007/978-3-319-90978-3_5

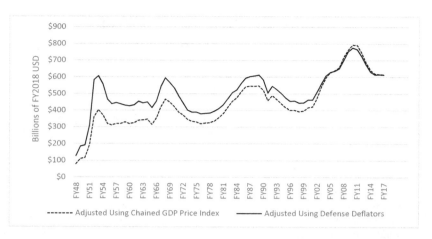

Fig. 1 United States total national defense outlays adjusted for inflation (billions of FY 2018 US Dollars). data generously provided by T. Harrison, director of defense budget analysis at the center for strategic and international studies

signify the end of our wars there. And President Donald Trump wanted our major European and Asian allies to contribute substantially more to their own defense, putting an end to their blatant freeriding. None got their way [3]. They were overruled by what a senior aide to President Obama called 'the Blob' [4], the Washington foreign policy establishment which is very much committed to the Primacy strategy and the requirement for continuous efforts at nation building, military interventions, and subsidizing the security of allies in the belief that these actions serve the longer run national interest [5].

This chapter examines the entrenchment of Primacy into American foreign policy, its origins, costs and future. Primacy rests on three pillars: the belief in its need and legitimacy, a mechanism for its low-cost maintenance, and little opposition at home and abroad. Counters to American dominance can be found. The question is whether the American people want to pay the price needed to overcome them.

2   The Road to Primacy

The United States entered the 20th Century powerful but seemingly without interest in global empire. Its colonial ambitions had fizzled in a costly insurgency in the Philippines and with the growing recognition of the incompatibility colonialism has with American experiences and values. By then, European powers had been chased out of the Western Hemisphere with small exception. Their distant rivalries mattered little until one seemed likely to gain dominance among them. The fear that Europe could be controlled by a single, likely hostile, nation drew American involvement in the First World War. But the Senate's unwillingness to abandon America's traditional isolationism kept the United States from helping enforce the peace that its own president had helped craft at the war's end. The United States was not a member of the League of Nations which was to be the forum for the world's disputes.

Although there was great reluctance to entering the Second World War, the United States did and was its main beneficiary. When the war began, there were several powers contending for global leadership, the United States not among them. The United Kingdom and France still had global empires. Nazi Germany was seeking to build a Reich that would last at least 1,000 years. Imperial Japan was seeking dominance in Asia. And the Soviet Union was seeking the global spread of Communism with itself as global central. The war destroyed or hobbled all of them. For the United States, the war shook off the debilitating effects of the Great Depression, gave it dominating military and economic power, and implanted the conviction that America had to manage global security as it could not avoid the consequences of distant wars.

This time the United States was going to be both the architect and the defender of global peace and prosperity. The United Nations, the successor organization to the League of Nations which the United States would not join, was designed at a conference held in San Francisco and then headquartered in New York City. The main global economic institutions are the International Monetary Fund and the World Bank, both of which trace their origins back to the Bretton Woods conference in New Hampshire and are based in Washington DC. And global security is anchored on an alliance system centered on the United States and led by one of its officers.

No longer was the United States hesitant about imposing its preferences on its friends and enemies. It controlled the pace of the war against Germany in the West and ran the war against Japan. Its late entry and reluctance to open a second front forced the bulk of casualties for crushing the Nazis onto its allies, particularly the Soviet Union, whose count for the war dead begins at 20,000,000 and was likely higher [6]. During and after the war, the United States undermined the efforts of its European allies to maintain their colonies in Asia and the Middle East. And as it became clearer that the Soviet Union was supporting the spread of Communism's influence in governments globally, the United States sought to frustrate that effort by intervening, covertly and openly, in many an election and civil war.

The result was the Cold War, a four decade plus global conflict, that pitted the United States against the Soviet Union. The Cold War pervaded American life, involved the United States directly in two bloody sub-wars, Korea and Vietnam, and cost trillions of dollars. Despite constant political turmoil over the extent of the threat and the required impingements on the rights of Americans, a broad consensus held that the struggle was necessary and worth winning. Internationally, the United States pursued two complementary strategies, containment and deterrence. Domestically, the strategy was moderation, tempering the cost of confronting the Soviets. Over the years, America prospered under this strategy, reducing greatly the relative burden of the Cold War on its citizens. Incomes rose, conscription ended, education levels increased, health services improved, and families thrived [7, 8]. It was this success as much as the unyielding military stance that caused the Soviet Union to collapse and the Cold War to end.

America normally demobilizes after its wars, maintaining a relatively small standing force and utilizing a handful of publicly-owned arsenals and shipyards for the development of new weapons. But with the Soviet challenge appearing so soon after the defeat of Germany and Japan, the United States did not fully demobilize, retaining significant military capabilities and keeping active much of the contractor and university network that had given America the technological edge in the war [9, 10].

America's European and Asian allies in the Cold War were initially too weak due to their Second World War experience to provide much assistance. They did offer, however, valuable real estate on which the United States created a system of bases that both surrounded the Communist world and gave the American military global reach. Preferring to keep the fight, were it to develop, over there, the United States forward deployed significant forces and ignored, or at least tolerated, the failure of most allies, even when they had fully recovered from the Second World War, to field proportional forces. What was conceived as a temporary necessity became the norm. The United States carried most of the burden and had most of the say. It was the champion of the West. And it had a gallery of sometimes cheering and sometimes criticizing fans.

The Cold War ended unexpectedly, bloodlessly and with two big questions: would the United States return home from its global mission and would any other nation or group of nations seek to replace it, even on a regional basis, as hegemon? The United States did reduce its overseas deployments, but only by half and not everywhere. Forward deployment of American forces was seen by senior government officials in the United States as a deterrent to the rise of a new peer competitor—a resurgent Russia or a rising China. And although there was trouble in the Middle East, ethnic conflict in the Balkans, and chaos in parts of Africa, no one stepped forward to take the United States' place as the security provider. The United Nations was a mostly feckless organization. The European Union was without an army and focused on its internal politics and economic interests. And the North Atlantic Treaty Organization (NATO) was the United States in a different guise. The United States was the last super-power standing and everyone's default setting, including itself, for global sheriff.

3 Why Primacy is Cheap

Americans are casualty adverse. They do not want their sons and daughters killed in wars. It is not that Americans love their children more than other people do, though they might, but rather that the United States is geographically isolated, living far from most fights, and is a strong democracy which means that its politicians are certain to pay a steep political price for involving the nation in distant, high casualty, inconclusive wars. Moreover, the United States has long been a land of labor scarcity, drawing in immigrants, but also practiced in substituting capital for labor, in this case bombs for people [11].

The appeal of airpower to win wars in this context is irresistible [12]. America's late entry into the First World War limited its losses to just over 100,000, but its allies paid dearly for years of trench warfare, their losses numbering into the millions. With aviation there was the promise of bypassing the gore of the battlefield to take the fight directly to an enemy's homeland to destroy its industrial capacity, transportation network, military stores, and will to fight. Many Americans became strong advocates for strategic bombing, offering as it did both a long reach to America's military power and the expectation of limited casualties.

The United States did use strategic bombing extensively during the Second World War, building tens of thousands of bombers and dropping millions of tons of explosives on Germany, Japan, Italy, France, Romania and other places, but with limited success. The problem stemmed from inaccuracies inherent in the attacks. Despite the use of improved bomb sights and navigation aids, it was nearly impossible to destroy critical targets or create transportation barriers. Bombing was essentially random with target misses measured in multiple thousands of feet.

The attacks were also costly. Over 50,000 American and British airmen lost their lives in the strategic bombing campaign in Europe. Tens of thousands more were killed doing similar missions elsewhere in the Second World War. The most valuable targets were often heavily defended by interceptors and anti-aircraft guns. Strategic bombing was a brutal proposition at both ends of the bomb bay doors [13].

Adjustments in tactics and weapons were made. Instead of seeking to destroy sets of factories making particular products—ball bearings, fuel or aircraft, the effort shifted to destroying the housing of factory workers where accuracies matter less, and the real target was their morale. Incendiaries were used to create firestorms that roared through German and Japanese cities. The raids and bombs got bigger. If a rain of 500-pound bombs could not do sufficient damage, then try a rain of 2,000 pounders. The Second World War ended with the development of the atomic bomb. With the atomic bomb missing by a mile was likely good enough.

American tolerance for inflicting civilian casualties diminished greatly after the Second World War. With nuclear weapons civilian casualties are essentially unavoidable, intended or not. But the value of these weapons lies mostly in their threat of intolerable casualties—their indiscriminate destructive force—not their surgical use. Military targets can be sited near civilian populations and the blast impact areas are wide. There have been significant accuracy improvements in the delivery of nuclear weapons, but mainly to destroy efficiently hardened targets, those protected by thick concrete or earth, most likely the enemy's nuclear weapons or command centers.

It is with conventional weapons, however, where the real revolution in accuracy has occurred, the main driver being the need to save aircrew members' lives. The United States has done a lot of conventional bombing since the Second World War, some of it against substantial air defenses. Over North Vietnam hundreds of pilots were killed or captured flying against these defenses. Important targets like the bridges in Hanoi required multiple missions, each with dozens of aircraft, to destroy. Given the precarious politics associated with these bombing campaigns—America's short run survival is not at stake, only its ability to influence events far from its shores—casualty avoidance becomes a political imperative. That is achieved best with accuracy, hitting the target with the first bomb or missile and reducing the exposure of pilots to defenses [14].

The development effort was large, complex and partially serendipitous, but the United States now bombs with precision. If a target can be identified and located, it can be destroyed. The means depends upon the circumstance, often weather related and platform availability determined, and include television, laser, and Global Positioning System (GPS) guided weapons. It is one target, one bomb or two to be certain. The United States has the means to make wars cheap in terms of its own personnel and even civilians, what is sometimes euphemistically called "collateral damage."

The Gulf War proved the point. Massed armies were sitting targets for precision weapons. With time, the United States got better and better at this, improving the range and capabilities of its target acquisition systems and weapons. Stealthy aircraft were developed so defensive systems could be penetrated and destroyed. Drones became a delivery system, so pilots did not have to be exposed at all to risks. Now terrorists are not safe even hiding in urban areas.

The United States has the found the means to police the world with near immunity. Good defenses are a hinderance, but not much of one and put in place by only a few countries. With forces not burdensome to maintain, it can protect its friends from their enemies and chase its own without paying much of a price [15].[2] Currently, the United States is bombing in seven countries and thinking about adding an eighth to the list.[3]

4   Hearing Only Crickets

The serious opposition to all of this is almost non-existent. At home, despite the American military being constantly in one fight or another since the end of the Cold War, there are no anti-war demonstrations, no marching in the streets, no sit-ins at colleges. There is also no conscription or special tax burden for these fights. Those at risk are volunteers, often more than once for combat unit assignments, and relatively well compensated for the exposure which is kept low by precision weapons. The fights are financed through borrowing. Some fights have been more popular than others and some have gone better others, but none have been so bloody or so costly as to cause total disengagement as happened in Vietnam. Failed missions, false justifications, limited interests, fears of entanglement, and corrupt allies has not kept the United States from continuing its involvement in places like Somalia, Libya, Iraq, the Balkans, Syria and Afghanistan.

Abroad there is near silence. Perhaps some grumbling in the cafes, but hardly any government complains. After all, the United States is the guardian angel for allies and friends, patrolling the global commons, hunting down terrorists and watching for trouble along their borders, and the protection is provided largely free. Most allies have been able to reduce defense spending, secure in the American shadow. Even Russia and China are beneficiaries of some of this, especially the terrorist hunting, as they both have Muslim populations that have radicalized elements and a history of rebellion.

There is acquiescence to American Primacy because it has been cheap to maintain and costly to overcome. The United States can meddle in conflicts across the globe without having to pay much of a price. For one or two percent of its GDP, it can buy the extra military might to intervene far from its shores. Casualties are light. Citizens do not have to become soldiers. Innocents are not being killed in large numbers. Taxes to pay for most of it are for some future generation. It is all borrowed money.

Russia and China, potential challengers, have been more concerned about asserting dominance among their close neighbors than they have in gaining global

---

[2] Of course, this does not mean it wins all of its wars.

[3] Libya, Syria, Yemen, Iraq, Afghanistan, Somalia, Pakistan and thinking about the Philippines.

responsibilities for themselves. Those who have tried to resist with regular forces—Saddam's Iraq, Serbia and Libya—have had their militaries shredded. Terrorist groups have persisted, but at a high price and are constantly on the run or in hiding.

5   What Might Change?

There are effective counters to America's power to intervene globally. One is nuclear weapons. Nuclear powers are rightly wary of each other. Non-nuclear powers are at their mercy. Nations get nuclear weapons for several reasons, but primarily because they have a very threatening enemy. Since the Treaty on the Non-Proliferation of Nuclear Weapons (NPT) came into force in 1970, four nations have acquired nuclear weapons of their own—Israel, India, Pakistan and North Korea. Israel is ringed by hostile nations. India has both China and Pakistan to fear. Pakistan worries most about India. And North Korea appropriately fears the United States [16].

Nuclear weapons do not solve all problems, but they certainly solve some. Libya gave up its efforts to build a nuclear weapon in 2005, two years after the United States invaded Iraq on the justification of stopping Iraq's efforts to acquire weapons of mass destruction, including the possible development of nuclear weapons. A little over five years later, NATO, led by the United States, was intervening in Libya's civil war and helping hunt down Qaddafi, something that would have been highly unlikely if Qaddafi's Libya had nuclear weapons.

After the 9/11 attacks, President George W. Bush made it clear that the United States reserved the option of resorting to preemptive attacks on nations harboring terrorists' groups and/or trying to obtain nuclear weapons, labelling Iraq, Iran and North Korea the Axis of Evil for their involvement in such activities. Iraq was attacked in 2003 by an American led coalition. North Korea withdrew from the NPT in 2003. Two years later, North Korea announced that it had become a nuclear weapon possessing state, likely escaping an American preemptive attack in large part because of America's preoccupation with wars in both Iraq and Afghanistan.

Iran, although remaining a party to the NPT, appears also to have increased its efforts to acquire nuclear weapons and their delivery systems after the Axis of Evil speech, earning citations for inadequate compliance with provisions of the Treaty and eventually severe economic sanctions for apparent violations. Fears that Iran was making progress toward a bomb despite the sanctions led to pressure within and outside the United States for preemptive action. President Barack Obama decided instead to seek negotiations with Iran and the members of the UN Security Council (all nuclear weapons states) plus representatives of Germany and the European Union which produced an agreement in 2015 that postpones Iran's ability to obtain a weapon for at least a decade. The temptation to go after Iran is still there among some in the United States and elsewhere. With nuclear weapons that temptation would be severely tempered, as the North Korean case proves.

Another counter to American global dominance is the proliferation of the very precision weapons and advanced sensors that gives the United States its conventional power. The United States wants to stop the spread of nuclear weapons because it found the mechanisms to destroy opponents' conventional forces with relatively inexpensive systems at low risk to its own forces. But what keeps Primacy cheap is itself proliferating. GPS guided weapons are now widely available. So too are drones, infrared-sensors, long-range missile systems and dozens of other elements of American power [17]. The underlying technologies, the kind that made the insiders in Microsoft, Apple, and Google billionaires, have globalized.

In fact, China has developed systems–ballistic missiles, satellites, etc.—intended to prevent the United States from approaching close enough to defend Taiwan and other allies near China. These blocking efforts, frequently referred to as Anti-Access/Area Denial (A2/AD), likely will proliferate, making it difficult for American forces to intervene against regional powers everywhere. Fighting to get to the fight is not what the United States is used to doing.

A third possible counter to America's interventions abroad is the opportunity cost —a domestic desire to spend money on other things, most likely health care. The American population is aging, increasing the need for health services. Health costs rise appreciably with age. The demand for health care is insatiable. As one wit put it: Defense and Health Care have the same goal; they are both against natural death. Not quite. America can avoid going to war. Its global policing is, it could be argued, a choice. Americans though cannot escape the fate of all humans.

Try they will though. The United States spends more than 18% of its GDP on health care, which is more than five times what it spends on defense. At the height of the Cold War, in the early 1950s, the United States spent about 14% of GDP on defense and 3 or 4% on health care. The lines crossed during the height of the Vietnam War when both were at about the 7% mark and the Medicare and Medicaid programs, key components of President Lyndon Johnson Great Society were put in place (Fig. 2) [18]. Defense declined as a percentage of GDP as America became ever more prosperous and health care increased as it filled out its welfare state.

It does not end. President George W. Bush initiated wars in Afghanistan and Iraq, but also a costly drug benefit for Medicare. President Barack Obama signed the Affordable Care Act which expanded access to health care to many who previously lacked health insurance by both mandating the purchase of insurance and subsidizing that purchase. Attempts by Republicans to repeal the Act have failed because benefit expansions are near impossible to retrieve. Despite its title, the costs of implementing the Affordable Care Act are certain to grow. So too will the demand for the expansion of benefits, increasing access and subsidies and reinforcing the quality of care.

Fully accounted to include the cost of care provided to service personnel and their dependents, veterans, and federal retirees as well as medical research and subsidies for private insurance, health care already absorbs a third of the federal government's budget. European governments explain their failure to spend more on their own defense by the burden of their welfare states. The United States has a less fully formed welfare state than those of its allies, but it is filling in by steps like the Affordable Care Act. It soon might think the burden of caring for its own citizens takes precedent over subsidizing the defense of others far from its own shores.

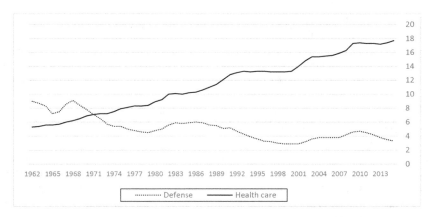

Fig. 2 United States spending on defense and health care as percent of GDP. Chart reproduced from Friedman, Benjamin H., and Sapolsky, Harvey M. (forthcoming 2018). Unrestrained: The Politics of America's Primacist Foreign Policy. In Benjamin H. Friedman, and Trevor Thrall (Eds.), *US Grand Strategy in the 21st Century: The Case For Restraint*. London: Routledge [18]

6 Why Change Is Unlikely

The wiser course for the United States might be to recognize that the costs of being the global manager of security are rising and to return home. The world wars showed the advantages of being behind rather than in front of allies. Without an American shield guarding their borders today, these allies would be certain to invest more in their own defense and perhaps seek a greater role in enhancing security in their own regions.

But it is unlikely that this will happen. Most Americans are uninformed about the details of American foreign policy, the promises embedded in their alliances, and their involvement in distant wars, and are happy with that lack of knowledge. Their concern in this sphere is mostly with the costs and risks as these costs and risks impinge on their daily lives. In contrast, American's role in the world is of crucial importance to the relatively small portion of the population that runs America's global security apparatus —the senior military, public officials, foreign policy specialists, and contractors who are Primacy's domestic beneficiaries and champions [19].[4] They fully believe in the links of distant conflicts with American security and will seek ways to mitigate Primacy's short run costs so the United States is not driven back into its traditional isolationist shell by the weak-willed and ill-informed majority. In that effort, they will have the support of allies who have learned well the advantages of freeriding. The call will be for the American leadership of old, the leadership that won the Cold War.

Wars are offense/defense struggles. Seeking to keep the fight away from its shores, the United States has acquired intimidating offensive capabilities with the logistical systems needed to support them globally. If nations build defenses to push American

---

[4] It is appropriate and only right at this point to thank Ben Friedman for his contribution. Ben's thinking had a big influence on this chapter as well as the joint chapter cited here.

forces away from their shores and turn precision weapons against them, they will likely see devastating attacks from different dimensions—cyber and space perhaps [20]. Robotic systems will limit American casualties. If nations acquire nuclear weapons and missile systems to thwart the United States' ability to intervene in their regions, they will be met by layered missile defenses, some of which are already being deployed.

Technological knowledge diffuses; it cannot be stopped. But the United States invests twice as much in military related research, development, test and evaluation, currently more than $70 billion a year, than the rest of the world combined, friend and foe [21, 22]. It has done so at an equivalent level for more than seventy years.[5] There have been periodic claims that others will catch up, and they have in particular technologies for a time, but the weight of the investment that the United States makes in military dominance is against them. Now the argument is that in the digital age that commercial advances are sufficient, but surely there is a translation cost to be paid which is why advanced weapon systems are so expensive. American Primacy is more technology based than is often acknowledged.

But what about the rising opportunity costs, the ever-increasing cost of health care and related components of the welfare state? Doubling the cost of Primacy, say from one and a half percent of GDP to three, would not be that expensive although it would add hundreds of billions of dollars to that effort. Compared to other industrialized nations, the share of society absorbed by government for all activities—defense, education, transportation as well as health care– and the tax burden imposed on citizens is low in the United States. There is room for the American government to grow. The question is whether Americans can be persuaded to devote that growth to influence affairs in places like the South China Sea or their own nursing home care. Or they could do both.[6]

References

1. Harrison T (2017) US defense spending. Center for Strategic and International Studies
2. Peter G, Peterson Foundation (2017) The United States spends more on defence than the next eight countries combined. http://www.pgpf.org/sites/default/files/0053_defense-comparison-full.gif. Accessed 13 Jan 2018
3. Abrams E (2017) Trump the traditionalist: a surprisingly standard foreign policy. Foreign Aff July/August 2017:10–16
4. Lake E (2016) Obama's foreign policy guru is the 'Blob' he hates. Bloomberg, 6 May 2017. https://www.bloomberg.com/view/articles/2016-05-06/obama-s-foreign-policy-guru-is-the-blob-he-hates. Accessed 13 Jan 2018
5. Rachman G (2017) How the Washington blob swallowed Donald Trump. Financial Times, 10 Apr 2017. https://www.ft.com/article-US-foreign-policy-gideon-rachman. Accessed 13 Jan 2018
6. Carleton G (2017) Russia: the story of war. Harvard University Press, Cambridge, MA

---

[5] With ratchet jumps up after Sputnik and in the Reagan years.

[6] That is the view of one of Primacy's strongest advocates. See Cohen, Eliot A. (2016). *The Big Stick: The Limits of Soft Power & the Necessity of Military Force*. New York: Basic Books.

7. Friedberg AL (2000) In the shadow of the garrison state: America's anti-statism and its cold war grand strategy. Princeton University Press, Princeton, NJ
8. Gaddis John Lewis (2005) Strategies of containment: a critical appraisal of postwar American National Security Policy. Oxford University Press, New York
9. Gholz E, Sapolsky HM (1999/2000) Restructuring the U.S. defence industry. Int Secur 24 (3):5–51
10. Gholz E, Sapolsky HM (Forthcoming) Many lines of defense: the political economy of defense acquisition
11. Sapolsky HM, Shapiro J (1996) Casualties, technology, and America's future wars. Parameters 26(2):119–127
12. Cohen EA (1994) The mystique of U.S. air power. Foreign Aff 73(1):109–124
13. Pape RA (1996) Bombing to win: airpower and coercion in war. Cornell University Press, Ithica, NY
14. Lambeth BS (2000) The transformation of American air power. Cornell University Press, Ithica, NY
15. Freedman L (2017) The future of war: a history. Public Affairs, Washington, DC
16. Sokolski HD (ed) (2016) Should we let the bomb spread?. Nonproliferation Policy Education Center, Arlington, VA
17. Steinbock D (2014) The challenges for america's defence innovation. The Information Technology and Innovation Foundation, Washington, DC
18. Friedman BH, Sapolsky HM (forthcoming 2018). Unrestrained: the politics of America's primacist foreign policy. In: Friedman BH, Thrall Trevor (eds) US grand strategy in the 21st century: the case for restraint. London: Routledge. Data from Office of Managegement and Budget (2017) Historical tables: table 8.4. WhiteHouse.gov. https://www.whitehouse.gov/omb/historical-tables/. Accessed 1 Feb 2018. Center for Medicare and Medicaid Services (2017) National health expenditure data: historical. CMS.gov. https://www.cms.gov/research-statistics-data-and-systems/statistics-trends-and-reports/nationalhealthexpenddata/nationalhealthaccountshistorical.html/. Accessed 1 Feb 2018
19. Friedman BH, Sapolsky HM (forthcoming 2018) Unrestrained: the politics of America's primacist foreign policy. In: Friedman BH, Thrall T (eds) US grand strategy in the 21st century: the case for restraint. London: Routledge
20. Kesling B (2017) Army set to broaden battlefield definition. Wall Street J, 9 Oct 2017:A-3
21. Office of Management and Budget (2016) Budget of the US government: fiscal year 2017. US Government Printing Office, Washington, DC
22. YouthXChange (2006) Military spending on R&D. http://www.youthxchange.net/main/ff4b265_military-spending-d.asp. Accessed 13 Jan 2018

NATO and NORAD
in the Sino-Russo-American Configuration
of Power

Alexander Moens[✉]

Simon Fraser University, Burnaby V5A 1S6, BC, Canada
moens@sfu.ca

Abstract. Both the North Atlantic Alliance (NATO) and the Canada-United States North American Air Defence Command, later Aerospace Defence Command, (NORAD) not only respond to specific threats but are also products of global great power relations. Important changes in these relations are in progress. The resurgence of Russian 'sphere of interest' politics in Eastern Europe and China's comprehensive march to great power status are chief among these. At the same time, we realize limits to power in both North America and NATO Europe. NATO, with Canada's active participation, is responding to its new threats. However, NORAD is struggling to address the full range of defence needs confronting North America. This chapter argues that Canada's own security logic of working closely with allies by means of integrated operations, which it has sought in NATO and NORAD since their beginnings, is increasingly at risk. The imbalance between Canada's pro-active approach in NATO and its self-limitations in NORAD do not serve Canada's security interests in an international system where the power of the United States is challenged by Chinese power and by Sino-Russian ad hoc cooperation.

1 NATO and NORAD: One Security Area with Integrated Military Operations

The North Atlantic Alliance has always been a function of the geopolitical logic of the international system. It not only serves the values and interests of the Euro-Atlantic region, but it takes on a politico-military role according to the strategic needs and opportunities that emerge from global great power relations. The Canada-United States North American Air Defence Command, later Aerospace Defence Command Agreement (NORAD) is also a function of this wider international security domain. Moreover, the 1958 NORAD text refers directly to how integrated command structures and operational control are part of NATO, and that the Canada-United States region is "an integral part of the NATO area" [1, p. 81]. The idea of "integrating headquarters exercising operational control" [2] very much connects at a political-strategic level with what Canada set out to do in both NATO and NORAD. Like NATO, NORAD has gone through various ups and downs, lulls and spurs, but for Canada two strands of

© Springer International Publishing AG, part of Springer Nature 2018
C. Leuprecht et al. (eds.), *North American Strategic Defense in the 21st Century:*,
Advanced Sciences and Technologies for Security Applications,
https://doi.org/10.1007/978-3-319-90978-3_6

logic stand firm. Canada works closely in the realm of security and defence with allies, none of whom are as important as the United States, and, secondly, integrated military operations give Canada both greater influence and more security efficiency. The 2006 NORAD Renewal Agreement reiterates that NORAD operates in one framework with the Alliance and that it contributes to the overall security of the Allies.

My point is this: Canada ended up during the first decade of the Cold War in a 12 plus 2 arrangement (NATO plus NORAD) that now is a 29 plus 2. They are side by side. They are separate. I am not suggesting bringing NATO into North America or NORAD into Europe. While they are meant to be separate, they also share two crucial factors that unite them in terms of purpose and effect. They both point towards the logic of one security area (North Atlantic and North America) and the importance of the practice of integrating military operations.

Today's international security revision is epitomized by Russia's return to a hard sphere of influence policy, an apparent ad hoc supportive policy between China and Russia, and the relentless rise of China as a political, economic and military great power. Great power change is taking place at the same time as the leading superpower of the international system is attempting to stave off nuclear weapon breakouts by North Korea and Iran and opportunistic actions by various extreme Islamist organizations to exploit political instability from West Africa to Southeast Asia. These power shifts and political threats are made more challenging by rapidly changing technology, especially in information and communication.

Particularly since 2014, NATO is trying to adjust to the latest international developments epitomized by Russia's return to a hard sphere of influence policy in Eastern Europe as well as the high potential of political chaos in the Middle East and North Africa. The latter impacts Europe especially in terms of refugee flows and terrorist attacks. Canada has taken on both NATO's eastern and southern threats as a serious and loyal ally. Canada is providing a share of the work in the Global Coalition against ISIS and NATO patrols in the Mediterranean. Even more so on the eastern front, Canada has stepped up to play a significant role as one of the four Framework Nations to lead an Enhanced Forward Presence operation in Latvia. Some 450 Canadian troops are committed to this Battlegroup for an indefinite period of time.

While Canada's articulation of current NATO threats and needed responses is well attuned, what about Canada's articulation of security threats and actions in North America? After all, it is in North America that Canada deploys an even larger day-by-day contingent of soldiers to NORAD and related tasks. By asking how both NATO and NORAD should assess and think about great-power changes in the international system and the threats to the North Atlantic and North American region, I am also asking how Canada is considering its interests and position in the NATO Plus NORAD logic it created in the 1950s. Is the government of Canada thinking clearly about the strong connection between the two regions, namely that they are one security area even more so now than in the 1950s? Is Ottawa pursuing the need to have integrated military operations as a prime piece of the puzzle not only in NATO but also in NORAD? Just as Canada is active on both NATO's eastern and southern area and diversified in terms of dealing with various threats, the question I raise is whether

Canada is equally active on the various 'fronts' North America faces. Since 9/11 we have seen a lot of attention on further cooperation against threats coming from aircraft, but what about missile-based, sea-borne, and cyber launched threats? By looking at changes in the international system, this chapter seeks to draw out discussion regarding threat assessments for both NATO and NORAD.

2 The International System

It is difficult to imagine now, but in the late 1940s, one of the biggest concerns among decision makers in the United States and Canada about creating the Atlantic Alliance was that it would undermine or violate the logic of collective security as formulated in the Charter of the United Nations [3, p. 54]. One can understand the strong urge for the ideal of collective security in the wake of two devastating wars. However, the gradual pursuit of Soviet domination over Eastern and Central Europe while rendering the UN Security Council incapable of action convinced the West that a collective defence alliance to complement the UN Charter was needed.

The rise of mutual nuclear deterrence between the United States and the Soviet Union, bipolar political and economic rivalry, and the American commitment to permanent alliances made NATO a strong feature of North Atlantic and European security and defence cooperation. So strong, in fact, that even the dynamic of European economic integration and eventually partial political integration in the form of the European Union could not replace it.

Just as it would have been impossible for individual Western European countries even when united in the Dunkirk Treaty or later the Brussels Treaty to stand with conventional forces against the Soviet Union, so it would have been impossible for Canada to shoulder the early warning and intercept requirements against Soviet bombers in the 1950s. After the North Korean invasion of the South, most Allies felt that the North Atlantic Alliance should set up an integrated command system and a much higher level of readiness to deal with potential communist aggression in Europe. The Soviet Sputnik breakthrough on rocket launchers and the growing capacity of both the United States and the USSR to deliver Intercontinental ballistic missiles in short order increased the pressure on American and Canadian forces to integrate the defence of North America, leading to the formal endorsement of the practice in 1958 through the establishment of NORAD.

The Atlantic Alliance also embodied another aspect of international security cooperation that the United Nations could not achieve or that superpowers could not impose if they wanted to do so, namely the shared foundation of liberal constitutional democracies around the core values embodied in the Washington Treaty's preamble: "[the parties to this treaty] are determined to safeguard the freedom, common heritage and civilisation of their peoples, founded on *the principles of democracy, individual liberty and the rule of law (italics added)*" [4]. We must keep in mind that the United Nations is essentially colour blind to the nature or quality of domestic governments. All it sees is whether the entity we call the state has sovereignty or not. Only in the most recent movement around 'Human Security' and towards the 'Right to Protect' has the UN moved in the direction of caring about the nature of justice inside a sovereign state.

Being a dictatorship or authoritarian democracy does not limit a state's rights in either the General Assembly or the Security Council. However, in NATO as well as in the 1958 Treaties of Rome constituting the European Communities, the added glue is that the members are Liberal-Constitutional Democracies who tend to see many international security questions in a similar light, based on the will of the people and the rule of law defined in their domestic politics. I am not suggesting that democratic values trump strategic interests in NATO consistently. For example, Portugal joined the Alliance because of the strategic importance of the Azores and the southern approach in the North Atlantic even though a right-wing dictatorship was still in place in Lisbon.

When the Soviet Union collapsed, the NATO allies and EU members had spent more than 40 years working on multilateral defence cooperation and combining politico-military policy making. Even though the core strategic interest (the Soviet threat) was gone, it was not desirable that the NATO allies should stop their alliance and re-nationalize their defence policy and military capacity. 'If no Soviet Union, therefore no NATO' was a simplistic and uninformed assessment of NATO back in 1992. Regardless of the Soviet Union, the idea of European cooperation even integration, rather than national competition was as dependent on NATO as it was on the EU. Moreover, now that Central and Eastern European countries obtained a real choice in how to manage their domestic and international affairs, they wanted *en masse* to join this conglomeration of European economic and security policy. How could the liberal constitutional democracies of the North Atlantic and the EU say 'no' to their aspiring neighbours?

It is seldom mentioned, but the foundation of NORAD is not simply that the United States and Canada need each other for dealing with the air-based or rocket threats from the Soviet Union or elsewhere. There is a deeper vein of compatibility. Both countries respect and expect responsible government from their partner because they share the values as articulated in the NATO Treaty preamble. The convergence of geography on the one hand and the vast asymmetry of power on the other are like opposing forces in their relationship. The political sinews of liberal democratic values and responsible governance institutions put some restraint on these centrifugal forces though they are no guarantee for the system to hold.

What NATO did in the 1990 to 2011 period—besides enlargement—can be best understood by realizing the twin strengths of the Alliance: continuous consultation among democracies who share many values and interests and who at the same time possess common military readiness and capacity to conduct integrated operations [5]. This helps us to understand why NATO got involved in crisis-management operations first in Southern Europe and then in Afghanistan and lastly in Libya. NATO becoming involved in non-collective defence operations inside and outside of its North Atlantic region was propelled by two additional factors. Despite the high expectations for a common security policy after the newly minted European Union Treaty in 1991, the Europeans were not ready politically and militarily to take on peace support operations in the Balkans and elsewhere. Second, United Nations peacekeeping experience in both Somalia and the Balkans in the early 1990s proved that the traditional so-called Blue Helmet nature of UN peacekeeping would need to be replaced by more robust forces and rules of engagement.

NORAD did not receive a new lease on life in the 1990s as NATO had in the form of crisis-management operations. Given that NORAD had always focused on the Soviet threat, the end of the USSR in 1991 put NORAD in a lower level security holding mode. NORAD's post-Cold War wake-up call came in 2001 amidst the airborne terrorist attacks in the United States. The re-invigoration of warning, patrol, and defence of the North American skies became an important task. However, in the decades since 9/11, it is becoming more apparent that while extreme Islamist terrorist attacks present serious regional threats, they do not at this point actually pose a systemic threat to world stability or a threat to the very survival of Canada and the United States. In other words, NORAD has become very good at keeping the skies safer—a task it needs to continue as the danger of drone attacks is growing—but it has not responded fully to larger strategic changes.

One reason NORAD has not done so is that Canada and the United States identified the threat of missile and nuclear proliferation, the need for ballistic missile defence, and the conception of how space should be used differently. James Fergusson has argued that Canada has diverged from American assessments on the need and development of missile defence on many occasions and that domestic political factors rather than strategic interest dominated Canada's decisions and indecisions. Avoiding and postponing was most often the explanation for Canadian inaction [6]. As a result, the original objective of NORAD, namely to employ integrated operations on shared security needs, has lived through decades of strain because the United States is committed by its own strategic assessment as well as by law to undertake missile defence. This wide gap is a more serious problem than most Canadians realize. It isolates and marginalizes Canada's defence and security position and capability. It translates into less cooperation by the two allies and less allied capability for Canada to draw upon. Given the renewed standoff with Russia and the rise of China as a full-fledged competitor to the United States, Canada will soon have to assess again whether its escapist position in North America alongside its participatory role in Europe really matches our values and security.

3 Russian Resurgence

After the end of Soviet containment, there was a genuine attempt by the First Bush and the Clinton Administrations to bring Russia into the global economy and to help Russia re-start liberal political development at home. IMF loans were extended as was membership in the G-7, and a Russia-NATO partnership. Arguably, the financial aid was not enough, and the challenge of reforming Russian law and institutions and preventing the rise of the oligarchs was underestimated. The sad end of the matter is that by the early 2000s both the Russian elites and most of the middle class felt vindicated that Western Liberalism was a failure and nothing more than a Western conspiracy to make Russia weak and subservient. The failure of liberalism in Russia (the second time if you add the attempt in the early years of the 20th Century) sowed the seeds of Putin's subsequent dictatorship which is still growing in power. Russia has returned as NATO's immediate threat. By threat, I mean the sizeable risk that Russia and NATO could come into direct conflict resulting from political turmoil in a NATO member state somewhere between the Baltics and the Black Sea or through a series of misperceptions and mishaps.

It is not factually correct to state that Russia is simply reacting to a broken promise made by the West not to enlarge NATO. This has become a much-peddled myth in the media and literature. Thanks to thorough research confirmed by recent archival access, we know that this does not match the record [7]. Giving Ukraine and Georgia a blanket unconditional promise of membership in NATO—as was done by NATO in Bucharest in 2006—was a diplomatic blunder. Even so, Russia's reaction to the Maidan crisis in 2014 in which it switched bait and took Crimea and continues to hold Donbas has set Ukraine and Russia at odds forever. Does NATO pose a threat of aggressive military action against Russia or does NATO threaten to take any Russian territory? The answer is unambiguously clear. The actual threat NATO poses to Russia is the combined threat of NATO and the European Union's way of life, that is to say, the threat that Russian citizens may also want to have the economic and political ways of living as does the West. Therefore, NATO is not a threat to Russia but to the authoritarian regime that governs Russia, likely with or without Vladimir Putin.

We are thus back at a strategic stalemate. The peoples and territories that feel threatened by Russia want the protection of NATO. At the same time, Russia wants to push back the political and economic cultures of Western Europe and North America and it wants to put Central and especially Eastern Europe back into a type of neutral zone in which the interests set by Moscow dominate or, at a minimum, neutralize the security choices of the region.

Since 2009, Russia has re-activated the stalemate by concentrating on two means: the robust build-up of conventional forces and a sophisticated investment in information warfare, cyber capability, and mass media manipulation. The Russian military build-up includes renewal and expansion of its capacity in the Arctic. While neither Russia nor North America are interested in linking the tension in Eastern Europe to the Arctic, the very nature of modern weaponry and technology is such that the capability of Russia to use force in the Arctic or to use the Arctic as a base for the use of force affects both NATO and NORAD security.

NATO and Russia have a shared interest of not stumbling into war. Though Russia violated key international agreements such as the Budapest Memorandum regarding Ukrainian nuclear weapon disarmament, the Russia-NATO Founding Act, and the OSCE's and UN's international prohibitions of violating national borders by force, Russia and NATO will eventually need to find a way to freeze their standoff and to resume substantial negotiations to lower the level of mistrust and misperception.

4 Chinese 'Restoration'

The new strategic confrontation between Russia and NATO is taking place in a very different geopolitical context than the Cold War. First, the international system in terms of economic, financial, and information power resembles a multipolar system. In the politico-strategic realm the main axis of any balance or preponderance of power is not between NATO and Russia, but between the United States and China. The rise of China, or what the government in Beijing prefers to call the "restoration" of China, is the most significant and largest strategic change of the last twenty-five years [8, p. 53].

The rise of China is taking place inside a larger phenomenon what Fareed Zakaria calls the "Rise of the Rest" [9]. Besides China and India, most economies in Asia have grown rapidly to make Asia a true economic powerhouse. Nevertheless, among all the economic power amassing in Asia, the growth of China is what will have the most immediate impact on the strategic and security realm as China is not only an economic phenomenon but a great power on the rise. Graham Allison argues that if the Chinese worker achieves the same level of productivity as the US worker—a reasonable expectation—the Chinese economy would then be four times the size of the American economy [10, p. 7]. We should expect China's economy to become sizeably bigger than that of the United States given the combination of population and the level of growth in domestic consumption. For nearly all the years after the launch of Deng Xiaoping's transformative policies, China's economy has grown robustly. Not many years after the economic engine fired up, Deng also allowed a military build-up to begin. In the last decade, and especially after the assertive leadership of President Xi Jinping, the other Asian countries near China have started to react. As a result, Asia is engulfed in various arms races and is on track to become the world's most powerful military continent. The re-election of Japanese Prime Minister Sinzhō Abe in late 2017 will mean further Japanese steps in this direction.

The 'Rise of the Rest' and the military build-up in Asia combined with a continual decline in real military spending in Europe and low levels of economic growth leaves the United States and its NATO Allies relatively weaker in the overall equation of global power. Multiple domestic challenges inside the United States suggest closing any power gap is unlikely. Richard N. Haass points to the "burgeoning debt, crumbling infrastructure, second-rate primary and secondary schools, outdated immigration system and slow economic growth," as the "most critical threat" facing the United States [11]. Some also argue that there is a long-term decline in American soft power; as a foreign policy and political brand, a popular social brand, and an economic example [12].

In a multipolar system, alliances and power-balancing become a critical feature of great power politics. We would expect the status-quo power (USA) to use its alliances as much as possible to offset the rise of the challenger (China). The American advantage, in terms of NATO, and the American hub-and-spoke system of bilateral defence arrangements in Asia make it a far more aligned great power than either China or Russia. At the same time, the history of American foreign policy shows that Washington does not always use its alliance potential to the fullest. This comes as a result of a sense of isolationism or exceptionalism or, as is the case in the early Trump administration, a case of excessive nationalism.

A potentially pivotal feature of the new international system is the growing trend of informal and ad hoc cooperation between China and Russia when it comes to challenging American policy and power. They provide each other diplomatic support in their respective 'near-abroad' by covering for each other's breaches of international law. Russia's economic power remains modest and prospects for growth outside of the carbon-based energy sector are low. But unlike nearly all of NATO, Russia has re-invested in military spending at a very high level starting in 2009. Its force modernization, restructuring, and higher readiness level is taking place in most areas of conventional and some nuclear arsenal and has continued even after the decline in oil prices. My point is this: Just as the USSR could build and maintain a superpower military with a very modest economy, so Russia is again putting all its economic assets into military power and may be able to sustain this for decades. Moreover, given China's strength in the economic sphere, should China and Russia come to cooperate more closely, the combined military and economic power they would bring to bear would be enormous.

China claims that it does not think in terms of military alliances the way the West does. While, in the logic of Westphalian international relations, sovereign national power and inter-state alliances are typical ways for states to exert power or defend ideas and territory, the Chinese insist that their relationship with other countries follows a different logic or model. China rejects military alliances per se, arguing they represent a Western concept of hegemony [13]. Instead, China thinks in terms of economic and political complementarity among states. The complementarity is not horizontally or equal as among sovereign states or perfectly two-way. The Chinese model includes hierarchy. Both the influence and benevolence that flows from China to other states in this logic exceeds what they can reciprocate. The one-Belt, one-Road (BRI) Initiative is the flagship of this Chinese paradigm of foreign relations. It is meant to be a gradual building out of economic ties and political exchanges, producing complementary relations. The dynamic derives from contiguous economic trading areas. The interlinked economic base is part of building a sphere of shared diplomatic thinking and practice.

In the case of China, we observe a strategic potential very different from Russia. First, it has the domestic components or ingredients of reaching superpower status. Second, it may forge a beneficial relationship with the main 'spoiler power' of international politics, Russia. Third, it may persuade a string of economically contingent and dependent states into a sub-society of international relations led by China. We know this string starts right around China (Cambodia comes to mind) and we do not know how far it will extend but likely will go all the way to Western Europe.

5   Sino-American Relations

The nature of Sino-American relations has never resembled the relationship between the United States and Russia/USSR. Regardless of the actual agenda President Trump has in mind regarding Russia, the relationship between Russia and America is the least likely to develop into anything constructive or aligned in terms of the economic and political-strategic realm. If China were to surpass the United States in military and economic power as well as global influence, the two lesser powers (America and Russia) would, in the raw logic of power politics, consider joining hands in order to balance against China. In my view, too many cultural, social, historical and other value gaps make this Russo-American alignment very unlikely. Possibly, another bilateral relationship with more counter-balancing potential is found in India and America. America's 'opening to India' which took place under George W. Bush has been followed consistently by both Obama and Trump.

The notion that the United States can or should contain China is not taken seriously for good reason: China is too big to contain and there are too many other American interests at stake for the United States to enter into a negative containment relationship. At the same time, should a transition of world dominance between America and China take place, no one expects a happy and mutually reinforcing follow-on relationship to develop between them such as did take shape between Great Britain and the United States after 1919 and especially 1945.

If both war and containment were avoided what kind of relationship could emerge between America and China? If it were peaceful competition, how stable would this system be and at what cost would it be maintained? How would the competition play out in terms of the ideas of the Liberal West and Authoritarian China and Russia? If the balance of power was swinging decisively towards authoritarianism, would we see a roll-back of democratic or Western influence? China is increasingly articulating a political rationale distinct from Western Liberal concepts. China is doing so assertively. China's recent attempts to influence the minds of Westerners includes subtle and overt coercion, leading to the new term "Sharp Power" [14, p. 13].

China's BRI is meant to produce a state of being 'beholden' to China. By means of the so-called 16 + 1 Initiative between China and sixteen East and Central European states created in 2012, China has begun both significant economic investment in these states and started a diplomatic dialogue with each [15]. Thus, China's politico-economic relationship model has already entered Europe.

It is in Europe that Russia is seeking to draw publics immediately on its western frontier away from the Liberal-constitutional model. Russia does not offer an economic option for these countries. At the same time economic growth in the European Union has been sluggish. It is China who may well have the best opportunity to fill in some of the economic vacuum.

The competition for the hearts, minds, and pocket books of Europeans, and especially Eastern Europeans, comes at a time when President Trump has spent his first year misfiring on Europe in his public diplomacy. It is fundamentally in America's interest to maintain close relations with NATO and to keep NATO and the EU working in harmony just as Dean Acheson perceived it at the birth of these organizations.

Is Trump simply misfiring on NATO or should we consider American policy towards NATO to have changed? To begin to answer this question, we examined Trump Administration statements on NATO (see Appendix 1). In the period between March 21, 2016, and October 17, 2017, we identified 35 publicly documented statements Donald Trump has made about NATO as quoted in the major US media.[1] We counted 21 that were clearly negative or mainly negative. Nine (9) were positive or

---

[1] I acknowledge the research work done by Cornel Turdeanu on the Trump Administration and NATO as well as the careful editorial review of this chapter by Alexandra Richards.

mainly positive, and four (4) were so mixed as to be neutral in overall impact. While the negatives appear to win the score, the *timing* of the comments adds another consideration. While almost all comments in 2016 were negative, the comments in the first four months of 2017 were near equal between positive, mixed, and negative. However, the comments from May 2017 to October 2017 were nearly all positive. Meanwhile, we counted and labeled 24 public statements by Secretary of Defense James Mattis between January 12 and November 9, 2017. Mattis scored 22 very positive statements and two mixed statements. While Secretary of State Rex Tillerson's four (4) public comments on NATO show no trend, Vice-President Mike Pence's nine (9) comments show a similar pattern to that of President Trump: negative early on but changing to positive after May 2017.

Based on this small (not definitive) sample of public pronouncements about NATO, we suggest that Trump's public policy on NATO has misfired. American policy and action in NATO has not changed from previous American administrations. During the election campaign and in the early weeks of his administration, Trump thought that his policy towards NATO was going to be revolutionary. However, as the advisory team, led by Mattis, wields more influence and Trump, by means of meeting NATO leaders, becomes more aware of all the stakes, Trump's NATO policy becomes evolutionary. The latter means that the Allies should do more, but also that the United States remains committed.

When it comes to influencing the hearts and minds of Europeans towards stronger North Atlantic ties and solidarity, the United States created its own public handicap. At the same time, Brexit has challenged solidarity and coherence within Europe. The likely departure of the British from the EU will make it more difficult for Western and Eastern EU members to work together on actual policy. Britain was the crucial counter-weight to the Franco-German engine, and without it, value differences between east and west are more difficult to bridge. If France and Germany move ahead with more EU-centered security and defence policy, the gap between what Eastern Europe hopes to achieve in NATO versus what Western Europe puts into NATO will widen.

The combination of negative Russian power (military and disruption power) and positive Chinese power (investment and trade) is putting more strain on a fragmenting Europe. Keeping Germany and France as well as Eastern Europe firmly placed in NATO is a prime American (and NATO) interest and it will require American leadership which always means a disproportionate share of US military and budgetary commitment to Europe. The default option is Western Europe doing defence mainly on its own and Eastern Europe becoming another US hub-and-spoke system of defence. This will produce more fault lines in Europe and it will leave Canada outside of any of the power relationships.

By acting like a revolutionary great power in the realm of trade, the United States is risking more than it can gain. China and Russia use military policy and economic dependence as a form of neo-mercantilism. If the United States has no alternative model of trade relations among developed economies, many of its allies will feel the need to join the new Chinese BRI model. Therefore, an evolutionary trade approach is needed whereby advanced and democratic economies agree together on how to reform or adjust international trade rules so that they can remain a coherent political and economic force in international relations.

Another key factor in a new multipolar international system is the question of the role of political values and principles. It must be kept in mind that when the Western democracies found common cause around the principles of democracy, liberty, and the rule of law, they also happened to be among the most powerful economic and military entities in the world. But if their combined power becomes less, will they still be drawn to cooperate or will the possible cost of doing so make them more interested in compromising and co-existing with the two big authoritarian powers, China and Russia? If that happens to our allies and trade partners in Europe, where does that leave Canada in North America?

6 Aligning Canada's Approach in NATO and NORAD

Canada has a strong interest in keeping the United States in NATO, but Canada also has a true interest in keeping the Europeans engaged with North America and would gain nothing from a European foreign policy aligned with China.

Canada took on an enhanced forward presence mission in Latvia and is committed to have about 450 troops involved as the lead nation with no specific end date on schedule. Obviously, Canada's stake in being able to re-supply our forces in Latvia, protect their work, and to cooperate with allies to create the highest level of security for these forces includes security in the North Atlantic. In addition, Arctic security means strong North Atlantic security. Besides North America, this is Canada's immediate security domain as well as part of our link to ground operations in Europe. If NATO is set to put a new focus on the North Atlantic, Canada needs both the capability and the decision-making power to be a key player there.

NORAD is not a separate strategic domain from the evolving relationship among the three great powers. Canada's efforts in NATO are not enough. How would assertive competitive relations between China and America impact the strategic calculation in NATO and NORAD? In an international system in which Chinese strength and Sino-Russian cooperation restrain American policy and actions, we should anticipate more emphasis on defence, including in North America. Even if such defence-oriented action is to offset higher risk in other areas of the world, the United States will need its allies to help it do so. If Canada is not that ally in a modernized defence of North America, it only leaves American unilateral action as an option. Such unilateralism means less security and less influence for Canada.

Appendix 1: Measuring Trump Administration Statements on NATO

Rex Tillerson	Mike Pence	James Mattis	Donald Trump
January 11, 2017—Positive	July 21, 2016—Mixed	January 12, 2017—Positive	March 1990—Negative
March 21, 2017—Negative	February 18, 2017—Mixed/ Mostly Positive	January 24, 2017—Positive	May 16, 2012—Neutral
March 31,2017—Positive	February 20, 2017—Mixed	January 24, 2017—Positive	March 21, 2016—Negative
October 15, 2017—Mixed	April 30, 2017—Negative	February 15, 2017—Mixed	March 21, 2016—Negative
	May 9, 2017—Positive	March 16, 2017—Positive	March 23, 2016—Negative
	June 5, 2017—Positive	March 23, 2017—Positive	March 24, 2016—Negative
	July 31, 2017—Positive	March 31, 2017—Positive	March 26, 2016—Negative
	August 1, 2017—Positive	May 9, 2017—Positive	March 27, 2016—Negative
	August 2, 2017—Positive	May 10, 2017—Positive	April 2, 2016—Negative
		May 17, 2017—Positive	April 4, 2016—Negative
		May 18, 2017—Positive	April 8, 2016—Negative
		May 28,2017—Positive	April 27, 2016—Negative
		June 3, 2017—Positive	June 6, 2016—Negative
		June 28, 2017—Positive	July 17, 2016—Negative
		June 28, 2017—Positive	July 20, 2016—Negative
		June 29, 2017—Positive	July 24, 2016—Negative
		July 10, 2017—Mixed	July 25, 2016—Negative
		August 9, 2017—Positive	July 27, 2016—Negative
		August 15, 2017—Positive	July 30, 2016—Neutral
		August 31, 2017—Positive	July 31, 2016—Negative
		September 19, 2017, Positive	August 15, 2016—Positive

(continued)

(continued)

Rex Tillerson	Mike Pence	James Mattis	Donald Trump
		September 21, 2017—Positive	January, 15 2017—Mostly Negative
		October 6.2017—Positive	January 27, 2017—Positive
		November 6, 2017—Positive	February 6, 2017—Positive
		November 7, 2017—Positive	February 6, 2017—Mixed
		November 9, 2017—Positive	March 17, 2017—MostlyPositive
			March 18, 2017—Mixed
			April 12, 2017—MostlyPositive
			May 25, 2017—MostlyNegative
			May 25, 2017 (Evening)—Negative
			May 27, 2017—Positive
			June 9, 2017—Positive
			July 6, 2017—Positive
			August 21, 2017—Positive
			October 17, 2017—Mixed

References

1. Blanchette AE (ed) (2000) Canadian foreign policy, 1945–2000: major documents and speeches. Golden Dog Press, Ottawa
2. Agreement between the government of Canada and the government of the United States of American concerning the organization and operation of the North American Air Defence Command (NORAD) 1958, E101015—CTS 1958 No. 9, Adopted 12 May 1958. http://www.treaty-accord.gc.ca/text-texte.aspx?id=101015. Accessed 10 Jan 2018
3. Kaplan LS (1984) The United States and NATO: the formative years. University Press of Kentucky, Lexington, Kentucky

4. The North Atlantic Treaty (1949), 4 Apr 1949 https://www.nato.int/cps/ic/natohq/official_texts_17120.htm. Accessed 10 Jan 2018
5. Moens A (2016) How NATO's values and functions influence its policy and action. Fellowship Monograph, 7. Rome: NATO Defense College. http://www.ndc.nato.int/news/news.php?icode=947. Accessed 21 Dec 2017
6. Fergusson J (2011) Canada and ballistic missile defence, 1954–2009: Déjà Vu All over again. UBC Press, Vancouver
7. Sarotte ME (2014) A broken promise? What the west really told moscow about NATO expansion? Foreign Aff 93(5):90–97
8. Lanxin X (2016) Xi's dream and China's future. Survival 58(3):53–62
9. Zakaria F (2009) The post-american world. W.W. Norton, New York
10. Allison GT (2017) Destined for war. Houghton, Mifflin, Harcourt, Boston, New York
11. Haass RN (2013) The world without America. Project Syndicate, 30 Apr 2013. https://www.project-syndicate.org/commentary/repairing-the-roots-of-american-power-by-richard-n–haass?barrier=accessreg/. Accessed 21 Dec 2017
12. Michel L (2017) US soft power and the trump presidency. Finnish Inst Int Aff 15(7):1–2. https://storage.googleapis.com/upi-live/2017/11/comment15_us_soft_power.pdf/. Accessed 18 Dec 2017
13. Xuetong Y (2011) Ancient chinese thought, modern chinese power. Princeton University Press, Princeton, New Jersey
14. Sharp Power. The Economist, 14 Dec 2017
15. Kuo MA (2017) China in Eastern Europe: Poland's perspective. The Diplomat, 19 Dec 2017. https://thediplomat.com/2017/12/china-in-eastern-europe-polands-perspective/. Accessed 27 Jan 2018

NORAD in an Age of Trump's Jacksonianism

Bessma Momani[1] and Morgan MacInnes[2(✉)]

[1] University of Waterloo, Waterloo, ON N2L 3G1, Canada
bmomani@uwaterloo.ca
[2] Centre for International Governance Innovation, Waterloo,
ON N2L 6C2, Canada
mmacinnes@cigionline.org

Abstract. The electoral successes of populist politics in America, culminating in the victorious presidential campaign of Donald Trump, have engendered uncertainty regarding US defence policy, and with it the security and stability of liberal internationalism. The Trump administration marks the ascendancy of the venerable Jacksonian tradition in US foreign and defence policy, which values robust military power, eschews international engagement for the sake of higher ideals or maintaining international order, and seeks to avoid the sort of international obligations which would constrain the country's ability to act unilaterally. While NORAD may benefit from the Trump administration's Jacksonian emphasis on core US interests and policy prioritization of increasing US military capabilities, the diminished global prospects for multilateralism are not in line with Canadian priorities and may aggravate the main security threats of concern to NORAD.

1 Trump's Jacksonian Defence Posture

Over the course of his bid for the Republican presidential nomination and subsequent presidential election, Donald Trump provoked apoplectic responses from the US political establishment and the country's foreign allies with a series of pronouncements which bluntly contradicted prevailing US defence doctrine. He has opined that NATO may be obsolete, insinuating that the US should not be obligated to defend treaty allies who fall short of NATO defence spending targets [1]. He expressed that Russian aggression in the Ukraine was a greater concern for Europe than America, and that European nations, rather than the US, should be responsible for confronting the Kremlin [2, p. 4]. Trump's campaign website declared that he would "end the current strategy of nation-building and regime change" in the Middle East [2, p. 7]. Some of his statements suggest that he thinks America's defence commitments are beyond its present capabilities: "When we did these deals, we were a rich country. We're not a rich country...We're not anymore" [3].

Although Trump has espoused a myriad of different positions depending on the audience at hand, many policy makers and members of the media have ascribed to Trump, based on this fragmentary evidence, a desire to see the US withdraw from the wider world. With mounting trepidation, they have identified Trump as the latest avatar of American isolationism. Council on Foreign Relations President Richard Haas charged Trump with reviving the desire to turn away from global engagement, returning to the "America first" attitude of those who sought to keep the US out of the Second World War [4]. Withdrawal from the Paris climate agreement and the Trans-Pacific Partnership has further contributed to the picture of an administration determined to turn inward. The fear is that the current international order, which has coincided with the least violent and most prosperous era in human history, will not survive without the hard power guarantee of the world's presiding military hegemon. However, to conceive of the constituency which propelled Trump to power as isolationist and opposed to foreign military involvement as a matter of principle would be to misdiagnose which strain of foreign and defence policy thought is truly in the ascendancy amongst the US electorate.

Walter Russell Mead identifies four traditions in US foreign and defence policy which he describes as being relatively stable and enduring throughout the country's entire history. The 'Wilsonian' school of thought holds that the US has a moral imperative to engage with the rest of the world, proselytizing democracy and standing up for individual liberties throughout the far corners of the world. This often entails cooperative engagement with other nations, and attempts to level the international Hobbesian Jungle and in its place construct international institutions to sustain a rules based global order [5, pp. 133–173]. The 'Hamiltonian' faction shares with the Wilsonian a desire for cooperative engagement with the wider world, but rather than being motivated by moral principles, the Hamiltonian's view this as a means by which to secure national prosperity. The US government should work with domestic business to advance their interests overseas, protect and extend the security and openness of global trade, and act as the lynchpin of a safe and orderly international economic system [6]. The Hamiltonians possess a realist view of geopolitics, believing in preserving a balance of power abroad through a network of allies across various regions of the world who can be supported to counter any emergent hegemon. It was the Hamiltonian and Wilsonian factions who jointly forged the existing foreign and defence policy consensus in the US, and presided over the construction of the post-war international order.

The 'Jeffersonian' tradition bares the closest resemblance to true isolationism. Jeffersonians believe that by becoming involved in the geopolitical maelstrom of petty regional squabbles and the megalomaniacal ambitions of tyrants, the US will end up putting itself through a lot of anguish which could easily be avoided. Additionally, a military sufficiently large to wield coercive force on the global stage would necessitate higher taxes and a larger state, which is ultimately the most serious threat to the liberty of US citizens. Jeffersonians are generally against foreign interventions, and desire to divert resources away from the military to domestic projects [5, p. 185].

Finally, the prickly and populist 'Jacksonians' often find common cause with the Jeffersonians, but are better understood as defensive or retaliatory rather than isolationist. In contrast to the other three schools of thought, Jacksonians find the binding force of American identity not in a set of political ideals, but in the social and cultural values held by a large portion of the US population; the US is conceived of as the nation state of the American people [7, p. 9]. The prime directive of US foreign policy should be promoting the safety and wellbeing of the US populace, and the government must be prepared to take all measures necessary to advance their political, economic, and security interests [7, p. 15]. To this end, entry into the sort of international agreements and organizations which limit the country's range of action is contemptible, and intervention in pursuit of some higher moral goal is generally eschewed. The international stage is accepted as Hobbesian, and each sovereign state must look to its own interests. A robust military, and the ability to act unilaterally must be maintained in order to respond to threats and attacks. During the Second World War, the Jacksonian constituency was largely unmoved by the death toll inflicted on Europe and Asia by Nazi Germany and Imperial Japan, but threw its full force behind the war effort after Japan attacked the US itself. In the wake of World War Two US policymakers were able to sell the electorally significant Jacksonian faction on the merits of International governance, a global alliance network, and free trade by invoking the threat of Communism [7, p. 19]. In the Soviet Union the US faced a polity sufficiently powerful to actually constitute a credible threat to the nation's physical safety, and in Communism, an ideational adversary sufficiently influential as to pose a credible threat to the way of life cherished by Jacksonians. With the Cold War over, the Jacksonian element in the US is questioning whether the country derives sufficient benefits from underwriting the world's current security architecture to justify the costs. Unable to discern any direct US interest, Jacksonians opposed intervention in Bosnia. However, they enthusiastically supported the effort to liberate Kuwait during the Gulf War, perceiving a threat to US economic vitality in the Iraqi seizure of its neighbor's vast oil supplies [8, p. 19].

Jacksonian thought places great emphasis on the effects of honor and reputation in international affairs, believing that the image a nation projects and the opinion other states have of its national character play a large role in how a nation is treated in the international arena. A nation must project an aura of strength or else be bullied and exploited. A nation must keep its word and honour its commitments in order to be treated fairly and respectfully by others [7, p. 16]. This ethos lies behind the scathing Republican criticism directed at President Obama for reneging on his threat to intervene in the Syrian civil war if chemical weapons were deployed. Jacksonians are often mistaken for isolationists due to their lack of enthusiasm for the global order agenda of the Wilsonians and Hamiltonians, but are willing to bear heavy costs from foreign operations if convinced it is truly in the national interest. Jacksonians conceive of the decision to wage war in binary terms; once conflict is initiated the country must mobilize all available resources and undertake any actions conducive to victory. Anything less than total unambiguous triumph could be perceived as weakness. Even in instances when those of Jacksonian persuasion were initially reluctant to get involved in a conflict, they have typically become advocates of increased commitments once hostilities commence [7, p. 23]. During the Kosovo war of 1998–1999, The Jacksonian faction at first opposed calls for intervention, but once the battle was joined they pushed for a bolder strategy including ground forces [7, p. 21].

Jacksonians possess a strong conviction in the virtues of common sense. Divergence between popular intuition and the positions of professional policy makers often leads to mistrust of whomever embodies the political establishment at a given time. Maintaining support among this constituency has in many ways been the most persistent challenge in US foreign policy. For the duration of the Cold War, relations between the proponents of the different foreign policy traditions were relatively harmonious, as the Jacksonian desire for proactive policies to counter the threat of Communism meshed well with the Hamiltonian and Wilsonian goal of constructing a liberal world order [9, p. 37]. With the Eastern Block vanquished, liberal internationalist policy makers are once again struggling to justify their mission to the Jacksonian constituency. The bloodshed committed by terrorist groups like ISIS rouse Jacksonian ire, but do not present the sort of imposing existential threat which would justify the burden of supporting a global order.

Mead characterises both the Tea Party movement and the successful presidential campaign of Donald Trump not as symptoms of isolationist sentiment, but a revival of the venerable Jacksonian tradition [10]. Although the Tea Party contained a whiff of Jeffersonian isolationism, it was the Jacksonian nationalist element which was dominant. A study conducted by Brian Rathbun found that isolationist attitudes were no more prevalent among those sympathetic to the Tea Party movement than the general populace. Rather, they held "militant Internationalist" views amenable to the use of force overseas if it served the national interest [11]. Donald Trump's speech to the UN general assembly, in which he extolled the virtues of inviolable national sovereignty, is exemplary of the Jacksonian rejection of multilateralism and strong international institutions as unwelcome restraints on national freedom [12]. The new administration's vehemence towards international institutions and the country's pre-existing agreements, should be interpreted not necessarily as a desire to sever contact with the wider world, but a desire to remain unencumbered by obligations to other parties which would restrict the government's range of action on the world stage.

The guiding principle of a Jacksonian influenced US foreign and defence policy would be preserving the freedom and capability to act in the interests of the American people. This would involve strengthening the implements of hard power through higher military spending. In contrast, the tools used to further national security in a broader sense, such as diplomatic capabilities, may end up neglected (as evidenced by the cuts to the State Department's budget exacted by the Trump administration). More Wilsonian and Hamiltonian administrations have confronted the imperial ambitions of powerful states, such as China's audacious claims in the South China Sea and Russian irredentism, by attempting to incentivize them to adhere to the rules of the liberal international order. An administration possessing a more Jacksonian perspective would likely cease to prevail upon rival states to join a system it is skeptical of itself, instead ignoring infractions which do not directly affect the US, while addressing those that do pragmatically on a case by case basis. A Jacksonian-influenced administration would also likely abandon President Obama's propensity to tie trade and military assurance to the fulfillment of democracy and human rights advancement as was the case throughout the Middle East [13].

2   Trump's Jacksonian Unilateralism in a Multipolar System

A strengthened Jacksonian sentiment in US defence and foreign policy would, in a certain sense, make it difficult to alter the nature of US relationships with other countries. Once another international actor has been identified as an enemy, Jacksonians will be mollified by nothing short of their defeat. This will place severe constraints on policy-makers looking to re-evaluate partnerships and rivalries in different regions of the globe. This can be seen in Donald Trump's repudiation of any sort of accommodation with Iran, and insistence on re-imposing economic sanctions, in spite of the fact that he has also pledged to not get entangled in the Middle East. The resumption of an adversarial stance towards Cuba, reversing the attempting reconciliation initiated by Obama, is also in line with the Jacksonian mentality. In contrast, Jacksonians may no longer regard Russia as an active adversary. The US "defeated" them during the cold war, and while Moscow's actions over the past decade have jeopardised a stable and predictable international system, any physical threat to US citizens or ideological threat to the American way of life ended with the Soviet Union. Though Russian actions in the Ukraine are the most blatant violations of the rules based international system, the Jacksonian constituency identifies economic competition with China as a more pressing concern to the wellbeing of the American people than Russia's thrashing against the constraints of the current world order. This may lead to a desire for a pragmatic accommodation with Russia in order to balance a rising China [13].

While the Jacksonian strategy of preserving the freedom to act in the national interest is a populist logic that garners US domestic support, in the context of a highly interconnected, multipolar world, this will likely prove maladaptive to many of the most pressing security challenges facing the US and Canada. This is further complicated by the reality that the international system today is better characterized as multipolar, with a rising China and India and confident and assertive Germany, France, and Russia. International relations theorists assumed that US unilateralism could occur under a unipolar international structure, but the populist rise of Donald Trump to the presidency upended this theory. Trump's unilateralist Jacksonian policy will not mesh with a multipolar world order.

Throughout modern history, the US sought to work within multilateral frameworks and reverted to unilateralism only as a last resort [14]. Indeed, the oft cited example of US unilateralism is the George W. Bush administration's decision to invade and occupy Iraq without a UN Security Council resolution. This unilateral policy was an aberration in US foreign policy often explained as a product of the brief *pax Americana*. Unilateralism certainly provides the US administration greater policy autonomy, and the US undoubtedly has the military capability of 'going it alone'. However, the common wisdom within the US foreign and defence policy community had been that there are inherent and high costs to unilateralism when conducted by a superpower like the US [15].

When the US is inclined to act unilaterally it absorbs higher costs in terms of both hard and soft power. A unilateral action invariably means the US will have to be ready with hard power assets, maintaining a large standing army replete with hardware that is globally dispersed with logistical capability to go it alone. In contrast, the benefits of a multilateral defence policy include unified war plans, interoperability of equipment, military specialization of tasks, economies of scale, and burden-sharing [16]. Unilateralism also comes at a cost of diminished soft power and influence particularly when done by a hegemon like the US. States in the international community do not react well to US unilateralism and prominent defence and foreign policy analysts have argued that it can lead weaker states to want to bind and rebalance American power through multilateral and institutional arrangements [17]. Structural realists posit that weaker states react to unilateralism by trying to counterbalance American hegemonic power in the international system [18, p. 87]. To do this, weaker states form their own coalitions, create alternative alliances and security arrangements, and enter strategic partnerships with rising powers. Hence, American realists often view multilateral engagement as a useful tool of US statecraft; multilateralism can signal a benign or benevolent hegemon and can effectively work to pacify weaker states' attempts to counterbalance US hegemony.

International relations literature portends that states will react to unilateralism by doubling-down on multilateralism, enhance their use of international organizations, strengthen diplomatic channels, and utilize economic statecraft as strategies to push back against a hegemon. Weaker states engage in 'soft balancing' "by actions that do not directly challenge U.S. military preponderance but that use non-military tools to delay, frustrate, and undermine aggressive unilateral U.S. military policies" [19]. Importantly, 'soft balancing' strategies can also be used by allies and friends, not just long time foes or adversaries. We have seen evidence of this in reaction to the Trump administration's unilateralist policies already, for example, in President Xi's promise to be the champion of globalization at Davos, in President Macron's promise to strengthen the Paris Climate Accords, countries signing on to China's AIIB and OBOR, and Japan's TPP-11 initiative. US defence allies can engage in 'soft balancing' through enhancing economic integration amongst themselves and by invigorating multilateral security arrangements like NATO [20].

3 Augmented NORAD Capability Amidst Global Uncertainty

American unilateralism should be cause for consternation among those who depend upon the existing liberal international order. This tendency will possibly undermine NORAD's unity of purpose while simultaneously augmenting its military capabilities. President Trump has publicly questioned the worth of NATO and Washington's commitment to that alliance. He has also mused that South Korea and Japan should look to their own defences, by way of nuclear weapons if need be [2, p. 20]. However, Trump's Jacksonian perspective does not preclude the notion of alliances and international institutions completely, accepting them when a direct benefit to the safety and prosperity of US citizens is apparent. While there is an argument to be made that as the world's largest economy the US benefits from a safe and predictable security environment that facilitates global commerce, any benefits thereof are indirect, nebulous, and hence difficult to quantitatively compare with the costs of universal security provision. In contrast, the benefits which the US receives through membership in NORAD are more direct and tangible. The Jacksonian faction has demonstrated an intense (some would say disproportionate) commitment to eliminating any threat capable of physically harming US citizens on their home soil, (hence the vehement fixation on radical Islamic terrorism). The threats which NORAD was designed to address likewise jeopardise the physical safety of Americans at home. NORAD's aerospace warning and control missions see to the neutralization of airborne attacks, and the new maritime warning mission likewise contends with potential attacks against US citizens within their home territory.

A renewed focus on core US interests under a Jacksonian influenced administration could well work to NORAD's advantage, in the sense that its mission pertains to the security of the home continent. As in the case of virtually all of its other defence commitments, the US has borne a disproportionate share of NORAD's costs, providing most of the funding for the requisite infrastructure in the Canadian arctic [21, p. 6]. However, Jacksonians are willing to shoulder incredible burdens if it is clearly in the national interest. While whatever stakes the US has in defending the Baltic States from Russian aggression or Taiwan from an emboldened China may not be obvious, none could question the need for a robust defence of North America. The US received a direct benefit from the formation of NORAD in the form of advanced threat detection and greater opportunities for interception of airborne attacks [21, p. 6]. While NORAD's purview extends beyond US borders to encompass Canada, physical proximity makes Washington's security relationship with Canada fundamentally different than any of its other allies. The US and Canadian economies are so tightly interwoven that any disruption to the Canadian economy would assuredly have a negative impact on the US economy as well, thus any attack on Canada is inherently a threat to US interests. As Washington is being increasingly compelled to question many of the elements of its 'forward defence' while simultaneously bolstering its hard power defensive capabilities, NORAD, as an organization could rise in relative importance owing to its focus on the physical defence of its core US interests.

NORAD's mission has relevance to four of the security challenges to which the Jacksonian constituency presently assigns great importance: North Korea, Iran, terrorism, and narcotics. This set of issues overlaps substantially with the '4+1' threat framework (referring to Russia, China, Iran, North Korea, plus international terrorism) currently utilised in US national security planning [22]. The hyperbolically belligerent ruling regime in North Korea attracts populist enmity with its blatant hostility towards the US. Donald Trump has consciously adopted a more confrontational line towards the Kim regime, amidst growing international apprehension that the efforts of the US and other countries to prevent North Korea's acquisition of nuclear armed intercontinental ballistic missiles will be in vain. Populist views of Iran are also highly adversarial. Iran's continuing efforts to develop intercontinental ballistic missiles could conceivably lead to another hostile party capable of launching an airborne attack on US home territory. NORAD's capacity to perform airborne threat assessment is highly relevant in confronting these risks. The trafficking of narcotics into the US is another issue which Trump has repeatedly raised, in which NORAD can play a constructive role through its capacity to interdict airborne drug smuggling. Finally, radical Islamic terrorism constitutes what is possibly the most salient security risk to the US in the minds of Trump's populist base. NORAD's mission extends to monitoring aviation security issues originating in North America, such as September 11th style hijacking attacks.

4 Unilateralism as an Impediment to Addressing Security Challenges

Whilst the relative importance of NORAD may be bolstered under a Trump administration influenced by Jacksonian principles due to the prioritization of the issues under NORAD's jurisdiction, the organization may be negatively impacted if the resultant unilateralism exacerbates some of the global security challenges which NORAD must contend with. The Joint Comprehensive Plan of Action, negotiated between the US, Iran, Russia, China, France, the UK, Germany, and the EU, produced an agreement in which Iran abandoned its nuclear weapons program in exchange for the lifting of economic sanctions imposed by the other partners. At the domestic level, Donald Trump has decertified the Iran nuclear deal to US Congress, in spite of the commitment of all other parties to the international deal remaining committed to its provisions, and the International Atomic Energy Agency vouching for Iran's adherence. Potential withdrawal from the JCPOA will breed increased Iranian antipathy towards the US, and politically strengthen the aggressive hardliner faction within Iran by seemingly vindicating their warnings of American deception. So long as the JCPOA's European members remain faithful to the terms of the international agreement, Iran may have an adequate incentive to refrain from resuming its nuclear weapons program. Never the less, US non-compliance weakens the agreement's integrity and Iran's incentive to remain compliant. As such, to the extent that Iran is capable of posing an airborne threat to North America, Jacksonian proclivities seem to be aggravating the risk.

Trump's unilateralism could also hinder efforts to neutralise terrorist organizations. ISIS, the most reviled terrorist organization of our time, has been pushed nearly to oblivion by the end of 2017, in large part due to an effective detente between the US and Iranian supported forces in Iraq and Syria. The Jacksonian's desire to pull out of the JCPOA jeopardises the prospects of continued collaboration against ISIS and the other Sunni extremist groups which have established themselves during the Mashreq's descent into anarchy.

NORAD is also involved in anti-narcotics trafficking operations in the capacity of monitoring aircraft suspected of illegal drug trafficking. Here too, a distaste for multi-lateralism in line with Jacksonian tendencies may frustrate efforts to deal with this security concern. The principal route through which narcotics are brought to the lucrative North American market is across the Mexican border, and the criminal syndicates responsible for this trade are based in Mexico, having taken root thanks to the relative weakness of the Mexican state. Thus far into his presidency, Donald Trump has taken a vitriolically confrontational approach towards Mexico, not only on the subject of drug trafficking, but also on the issues of immigration and trade. As a consequence, relations between the two countries have reached a low point, severely diminishing prospects for collaborative measures to combat the illicit drug trade. Moreover, the rise of a left wing populist in Mexico contending for the Presidency in 2018 that is vehemently anti-American and anti-Trump, will aggravate an already tense relationship.

5 US-Canadian Relations

While threats which NORAD was built to address may be prioritized by a Jacksonian influenced administration, frictions may arise as Canada is asked to make greater contributions to the joint defence effort. Canada may feel the need to reverse the decision made in 2005 to participate in ballistic missile defence (though conducting this mission would not necessarily fall under NORAD's jurisdiction) [21, p. 32]. It is likely that Canada would be asked for a more substantial contribution beyond the mere provision of land as in previous cases, and Canada may have to shoulder much of the burden of repairing or replacing the Northern Warning System [21, p. 38] Since Canadian participation in such an initiative is largely conceived as a matter of national sovereignty, and opinions of the Canadian public a function of attitudes towards the current US administration, Canadian contribution will be less politically feasible under President Trump than at any other time.

Trump's emphasis on unilateralism will clash with Canada's strategic commitment to operating within multilateral/bilateral frameworks. It will be imperative for Canada and the NORAD alliance to not allow enemies to sense a division of purpose. It is key that Canadian foreign and defence policy announcements are carefully messaged and crafted to always portray resoluteness. 'Living near the elephant' is a fine balancing act which Canada has managed well historically, and will likely continue to do so despite potential differences in foreign policy frameworks.

While the US is likely to allocate more funding to homeland defence, this may not result in deeper integration of continental defence arrangements. Under NORAD, the US' strong preference for unilateralism could prove a grave hindrance to addressing bilateral security issues while pressuring Canada to augment its bilateral defence commitments. Canadian Foreign Minister Chrystia Freeland's address to parliament outlined a hybrid approach to maintaining Canadian commitment to liberal internationalism while committing more spending to defence [23]. Pressuring Canada to commit even more defence spending in a Trump administration's 'America First' strategy may not be greeted favorably by Canadians and the Trudeau government is unlikely to commit additional defence spending beyond its 2017 announcements. Canada will face a political challenge both at home and in its bilateral relationship with the US in attempting to balance the concerns of Canadian public opinion while preserving friendly diplomatic relations. Canada would be wise to use the same strategy it did during the Bush administration when pressured to commit Canadian troops to the Iraq invasion of 2003. At that time, Canada agreed to send troops only if a United Nations resolution was achieved. The US was unable to convince the United Nations Security Council of a threat to world order and Canada was able to bow out of the disastrous Iraq war without appearing to cower from conflict. Reiterating a commitment to mulitilateral frameworks is a helpful means of ensuring that Canada keeps good ties with its US allies while not jeapordizing its own values.

The trend toward deeper integration of bilateral homeland security (encompassing intelligence sharing, border crossings, and law enforcement), with weaker integration of the bilateral homeland defence cooperation which most affects NORAD's institutional capability, may experience a reversal under the Trump administration [24]. With a more obsequious presence on the world stage, and hence fewer state actors which they can count as enemies, Canada is far more concerned with homeland security on issues like climate change and homegrown terrorism that are not addressed through enhanced defence integration. Either Iran or North Korea perpetrating an airborne attack on Canada is considered extremely unlikely, but fears of homegrown terror plots are of greater importance. Canada has a stake in addressing these country's airborne offensive capabilities only in so far as an attack against the US would not be in Canada's interests. Canada's main incentive in addressing Iran and North Korea's airborne threat capabilities may be to maintain good relations with its principal economic partner by helping the US improve their defensive position. Lacking the imposing security threats felt by many US allies such South Korea and the Baltic states, Canada has comparatively less to lose should the US prove unwilling to engage in universal security provision. However, it would behoove Canada to mollify the ascendant Jacksonian's concerns about free-loading allies in order to mitigate demands for concessions regarding trade. To this end, the incumbent Liberal government has pledged to increase the armed forces budget by more than 70% over the coming decade, including plans to expand the number of fighter planes to be purchased beyond what the previous Conservative government had pledged (specifically citing the need to meet its commitments under NORAD), as well as participating in the refurbishment of the North Warning System [25].

Canada has not been nearly as concerned with potential threats from the Asia-Pacific region and when the pivot and rebalancing of forces toward Asia was taking place under President Obama, Canada did not follow suit. Under the Trump administration the hardened policy lines towards North Korea, and to a certain extent China, will again put Canada in a differing position. While the Asia-Pacific is seeing the proliferation of nuclear capability and the redrawing of spheres of influence, the US under Trump has ratcheted up its rhetoric while Canada has pushed for working within multilateral dispute resolution forums. Canada's pursuit of a China-Canada free trade agreement may also be seen as a soft-balancing against increased US hegemony. That said, clearly Canada is the forward defence line for NORAD. Having strong defence capability at Canadian borders, waters, and airspace is the best strategy for defending the American continent from Asia-Pacific or Russia.

6   Conclusion

An enduring feature of the American political landscape, the Jacksonian constituency was sold on the merits of supporting the construction of an international order to combat the existential threat posed by the Soviet Union. The foreign policy consensus forged during the heat of the Cold War, which was sustained through the years of the *pax Americana,* is coming to an end as the Jacksonian school of American foreign policy breaks with established doctrine, questioning whether it is in the national interest to uphold the existing world order. Although the election of Donald Trump presents an especially jarring manifestation of the Jacksonian will, the distinct features of this school of thought will likely become a more salient presence in US foreign policy in the decades to come than was the case in the latter half of the twentieth century. Accordingly, Canada will have to plan for a persistent shift in the foreign policy perspective of the US. Rather than isolationism, the ascendancy of the Jacksonians within the halls of power will mark a shift towards a more unilateralist US foreign policy, distinguished by the desire to remain unencumbered by multilateral obligations which would restrict policymaker's ability to act in the national interest. While this will be to the general detriment of multilateral institutions, NORAD may ultimately be a beneficiary of the Jacksonian emphasis on the physical security of core US interests. However, it is likely that a more unilateralist approach to American foreign policy will inject a certain degree of turbulence into the Canada-US relationship, as well as exacerbate a number of the security challenges which NORAD is tasked with confronting.

References

1. The Economist (2017) Donald Trump seems to see allies as a burden, 14 Feb 2017. https://www.economist.com/news/united-states/21716034-nato-leaders-make-pitch-president-donald-trump-seems-see-allies-burden
2. Smith B, Brook-Holland L, Page R (2016) Donald Trump on foreign and defence policy. House of Commons Library. http://researchbriefings.files.parliament.uk/documents/CBP-7780/CBP-7780.pdf. Accessed 7 Feb 2018
3. Haberman M., Sanger D (2016) Transcript: Donald Trump expounds his foreign policy views. The New York Times, 26 Mar 2016. https://www.nytimes.com/2016/03/27/us/politics/donald-trump-transcript.html. Accessed 7 Feb 2018
4. Haas R (2016) The isolationist temptation. Wall Str J, 5 Aug 2016
5. Mead W (2001) Special providence: American foreign policy and how it changed the world. Alfred A. Knopf, New York
6. Mead WR (1996) Hamilton's way. World Policy J 13(3):89–106
7. Mead WR (1999) The Jacksonian tradition: and American foreign policy. Natl Interest 58:5–29
8. Clarke M, Ricketts A (2016) Understanding the return of the Jacksonian tradition. Orbis 61 (1):13–26
9. Mead WR (2011) The tea party and American foreign policy: what populism means for globalism. Foreign Aff 90(2):28–44
10. Mead WR (2017) The Jacksonian Revolt: American populism and the liberal order. Foreign Aff 96(2)
11. Rathbun B (2013) Steeped in international affairs? The foreign policy views of the tea party. Foreign Policy Anal 9(1):21–37
12. Trump D (2017) Speech to the UN general assembly. CNN. http://www.cnn.com/videos/us/2017/09/19/trump-united-nations-full-speech.cnn. Accessed 7 Feb 2018
13. Jones D, Khoo N (2017) Donald Trump and the New Jacksonians. Policy J Public Policy Ideas 33(1):42–49
14. Brooks SG, Wohlforth WC (2005) International relations theory and the case against unilateralism. Perspect Polit 3(3):509–524
15. Hoffmann S (2002) Clash of globalizations. Foreign Aff 81(4):104–114
16. Abbott KW, Snidal D (1998) Why states act through formal international organizations. J Confl Resolut 42(1):3–32
17. Monten J (2007) Primacy and grand strategic beliefs in US unilateralism. Glob Gov Rev Multilater Int Organ 13(1):119–138
18. Stephen W (1987) The origins of alliances. Cornell University Press, Ithaca
19. Pape RA (2005) Soft balancing against the United States. Int Secur 30(1):7–45
20. Oswald F (2006) Soft balancing between friends: transforming transatlantic relations. Debatte 14(2):145–160
21. Charron A, Fergusson J, Huebert R, Jockel J, Malone E, McGuire S, Sokolsky J, Stephenson A, Trudgen M, Tucker D, Aseltine P (2014) NORAD in perpetuity? Challenges and opportunities for Canada. Centre for Defence and Security Studies, University of Manitoba
22. Dews F (2017) Joint chiefs Chairman Dunford on the "4+1 Framework" and meeting transnational threats. Brookings Institution. https://www.brookings.edu/blog/brookings-now/2017/02/24/joint-chiefs-chairman-dunford-transnational-threats/. Accessed 9 Feb 2018

23. Freeland C (2017) Address by Minister Freeland on Canada's foreign policy priorities. Global Affairs Canada. https://www.canada.ca/en/global-affairs/news/2017/06/address_by_ministerfreelandoncanadasforeignpolicypriorities.html. Accessed 9 Feb 9 2018
24. Jockel J, Sokolsky J (2016) Ten years into forever: NORAD's place in Canada-US defence relations. In: Fergusson J, Furtado F (eds) Beyond Afghanistan: an international security agenda for Canada. UBC Press, Canada
25. Canada, Department of National Defence (2017) Strong secure engaged: Canada's defence policy

Canadian Defense Policy

New Wineskin, Old Wine: The Future of Canadian Contributions to North American Security

Kim Richard Nossal[✉]

Queen's University, Kingston, ON K7L 3N6, Canada
nossalk@queensu.ca

Abstract. Putting "old wine in a new bottle" is a well-known expression for any effort to present an existing concept, policy, or idea as though it was new. It derives from a New Testament parable based on a contemporary saying that new wine must be put in new bottles. However, the original biblical saying probably makes little sense to most modern readers, since it is not at all clear why new wine cannot be put in *old* bottles. The problem lies with the word "bottle," which is how the New Testament Greek ἀσκός (*askos*) is often translated. For most modern readers, the word "bottle" connotes a vessel made of glass. However, a more correct translation of *askos* is a wineskin or leather bottle. Wineskins in which wine had fermented tended to become stretched and brittle, increasing the likelihood that, were the wineskin to be reused and filled with new wine, it would burst, both spilling the wine and destroying the leather bottle itself. That is why the saying had it that new wine had to be put into a new *askos,* or leather bottle—though in modern parlance the "leather" was eventually dropped in both the new wine saying and the old-wine-new-bottle expression which derived from it. How one translates *askos* is central to the argument of this chapter. For I argue that Canada's new defence policy announced by the Liberal government of Justin Trudeau in June 2017—entitled *Strong, Secure, Engaged*—is indeed a case of "old wine" (an established and largely unchanging Canadian defence policy) in a "new bottle" (a new defence policy statement).

1 Introduction

Putting "old wine in a new bottle" is a well-known expression for any effort to present an existing concept, policy, or idea as though it was new. It derives from a New Testament parable based on a contemporary saying that new wine must be put in new bottles. However, the original biblical saying probably makes little sense to most modern readers, since it is not at all clear why new wine cannot be put in *old* bottles. The problem lies with the word "bottle," which is how the New Testament Greek ἀσκός (*askos*) is often translated. For most modern readers, the word "bottle" connotes a vessel made of glass, and thus most modern readers will miss the crucial reason why two thousand years ago new wine had to be put in new bottles. However, a more correct translation of *askos* is a wineskin or leather bottle. Wineskins in which wine had fermented tended to become stretched and brittle, increasing the likelihood that, were

C. Leuprecht et al. (eds.), *North American Strategic Defense in the 21st Century:*,
Advanced Sciences and Technologies for Security Applications,
https://doi.org/10.1007/978-3-319-90978-3_8

the wineskin to be reused and filled with new wine, it would burst, both spilling the wine and destroying the leather bottle itself. That is why the saying had it that new wine had to be put into a new *askos,* or leather bottle—though in modern parlance the "leather" was eventually dropped in both the new wine saying and the old-wine-new-bottle expression which derived from it.

How one translates *askos* is central to the argument of this chapter. For I argue that Canada's new defence policy announced by the Liberal government of Justin Trudeau in June 2017—entitled *Strong, Secure, Engaged*—is indeed a case of "old wine" (an established and largely unchanging Canadian defence policy) in a "new bottle" (a new defence policy statement). To be sure, the Trudeau government presented the policy to us as though it contained, as the statement puts it, a "bold new vision" for Canada [1, p. 11]. And certainly *newness* is a pervasive theme in the 2017 defence policy: the word "new" appears fully 219 times in a 113-page document. But I suggest that we should think of the new defence policy statement—the vessel—as a wineskin (ἀσκός, *askos*) rather than a bottle, since one can readily put wine into an old *glass* bottle without fear of it bursting. But if instead we think of *Strong, Secure, Engaged* as a *wineskin*, we can see why the metaphor is so very apt in the case of Canadian defence policy. I will argue that governments in Ottawa have treated defence policy statements over the years as little more than wineskins that become stretched and brittle after a period of fermentation and need to be replaced. But the wine, I will argue, rarely changes. Certainly, this is the case of the 2017 defence policy statement: the new defence policy does not significantly change Canada's contribution to North American security.

2   Canadian Defence White Papers: A Brief History

Unlike many other countries, Canada rarely reviews its defence policy. In the last half-century, despite the dramatic changes that have marked global politics, there have only been seven defence reviews. By contrast, the United States reviews defence every four years with its Quadrennial Defense Review, and many other Canadian allies review their defence policies much more frequently than in Canada. However, the rarity of the process should not blind us to the reality that the process of reviewing defence policy in Canada is actually very regular—indeed, it is as regular as clockwork. It is just that Canadian defence-review clocks do not measure time in a normal way, by hours or years. Rather, in Canada there is another regularity at work—and the years in which Canadian defence reviews were published gives away the nature of that regularity: 1964, 1971, 1987, 1994, 2005, 2008, and 2017. In other words, when Canadians get a new prime minister, it is time for a new defence review. Lester B. Pearson published a defence review in 1964 after the Liberals won the 1963 election. After he won the leadership of the Liberal party in 1968, Pierre Elliott Trudeau published a foreign policy review in 1970 and a defence policy in 1971. When the Progressive Conservative party won the September 1984 elections, Prime Minister Brian Mulroney published a foreign policy review in 1985 and a defence policy in 1987. After the Liberals regained government in 1993, Jean Chrétien issued foreign and defence policy reviews in 1995. His successor, Paul Martin, Jr. published his *International Policy*

Statement in 2005 that incorporated reviews of foreign policy, defence policy, trade policy and development assistance policy. Stephen Harper's Conservative government published a defence policy in 2008, but broke the tradition of launching a foreign policy review: at the outset, Harper decided that there was no need for a foreign policy review.

In theory, articulating periodic statements of a country's defence policy makes a great deal of sense, even for a non-great power like Canada. After all, world politics is in a constant state of evolution, and subjecting policy to a formal review provides an opportunity to take account of changes and to subject the accepted verities of one period to scrutiny. Policy reviews set up a feedback loop that enables a government to adjust its international policies to ensure that its global strategy—and its spending— will keep pace with change.

This might be the theory, but all of the defence policy reviews launched by Canadian leaders since the 1960s—and the statements of policy issued at the end— were not designed for any strategic purpose. That much is clear from the fact that not a single prime minister between 1964 and 2015 ever revisited the foreign or defence policy reviews launched at the outset of their ministries, even though Pierre Trudeau was in office for sixteen years, Chrétien in office for ten years, and Mulroney and Harper for nine years. Rather, the primary purpose of these reviews was *purely* political: to demonstrate just how different the new government was from its prede-cessor in defence policy. Pearson's 1964 review was aimed at establishing distance between the disastrous defence policies pursued by the Diefenbaker government; when he took over the Liberal leadership from Pearson, Trudeau *père* used his 1971 white paper on defence, *Defence in the 70s,* to signal how different he was from the previous government; Mulroney's 1987 defence policy review, *Challenge and Commitment,* was aimed squarely at Trudeau. In a similar fashion, Chrétien took aim at Mulroney. When Martin finally seized the Liberal leadership from Chrétien in 2003 after a bitter civil war, he needed to establish policy distance from Chrétien, just as Trudeau *père* had sought to do with Pearson in the late 1960s: his *International Policy Statement,* published in April 2005, just months before the Liberals were defeated in the January 2006 elections, was designed to mark his approach to defence. Likewise, Harper's 2008 defence review, *Canada First Defence Policy,* was designed to distance the Conservative government from the Liberal governments of Jean Chrétien and Paul Martin.

During the 2015 general election campaign, the Liberals under Justin Trudeau promised that a Liberal government would pursue a very different foreign and defence policy than the Harper Conservatives. The Liberal platform devoted just ten pages of their 88-page platform to international policy [2]. While there was no foreign policy section per se, the Liberals did promise to "restore Canada as a leader in the world" [2, p. 68]. This general promise to restore Canadian leadership in the world was accom-panied by a range of other promises. On peace and security, the platform committed a Liberal government to renew Canada's commitment to peacekeeping operations and to allocate resources to the United Nations (UN), particularly on civilian police training and peace operations. On defence, the Liberals committed to maintain current spending levels and to launch a review of defence policy. The platform did, however, embrace three very specific promises. One focused on the replacement for the fleet of CF-18

Hornet jet fighters: "We will not buy the F-35 stealth fighter-bomber." Instead, a Liberal government would "immediately launch an open and transparent competition" to replace the existing CF-18 fleet, but would not allow Lockheed Martin to compete. (How it was possible to run an "open" competition while refusing to allow one of the primary competitors to compete was not addressed.) The second specific promise related to the Canadian operations in Iraq and Syria against Islamic State in Iraq and the Levant (ISIL, also known as ISIS, Islamic State in Iraq and al-Shām, or *Daesh*, its Arabic acronym): a Liberal government would end Canadian combat contributions to the Global Coalition to Counter ISIL. In particular, the CF-18s, which had been engaged in bombing attacks against ISIL in Iraq and Syria, would be withdrawn. Instead, a Liberal government would "refocus Canada's military contribution in the region on the training of local forces, while providing more humanitarian support," and admit 25,000 Syrian refugees immediately. Third, the platform promised to remain "fully committed" to the existing military contributions to the North Atlantic Treaty Organization (NATO) assurance measures in Central and Eastern Europe [2, pp. 69–71].

Once in power, the new government moved to implement a number of its defence policy promises. The CF-18s were duly withdrawn from Iraq and Syria in February 2016, although the government did seek to soften the blow somewhat by leaving key air assets—a CP-140 Aurora and a CC-150T Polaris air refueller—in theatre, and by embracing a significantly increased ground presence. Reflecting the Liberal promise to return Canada to its mythical peacekeeping past, the new government began bruiting the idea of a major deployment of peacekeeping troops to an operation in Africa, widely anticipated to be Mali.

It started to make good its promise not to acquire the F-35 as the replacement for the CF-18 Hornet. While Trudeau quickly backed away from his promise not to even allow Lockheed Martin to participate in the CF-18 replacement competition on the advice of the government's lawyers, the prime minister nonetheless continued to openly denigrate the F-35, claiming in Parliament, for example, that the F-35 "does not work and is a long way from ever working."[1] His minister of national defence, Harjit Sajjan, quickly found a way to defer a decision on the CF-18 Hornet replacement. He declared that the existing fleet of seventy-six CF-18s would not be enough if for some reason Canada were called on to fulfill all its military commitments at once. The only way to overcome this "capability gap" in fighter aircraft strength, Sajjan declared, was to purchase an interim fleet of eighteen Boeing Super Hornets, and defer a decision on a long-term replacement for the CF-18 Hornet fleet until the early 2020s.

This was an exceedingly neat piece of political legerdemain, and it might have worked had Boeing Co., the manufacturer of the Super Hornet, not launched a trade complaint against Bombardier Inc. of Montréal, claiming that Bombardier had dumped its C-series airliner in the United States market. In September 2017, the United States imposed a duty of 200% on the C-series. Trudeau, furious at the harm being done to

---

[1] Trudeau was speaking in French, claiming that the Conservatives "se sont accrochés à un avion qui ne fonctionne pas et qui est loin de pouvoir fonctionner," which Hansard translated as "The Conservatives threw in their lot with a plane that does not work and is a long way from ever working": Canada, House of Commons, *Debates*, 42nd Parl., 1st Sess., 7 June, 14 h 20.

Bombardier, walked back the Super Hornet plan, promising that Canada "won't do business with a company that's busy trying to sue us and put our aerospace workers out of business" [3].

In Europe, the Trudeau government continued the policy that had been pursued by the Conservatives. In March 2017, the government extended its military training commitment to Ukraine for a further two years. In Central and Eastern Europe, the Trudeau government decided to ramp up its commitment to the reassurance mission, announcing in July 2016 that Canada would lead a multinational battlegroup in Latvia [4]. In June 2017, Enhanced Forward Battlegroup Latvia was stood up, with 450 Canadian forces joined by forces from Albania, Italy, Poland, Slovenia, and Spain.

But the key initiative was the launching of a review of defence policy. (Like Harper, Trudeau chose not to launch a foreign policy review.) In early 2016, it looked as though history was going to repeat itself. The timeline established at the outset was compressed: public consultations would be held across the country during the summer of 2016, and the review would be published in the fall of that year. The new defence review, in glossy four-colour format and featuring catchy slogans ripped from a *Mad Men* episode, would prominently adorn desks in National Defence Headquarters—and then, like all the previous Canadian defence reviews, it would be promptly forgotten for the remainder of the Trudeau *fils* ministry.

3 The Rise of Trump

That normal trajectory was, however, disrupted by the rise of Donald J. Trump in the United States. Trump's hostile takeover of the Republican Party in May 2016 was followed by his election as president in November. There is little doubt that the Trudeau government saw the Trump insurgency as a major threat to Canadian interests. For during his candidacy, Trump promised to overturn the key pillars of Canada's approach to global politics since the end of the Second World War in 1945. Of considerable concern was Trump's constant slagging of the North Atlantic Treaty Organization as "obsolete" during the election campaign; his disparagement of traditional American friends and allies for "ripping off" the United States by not spending enough on defence; and his denigration of international trade in general and the North American Free Trade Agreement (NAFTA) in particular as "the worst trade deal maybe ever signed, anywhere," as he put it during the first presidential debate in September 2016 [5].

The response of the Liberal government in Ottawa to Trump's election was immediate. Trudeau shuffled his cabinet. Stéphane Dion, was who widely seen as not having the right personality for a Trump White House, was appointed to a diplomatic post in Europe. In his place, Trudeau appointed Chrystia Freeland, the trade minister. Not only did Freeland have a solid grasp on the trade file that was seen as a key issue, given Trump's highly negative views of NAFTA, but she also had extensive contacts in the United States from her time with the *Financial Times* and Thomson Reuters. Trudeau also sought out a number of former policy-makers in the formulation of policy towards the United States. For example, he consulted Brian Mulroney, who as prime minister had been the driving force behind both the Canada-United States Free Trade

Agreement that had gone into force in 1989 and the trilateralization of free trade talks that had led to NAFTA. Trudeau also consulted Derek Burney, Mulroney's chief of staff from 1987 to 1989 and then Canadian ambassador in Washington from 1989 to 1993.

Importantly, the Liberal government deployed Canada's diplomatic and political assets widely across the American political system, embracing not only both houses of Congress, but state and municipal governments in what one observer called Canada's "doughtnut strategy"—in other words, working around the "hole" that was the Trump White House [6]. Trudeau even reached out to Ivanka Trump, the president's daughter, in what was described as "daughter diplomacy" (prompting John Higginbotham, who had been the minister in the Canadian embassy in Washington from 1994 to 2000, to observe, "It is just so *Game of Thrones*") [7].

Importantly, the rise of Trump also had an impact on the defence review. The Trudeau government slowed the review down to a crawl as it sought to assess the likely impacts of a Trump presidency on global politics in general and Canadian policy in particular. The timing of the defence review release was pushed back, first beyond Trump's inauguration in January, when the new president made it very clear in his inaugural speech that his America First rhetoric in 2016 was not just a campaign shtick, and then again after Trudeau and Trump had their first summit meeting at the White House in February 2017.

In the meantime, the Trudeau government simply took the idea of a major Canadian contribution to a peacekeeping operation in Africa off the agenda by deferring an announcement and refusing to accept offers of leadership positions in UN missions being bruited by the United Nations and other allied governments. While it was never overtly stated by the Trudeau cabinet, it was clear that there was a hesitation to commit a significant force to a peace operation before it was clear how Ottawa was going to respond to the demands being made by the incoming administration about increased defence spending by America's allies. Instead, the government in Ottawa moved ahead with a major deployment to Latvia as part of a broader effort by NATO at reassurance in Central Europe. And while it withdrew Canada's CF-18s from combat missions in Syria and Iraq, it continued a major operation in Iraq with the Global Coalition to Counter ISIL.

It was not until four months after Trump's inauguration that the Trudeau government judged that it was an appropriate time for the defence review to be released. However, the government decided that before the defence review was released, it needed to be placed in a broader foreign policy context. As a result, on 6 June, two days before the release of the new defence policy, the minister of foreign affairs, Chrystia Freeland, rose in the House of Commons to deliver a major foreign policy speech that sought to frame Canada's broad approach to global politics in an era when American leadership and support for the liberal international order could no longer be taken for granted [8].

Then, on 8 June, the minister of national defence, Harjit Sajjan, unveiled the government's defence policy. To be sure, the *Mad Men* approach was still evident— Canadian defence, the review assured us, as all about being *Strong, Secure, Engaged* ("strong at home, secure in North America, engaged in the world").

4 Strong, Secure, Engaged

Because Canadian defence white papers or policy statements are driven by domestic political needs rather than proper strategic considerations, they invariably repackage long-lived and enduring verities about Canadian defence policy, putting them in new wineskins after the wineskin embraced by the previous prime minister, sometimes more than a decade before, had become stretched and brittle. In this respect, *Strong, Secure, Engaged* is just like all its predecessors. The broad lines of policy outlined in the 2017 policy do not differ much from previous statements: after all, Canadian defence policy is deeply and structurally fixed by its relations with the United States and its membership in the North Atlantic Treaty Organization (NATO). Since the 1950s, Canadian defence policy has always stressed home defence, continental defence cooperation with the United States, and military engagement beyond the North American continent. So it was not at all surprising that the defence policy of the Trudeau Liberal government embraced as its guiding slogan: "Strong at home, secure in North America, engaged in the world." The previous defence reviews said much the same thing, even if the language used was slightly different.

To be sure, the Trudeau government's new defence policy did have some new elements. For example, as Stéfanie von Hlatky and I have argued [9], one major departure was the embrace by the Trudeau government of the idea that military personnel is a crucial part of defence policy. To be sure, the phrase "people are our most important asset" has the makings of a cliché, but crafting a comprehensive strategy to improve the environment for the professional military was notably absent from the 2008 *Canada First Defence Strategy* put out by the Conservative government of Stephen Harper. The Trudeau government's new defence policy, in contrast, promises "unprecedented support to our people and their families." More than half of the defence budget is already set aside for military personnel. The policy creates new resources to address mental health issues, to better plan for military-to-civilian military transitions and to make military service easier on families. Moreover, the theme of diversity can be felt across the various personnel-focused objectives. This promises to contribute to repairing the military's reputation after the damaging report on sexual misconduct in the military by Marie Deschamps [10]. For example, the policy launches new recruitment efforts for women, to reach the goal of 25% of women in the armed forces by 2026 (the CAF currently has about 15%).

More broadly, a diverse CAF is about building a military that resembles the population it serves: more women, more visible minorities, more indigenous peoples, etc. Beyond diversity, the CAF also wants to be an employer of choice, since it needs to compete for talent with other sectors, offering better compensation for deployments and more flexibility to servicemen and women who want to alternate between military service and other pursuits, professional or personal. What remains to be seen is how this will be communicated to Canadians and whether this will have an impact at the recruiting centres.

A second major departure was the way that the 2017 defence policy sought to cost out as explicitly as possible its future planned capital acquisitions. In the past, it was common for Canadian defence reviews to identify key weapons systems needed for the future. For example, in 1987, the key weapons system identified by the Progressive Conservative government of Brian Mulroney was a new fleet of twelve nuclear-powered submarines. Likewise, the 2008 *Canada First Defence Strategy* had a long shopping list of capital items that the Harper Conservatives were promising to purchase for the Canadian Armed Forces. But there was usually little in the way of indicating what the costs were and how they were going to be paid. The 2017 review was like its predecessors in outlining the reinvestment that the government intended to make in the core capabilities of the Canadian Armed Forces. Indeed, the reinvestment was as close to full-spectrum as one could imagine in a Canadian context. For the Royal Canadian Navy, the government promised to acquire fifteen surface combatants, two joint support ships, five to six Arctic offshore patrol ships, a modernized *Victoria*-class submarine fleet, with enhanced intelligence, surveillance, reconnaissance and armament systems. For the Canadian Army, the government promised modernization across systems, with a commitment to increase Arctic mobility and ability to operate in remote regions. For the Royal Canadian Air Force, there was the promise of a new fighter fleet of eighty-eight aircraft, fully twenty-three more than the sixty-five that had been the previous size of the fleet promised by the Conservatives in 2008. In addition, next generation multi-mission planes to replace the CP-140 Auroras and new air-to-air tankers, new utility transports, and new remotely piloted systems were added. New joint capabilities were promised. And the defence review outlined plans to recapitalize and modernize Canada's Special Operations Forces.

But unlike previous reviews, the Trudeau government provided a full costing of these programs for modernization and reinvestment. The defence statement proposed to increase Canada's annual defence spending on a cash basis from $18.9 billion in 2016–17–$32.7 billion by 2026–27, a massive increase of 70%, unprecedented in times of peace. Importantly, a total of $33.8 billion was committed for the acquisition of capital assets over the twenty years from 2017–18 to 2036–37. Another departure from past practice was that this massive reinvestment was carefully costed out, with the review at pains to demonstrate the differences between funding on an accrual basis versus a cash basis.

However, it is important to recognize that although at first blush the overall defence reinvestment numbers *sounded* good, the Trudeau government was in fact engaging in yet more legerdemain. It is possible that the Liberal cabinet embraced a robust reinvestment plan for the CAF in the hope that the reinvestment numbers might sound good to a United States president who had spent the better part of the previous year slagging America's allies for their cheapness in defence spending, and claiming that allies "owed" the United States vast sums of money for past protection provided by the US. It is also possible that the Liberal government was counting on Trump not noticing the Canadian legerdemain. For the recapitalization of the CAF announced in June 2017 was all loaded far into the future, and well beyond the next election, scheduled for 21 October 2019. Populating an Excel spreadsheet with twenty years' worth of columns, and then filling them with impressive-sounding numbers is easy: promising in 2017 that the Canadian defence budget in 2031–31, for example, will be $30 billion is little more than a 6/49 "imagine the freedom" exercise, divorced from the reality that it will be the government elected (or re-elected) in 2019 that will have to grapple with the huge deficits run by the Trudeau government in its first term. Previous governments had written big defence shopping lists—for example, the Mulroney government's promise to buy twelve nuclear-powered submarines, or the Harper government's 2008 *Canada First Defence Strategy* shopping list—but they never wrote shopping lists that were so unambiguously to be paid for by some future government.

5 Implications for North American Security

While *Strong, Secure, Engaged* does not substantially alter the Canadian government's overall approach to defence, there are two aspects of the Trudeau government's policy that do have implications for North American security in the medium term.

The first is that the Trudeau government's approach to the replacement of the CF-18 Hornet fleet promises to affect the future of North American security in the air domain. While *Strong, Secure, Engaged* commits Canada to interoperability with the United States Air Force, we are likely to see an emerging divergence between the capabilities of the USAF and RCAF in the air defence of North America in the 2020s. Because the Trudeau government has chosen to play such political games with the CF-18 fleet replacement, Canadian fighter capability into the 2020s will be limited by the decision to fly the CF-18 Hornets until the early 2030s. A new fighter fleet is not scheduled to come into service until the late 2020s, and it is not clear at this juncture that the Canadian government will select the F-35, the only fifth-generation fighter on the market. In the meantime, however, the United States will soon be deploying only fifth-generation fighters in its regions of NORAD. The significant discrepancy in capabilities that may emerge will have considerable impact on North American security.

The second facet of the Trudeau government's North American security policy that will have a significant impact on defence relations between Canada and the United States is the continued unwillingness of the Canadian government to join the US ballistic missile defense (BMD) scheme. Since the 1990s, successive Canadian governments have refused to accept American invitations to join BMD. The Liberal government of Jean Chrétien (1993–2003) was firmly opposed to BMD. When Paul Martin was seeking the Liberal leadership in 2002 and 2003, he promised that if he became prime minister, he would join BMD. However, after he became prime minister in December 2003, he reversed course when he realized how much domestic political opposition there was, eventually deciding in February 2005 that Canada would not participate in BMD [11]. At the time, the leader of the Conservative opposition was Stephen Harper, who was quick to promise that a Conservative government would join BMD. But when the Liberals were defeated in the January 2006 elections and Harper became prime minister, he spent the next nine years in power actively avoiding a decision on BMD. By the time that Justin Trudeau and the Liberals were elected in 2015, there was some speculation that the new government would take the opportunity to use the defence review as a way to revisit the BMD issue. However, like Harper, Martin, and Chrétien, Trudeau steered well clear of the BMD issue: *Strong, Secure,*

Engaged announced unambiguously that "Canada's policy with respect to participation in ballistic missile defence has not changed" [1, p. 90]. But this continuation of a twenty-year avoidance of BMD will pose increasing problems for Canada in an era when the Democratic People's Republic of Korea increases its ballistic missile and nuclear capabilities and the United States is inclined to respond more assertively than in the past.

6 Conclusion

The 2017 defence policy embraced by the Trudeau Liberals contained few new elements about North American security and defence. The defence statement could have been an opportunity to rethink Canadian defence policy in a global environment that is in the midst of dramatic changes, the result of the rise of China as a global power, the willingness of the Russian Federation to play a disruptive role globally, and the tendency of an American president who seems to care little for the maintenance of United States global hegemony. However, *Strong, Secure, Engaged*, like all its predecessors, had no *strategic* purpose at all; it was written for purely domestic political purposes: to demonstrate to Canadian voters that Justin Trudeau had a different approach to defence policy than his predecessor, Stephen Harper.

To be sure, it is possible that at least one part of the 2017 defence policy—the promise of a massive reinvestment in the CAF—may have been added to appease Donald J. Trump, at least in the short term. Indeed, the fact that the vast majority of the promised increases occur well after 2019–20 is likely no coincidence. In other words, the large-scale spending promised by the 2017 defence policy occurs well after the mid-term American elections in 2018, when it is possible that the voters may produce changes in the American political scene. It may be that the Trudeau government simply decided to offer up pleasant-sounding numbers to the Trump administration in the short term, while kicking the longer-term issue of actually finding the funds to make good on the promises down the road.

In sum, *Strong, Secure, Engaged* works well enough as a replacement for the old wineskin put out by the Conservatives in 2008. The 2017 policy certainly looks the part, particularly its constant claims of *newness*. But in fact the wine in this new wineskin is old: the 2017 defence policy embraces the same ideas that have been embraced for the last fifty years. Moreover, it does not address the twin challenges posed to North American security and defence posed by the Trudeau government's unwillingness to replace the aging CF-18 Hornet fleet and its unwillingness to address the problem caused by Canada's refusal to participate in ballistic missile defence. Finally, *Strong, Secure, Engaged* does not begin to address the reality that Canadian Armed Forces are in need of a major reinvestment and modernization in the short term, not the longer term. Although the 2017 defence policy promises a lot, it in fact does not provide the CAF with the capabilities that it needs in the short to medium term to be strong at home, secure in North America, and engaged in the world.

References

1. Canada, Minister of National Defence (2017) Strong, secure, engaged: Canada's defence policy
2. Liberal Party of Canada (2015) Real change: a new plan for a strong middle class, 5 Oct 2015.   https://www.liberal.ca/wp-content/uploads/2015/10/New-plan-for-a-strong-middle-class.pdf. Accessed 15 Feb 2018
3. Sheetz M (2017). Justin Trudeau says Canada will not buy from Boeing while it is 'busy trying to sue us'. CNBC.com, 18 Oct 2017. https://www.cnbc.com/2017/09/18/justin-trudeau-says-canada-will-not-buy-from-boeing-while-it-is-busy-trying-to-sue-us.html. Accessed 15 Feb 2018
4. Berthiaume L (2016) Canada to send 450 troops to Latvia as NATO faces off against Russia. Globe and Mail, 8 July 2016. https://www.theglobeandmail.com/news/politics/trudeau-pledges-troops-frigate-jets-as-nato-faces-off-against-russia/article30816617/. Accessed 15 Feb 2018
5. Blake A (2016) The first Trump-Clinton presidential debate transcript, annotated. Washington Post, 26 Sept 2016. https://www.washingtonpost.com/news/the-fix/wp/2016/09/26/the-first-trump-clinton-presidential-debate-transcript-annotated/?utm_term=.ec5c306a7200. Accessed 15 Feb 2018
6. Fisher M (2017). Canada's Trump strategy: go around him. New York Times, 22 June 2017. https://www.nytimes.com/2017/06/22/world/canada/canadas-trump-strategy-go-around-him.html. Accessed 15 Feb 2018
7. Dale D (2017) Daughter diplomacy: Trudeau's unorthodox play for Donald Trump's approval. Toronto Star, 16 Mar 2017. https://www.thestar.com/news/world/2017/03/16/daughter-diplomacy-trudeaus-unorthodox-play-for-donald-trumps-approval.html. Accessed 15 Feb 2018
8. House of Commons (2017) Debates. 42nd Parl. 1st Sess., 10 h 25, 6 June 2017
9. von Hlatky S, Nossal KR (2017) Canada's new defence policy: the short version. In: Conference of Defence Associations Analysis, July 2017. http://cdainstitute.ca/wp-content/uploads/2017/07/CDA-Institute-Analysis-vonHlatkyNossal-July-2017FINAL-3.pdf. Accessed 15 Feb 2018
10. Deschamps M (2015) External review into sexual misconduct and sexual harassment in the Canadian armed forces. External Review Authority, Ottawa, 27 Mar 2015. http://www.forces.gc.ca/assets/FORCES_Internet/docs/en/caf-community-support-services-harassment/era-final-report-(April-20-2015)-eng.pdf. Accessed 15 Feb 2018
11. Barry Donald (2010) Canada and missile defence: saying no to Mr Bush. J Mil Strateg Stud 12(3):12–44

Canada's New Defence Policy and the Security of North America

Allen Sens[(✉)]

Department of Political Science, University of British Columbia,
Vancouver, BC V6T 1Z1, Canada
asens@mail.ubc.ca

Abstract. Since the end of the Cold War political and technological developments have presented an increasingly diverse array of old, resurgent, and new
security threats to North America. Canada, Mexico, and the US have responded
by creating an equally diverse constellation of bilateral and trilateral agreements
addressing these threats. This architecture, if it can be called that, is the sum of
decades of reactive, incremental additions and renovations to existing security
arrangements. However, there is no formal or informal focal point for deliberation, analysis, or management of North American security cooperation. In an
era of complex and interrelated security threats, North American security
cooperation is curiously headless and lacking a capacity for strategic mindfulness, assessment and guidance.

1 Introduction

Since the end of the Cold War political and technological developments have presented
an increasingly diverse array of old, resurgent, and new security threats to North
America. Canada, Mexico, and the US have responded by creating an equally diverse
constellation of bilateral and trilateral agreements addressing these threats. This
architecture, if it can be called that, is the sum of decades of reactive, incremental
additions and renovations to existing security arrangements. However, there is no
formal or informal focal point for deliberation, analysis, or management of North
American security cooperation. In an era of complex and interrelated security threats,
North American security cooperation is curiously headless and lacking a capacity for
strategic mindfulness, assessment and guidance.

On 6 June 2017 the government of Canada released its defence policy statement,
titled *Strong, Secure, Engaged: Canada's Defence Policy*. Like most documents of its
kind, *Strong, Secure, Engaged* serves as one part strategic assessment taking stock of
the security environment facing the country, one part policy plan identifying defence
priorities and the roles of the Canadian military, and one part political showcase
demonstrating the veracity of the government's approach to defence. A review of
previous defence policy statements reveals an enduring, consistent Canadian strategic
approach to defence based on three fundamentals: the security of Canada; the security
of North America; and the security of Canada's interests abroad.

© Springer International Publishing AG, part of Springer Nature 2018
C. Leuprecht et al. (eds.), *North American Strategic Defense in the 21st Century:*,
Advanced Sciences and Technologies for Security Applications,
https://doi.org/10.1007/978-3-319-90978-3_9

This chapter focuses on *Strong, Secure, Engaged* and the future of North American security cooperation, and makes several interrelated arguments. First, *Strong, Secure, Engaged* is the latest in a long line of Canadian defence policy statements that reflect an enduring Canadian grand strategy in world affairs. Second, *Strong, Secure, Engaged* confronts the same political challenges that largely compromised its predecessors. Third, the record of Canada-US security cooperation suggests the existence of a common Canada-US security and defence identity. However, a more comprehensive governance framework than that envisioned in *Strong, Secure, Engaged* must be developed if the diverse range of threats to North America are to be effectively met in the future.

2   Canadian Defence Planning: A Canadian Grand Strategy?

Like all statements of its kind *Strong, Secure, Engaged* was not composed in a vacuum. The document is faithful to a grand strategic narrative that has dominated discourse on Canada's place and role in the world. Grand strategy is most often associated with great powers, but countries with more modest capacities and influence in world affairs can have grand strategies. *Strong, Secure, Engaged* is not strictly speaking a grand strategic document, but within its pages are expressions of grand strategic thinking, even if Canadian governments and Canadians have difficulty associating such lofty allusions (illusions?) with Canada. Canada does have a grand strategy: it is just not very grand, relatively speaking.

What are the core features of Canada's grand strategy in world affairs? The first is the role geography exerts on the country's outlook. Canada is located right next door to the US, requiring Canadian governments to manage a close political, economic, and societal relationship with the US while at the same time maintaining the country's sovereignty and distinctiveness. In practice, this has led Canadian governments to seek counterweights in relations with other countries and multilateral institutions to balance the influence of the US and exert foreign policy independence. The balance between maintaining close relations and maintaining independence is a delicate one: governments have been criticized for getting too close to the US (Brian Mulroney's Conservatives) or too distant (Jean Chrétien's Liberals).

Canada's vast geographic space complicates its strategic calculus. The country spans 9,984,670 km^2 (3,855,103 square miles). The distance from Canada's west coast to its east coast is over 5,000 km (3,100 miles). The border with the US stretches for 8,900 km (5,530 miles) including the 2,500-km (1,550 mile) border with Alaska. Canada's saltwater coastline extends for 243,797 km (151,488 miles). Of special concern is Canada's Arctic, a vast area composed of 36,500 islands and 1.4 million km^2 (870,000 square miles). Canada faces an eternal paradox in the Arctic: its most important security and trade partner is simultaneously the most serious threat to Canadian sovereignty over the region. In the future, the strategic significance of the Arctic will continue to increase due to climate change impacts.

A second core feature of Canada's grand strategy is a search for influence in world affairs. Successive Canadian governments have sought a voice and seat at the table, where they could participate in joint decision-making. This interest was so crucial to

Canada that it took on the status of a dogma known as the functional principle, originally outlined in the House of Commons by Prime Minister Mackenzie King in 1943. The functional principle holds that the influence of countries in international affairs should depend on their contributions: countries that make contributions should get a voice, with some expectation of influence over outcomes. The functional principle implied selectivity: it was never envisioned that Canada would be everywhere or do everything. Rather, Canadian governments had to define priorities, an inherently strategic task.

A third core feature of Canada's grand strategic approach is multilateralism in general and multilateral institutions in particular. It is taken as an axiom that Canada cannot decisively influence world affairs on its own, and must therefore do so in concert with other like-minded countries in formal or informal arrangements. This explains the long pattern in Canadian diplomacy of active engagement in institutions such as the United Nations (UN) and the North Atlantic Treaty Organization (NATO), and a wide range of international treaties, trade agreements, and informal arrangements such as the G7 and G20. Canada has thus been a proponent of liberal internationalism, a diplomatic outlook associated with institution building, free trade, the promotion of the rule of law and democracy, and good governance.

A fourth core feature of Canada's strategic outlook is the importance of global stability. To this end, Canadian governments have always professed support for international peace and security, a now iconic phrase in Canadian foreign and security policy discourse. A stable international system prevents the emergence of threats to Canada's physical security, reduces the need for Canadian expeditionary operations abroad, and is the precondition for rules-based international system suited to a less powerful, trade-dependent country.

Taken together, these elements constitute what might be called Canada's grand strategy. They are cornerstones of a Canadian self-identity in world affairs, which revolves around the idea of the middle power. The middle power model, as it has come to be known in Canada, posits the existence of a set of countries that do not have the assets and interests of great powers, but have a larger role to play than small states. The model continues to attract criticism, but in general these core concepts have been entrenched in the mainstream of Canadian political leadership, officialdom, and the foreign and defence policy community for many decades. It is in this larger context that Canada's defence statements and approaches to North American security must be understood.

3   Canada's Defence Statements

Known variously as Defence White Papers and Defence Reviews, Canadian governments have produced Defence Statements at irregular intervals. The statements are the product of a lengthy internal review process conducted by the Department of National Defence (DND). This process engages other governmental departments, stakeholders in industry, and usually is accompanied by a public consultation process that includes academia, civil society groups, and members of the public. Defence Reviews are not conducted in accordance with a mandated, regular schedule (such as the Quadrennial

Defence Reviews in the US). New governments have generally produced new defence statements, or done so when the relevancy of the current statement has been called into question.

For the early part of the Cold War, foreign and defence policy statements were thematically consistent. The 1964 defence statement captured the fundamentals of defence policy in this period:

> The objectives of Canadian defence policy, which cannot be dissociated from foreign policy, are to preserve the peace by supporting collective defence measures to deter military aggression; to support Canadian foreign policy including that arising out of our participation in international organizations, and to provide for the protection and surveillance of our territory, our air-space and our coastal waters [1, p. 5].

In 1970 the government of Pierre Elliot Trudeau produced *Foreign Policy for Canadians*. This six-booklet set was billed as a fundamental reassessment of Canada's foreign policy priorities in the world, and was followed by the release of a defence statement in 1971. Although the Trudeau government had envisioned a significant departure from Canada's Cold War foreign and defence policy, by the end of Trudeau's tenure there had been little change to the fundamentals of Canada's foreign and defence policy orientation. In 1987, the Conservative government of Brian Mulroney produced *Challenge and Commitment: A Defence policy for Canada*. The glossy document was intended to reinvigorate the Canadian military after decades of neglect, and featured the purchase of a fleet of nuclear-powered attack submarines. However, the end of the Cold War rendered much of the statement obsolete.

Despite significant variations in governmental approach and an evolving security environment, Canadian defence policy during the Cold War was characterized by fundamental continuities. These included domestic aid of the civil power roles, the defence of North America, and the defence of Western Europe through NATO, which featured the commitment of stationed forces in Germany. Peacekeeping played a prominent role through the Cold War but despite its high public profile and approval ratings within Canada, the peacekeeping role was always considered secondary to the warfighting missions of the Canadian military.

Since 1987, major Canadian defence statements have been released in 1994, 2005, 2008, and 2017. The 1994 White Paper on Defence was the first review of defence policy in the wake of the Cold War. The 1994 White Paper identified a number of international security concerns (eschewing the language of threats) including global pressures, failed states, the resurgence of old hatreds, and weapons proliferation. The Paper struck a cautionary tone about the future:

> …it seems prudent to plan for a world characterized in the long term by instability. Canada's defence policy must reflect the world as it is, rather than the world as we would like it to be. Under these conditions, the most appropriate response is a flexible, realistic, and affordable defence policy, one that provides the means to apply military force when Canadians consider it necessary to uphold essential Canadian values and vital security interests, at home and abroad [2, p. 8].

The 1994 White Paper established a trifecta of roles for the Canadian military that would endure in subsequent defence statements. The missions were: the Protection of Canada; Canada-US Defence Cooperation; and Contributing to International Security.

In 2005 another review produced the 2005 International Policy Statement, titled *A Role of Pride and Influence in the World*. The statement came in the form of five booklets, consisting of an overview followed by booklets on Defence, Diplomacy, Commerce, and Development. By this time, the language of threats to Canada's well-being, interests, and values had returned, specifically in the form of failed and failing states, global terrorism, proliferation of weapons of mass destruction, and intra-state and inter-state conflict. The missions of the Canadian military were identified as: Protecting Canada and Canadians; Maintaining a strong Canada-US defence relationship; and Contributing to a safer and more secure world.

In 2008, after a largely internal review process, the Conservative government of Stephen Harper released the *Canada First Defence Strategy*. The government contended that previous governments had failed to provide the Canadian military with sufficient resources. The Harper government was less sympathetic to UN peacekeeping roles and sought to restore pride in Canada's military history. Despite significant differences between the new government and previous Liberal governments, the fundamentals of Canada's defence policy remained largely intact: Defending Canada: Delivering Excellence at Home; Defending North America: A Strong and Reliable Partner; and Contributing to International Peace and Security: Projecting Leadership Abroad.

Successive defence policy statements have all reflected the enduring, grand strategic calculus that has dominated Canadian approaches to security and defence. Since the end of the Second World War Canadian concepts of national defence have been based around three concentric circles: the defence of Canada, driven by the need for territorial security and defence against external threats; the defence of North America, driven by the interest in North American security and the need for cooperation with the US; and contributing to international security and stability, driven by the logic of the functional principle, the desire for counterweights, and interest in a peaceful, rules-based international order. *Strong, Secure, Engaged* is the latest in this lineage of defence statements.

4   *Strong, Secure, Engaged*: Canada's 2017 Defence Statement

Released on 6 June 2017, *Strong, Secure, Engaged: Canada's Defence Policy* exhibits a high level of continuity with previous Canadian defence statements. The fundamentals of Canada's strategic interests and the missions of the Canadian Armed Forces (CAF) remain largely unchanged from previous decades. The paper offers a strategic vision in which Canada is: Strong at home; Secure in North America; and Engaged in the world. *Strong, Secure, Engaged* recognizes changes in the threat environment and emphasizes the need to anticipate emerging threats and challenges, adapt to the rapid pace of change, and act decisively with effective military capability.

The statement identifies a number of key trends that will drive Canadian defence policy planning. First, the evolving balance of power is characterized by shifts in the relative power of states and the re-mergence of major power competition. Second, the nature of conflict has changed significantly. Conflict drivers are increasingly associated with the complex interaction of economic inequality, demographics, migration, and climate change. Furthermore, states and non-state actors are making increased use of hybrid methods in the grey zone just below the threshold of violent conflict. Third, the rapid evolution of technology will make the future of defence vastly different than it is today, with a number of technologies—especially in the cyber domain and space—holding the potential for a fundamental change in military operations.

Strong, Secure, Engaged opens with a focus on people and a number of new initiatives aimed at improving care, services, and support. This is significant in light of public revelations concerning insufficient services for military personnel and their families, challenges faced by veterans, mishandling of sexual offences, and obstacles to recruitment and retention. The next chapter of *Strong, Secure, Engaged* is titled Fixing Defence Funding. The plan provides for C\$62.3 billion in new defence spending over 20 years. As a result, annual defence spending will rise from \$18.9 billion in 2016–2017 to C\$32.7 billion in 2026–27. Total defence spending as a percentage of gross domestic product will increase to 1.4% by 2024–2025. The spending plan devotes considerable attention to new equipment procurement, including the provision of C\$33.8 billion (on an accrual basis) for 52 new capital projects. When combined with existing projects, the total funding commitment to capital equipment in *Strong, Secure, Engaged* is C\$108 billion.

Strong, Secure, Engaged envisions a significant investment in the modernization, renewal, and restoration of the CAF. The statement emphasizes the importance of intelligence and cyberwar opertions, along with an ambitious procurement program designed to ensure the military can operate across the spectrum of conflict, is interoperable with Canada's allies, and maintains an operational advantage over current and future threats. To this end, the Royal Canadian Navy, the Canadian Army, the Royal Canadian Air Force, and the Canadian Special Operations Forces Command will embark on significant new capital investment projects, including the acquisition of 15 new Canadian Surface Combat ships and a fleet of 88 future fighter aircraft, along with a commitment to the purchase of an interim fighter capability as a bridge to the future fighter program.

Strong, Secure, Engaged received widespread support, even from sectors of Canada's security community that are generally critical of Liberal governments. The challenges facing the statement are not conceptual, but political. The implementation of *Strong, Secure, Engaged* will encounter the same three challenges faced by previous Canadian defence policy statements. First, the history of Canadian defence policy is characterized by the failure of governments to meet the defence spending requirements of their own statements. The result is a long list of delayed or cancelled procurement projects, unrealized force size targets, and difficult spending tradeoffs between new equipment, operations and maintenance, personnel and training, and infrastructure. Second, Canada's famously byzantine procurement system has produced a form of political paralysis when it comes to major procurement programs, especially ships and aircraft. Third, Canada's military has confronted a systemic commitment-capability gap between the demands placed on the military by successive governments and the capacities of the military.

The political implications of these problems are significant. While the functional principle in the Canadian strategic outlook was built on the idea that those countries who make contributions to multilateral efforts should receive a voice and some expectation of influence, the truth was the equation also worked in reverse: if a country could not make a contribution, or the contribution was a token one, then no voice or influence would be extended, or expected. As former Prime Minister Stephen Harper observed: "...if you don't have the capacity to act you are not taken seriously. Nobody takes your views seriously unless you can contribute to solutions, and it's very difficult to contribute to solutions unless you can contribute across the range of capabilities, up to and including military capabilities" [3]. This principle has informed decades of Canadian security policy, including approaches to the security of North America.

5 North American Defence Planning in Context

In Cold War Europe, the combination of the Soviet threat and ambivalence (at least in some countries) about overreliance on the US led to a decades long effort to encourage the development of a European security and defence identity. Although rarely defined in such terms, it is possible to speak of a North American security and defence identity, especially between Canada and the US. The core features of this identity rest on two political fundamentals: both Canada and the US recognize that North American security is a common problem best secured through cooperation; and both Canada and the US have political reasons to limit the extent of that cooperation.

The formation of this identity extends to the years before World War Two and the growing threat of Nazi Germany, when both countries agreed that the defence of North America should be a shared responsibility. In a speech at Queen's University in Kingston Ontario on 18 August 1938, US President Roosevelt pledged the following: "The people of the US will not stand idly by if the domination of Canadian soil is threatened by any other Empire." Prime Minister Mackenzie King responded two days later with a reciprocal pledge: "We too, have our obligations as a good friendly neighbor, and one of these is to see that... our country is made as immune from attack or possible invasion as we can reasonably be expected to make it, and that, should the occasion ever arise, enemy forces should not be able to pursue their way by land, sea, or air, to the United States across Canadian territory." Together, these statements came to be called the Kingston Dispensation [4, p. 22]. This understanding was formalized in the Ogdensburg Agreement of 1940, which created the bilateral Permanent Joint Board of Defence (PJBD), a military and civilian body charged with policy-level consultation on defence matters.

After WWII, the primary threat to North America came in the form of the USSR. This shared threat led to the creation of the bilateral Military Cooperation Committee (MCC) in 1946, designed to increase cooperation and planning at the operational military level. The creation of NATO in 1949 established the Canada–US Regional Planning Group (CUSRPG) to coordinate the defence of North America within the NATO framework. The Soviet Union's first nuclear test in 1949 and the development of Soviet long-range aviation led to the creation of the Distant Early Warning (DEW) Line in 1954, and subsequently the signing of the North American Aerospace Defence Agreement (NORAD) of 1958. Cooperation between the two countries also extended to defence production and weapons testing.

The Canada-US security relationship has always been difficult for Canada to navigate. Virtually all continental security and defence cooperation programs and initiatives with its superpower neighbor raise the issue of Canadian sovereignty and independence in world affairs. At the core of this deliberation is an eternal question: does cooperating with the US, or not cooperating with the US, better serve Canadian sovereignty? Critics have charged that cooperation undermines Canadian autonomy and independence, and threatens Canadian control over its territory and military forces. Defenders of increased Canada-US military co-ordination have argued that Canadian sovereignty is best protected through co-operation with the US, by securing political and military access and a voice rather than facing exclusion from US decision-making.

Canadian governments must also confront the reality that American governments will defend North America with or without Canada. Canadian governments have largely responded by committing Canada to bilateral cooperation. This phenomenon was characterized by Nils Ørvik as "defence against help," by which a mid—or small-sized state would engage in security cooperation with a more powerful state largely to avoid unwanted engagement from the more powerful state in and around its own territory [5]. Defence against help raised its own concerns: the contributions of the smaller state were necessarily asymmetric, raising questions about how much was enough to secure a meaningful voice and avoid charges of free riding. Furthermore, as the smaller state, Canada is essentially trapped within the world of US threat perceptions which drive the North American security agenda.

The end of the Cold War removed most of the urgency from the Canada-US security relationship. This changed after September 11, 2001, when the terrorist threat to North America displaced all other Canada-US issues. The September 11 attacks complicated Canada's relationship with the US with respect to security, sovereignty, and trade. A sudden focus on homeland security increased US government concerns about Canada as a possible base for terrorists and brought more attention to the security of the Canada-US border. An uncomfortable amount of US government scrutiny was directed at domestic Canadian policies and practices. For example, the US State Department's 2002 report on global terrorism, while generally praising Canada-US terrorism cooperation, identified inadequate funding and restrictive privacy legislation as two shortcomings in Canada's ability to combat terrorism [6, pp. 74–75]. A subsequent Library of Congress report accused Canada of being a "favoured destination" for terrorists because of lax law enforcement and immigration laws, and high levels of protection for civil liberties [7].

The September 11 border shutdown vividly illustrated the dependence of the Canadian economy on an open border. In subsequent discussions of border security, Canadian and US interests had different points of emphasis: Canada was interested in keeping the border as open as possible, while the US was interested in keeping it as secure as possible. Canadian concerns about a hardening of the border were realized in the form of the 2009 Western Hemisphere Travel Initiative, a US law requiring travelers from Canada (and Mexico and Bermuda) to have a passport.

After September 11 Canadian sovereignty was challenged in new and more intimate ways. The call for a security perimeter around North America in response to the terrorist threat was accompanied by the call for increased harmonization of customs, immigration, and security laws. Seldom has the sovereignty/security and trade/security linkage appeared so starkly in Canada-US relations. The Canadian government resisted the idea of harmonization and a perimeter, concerned that this would imply the convergence and standardization of laws and regulatory regimes across the two countries. To Canadians, the call for the harmonization implied Americanization. Yet ultimately the government had little choice but to pursue some enhanced forms of cooperation and some harmonization, given the alternative was a more tightly controlled Canada-US border that would have compromised trade.

In subsequent months and years Canada would participate in the negotiation of a series of security agreements with the US, including the Smart Border Declaration in December 2001, to facilitate the flow of people and goods across the border while enhancing security co-ordination. In addition, Canada undertook many national initiatives driven at least in part by concerns about the terrorist threat to the US. These included the Anti-Terrorism Act in December 2001 and the Immigration and Refugee Protection Act in June 2002. While there was strong domestic political support for improved security measures, anti-terrorism legislation provoked considerable controversy over the implications for civil liberties, particularly in light of the US Patriot Act.

Canada also found itself reacting to American initiatives to reorganize government and military structures. The creation of the Office of Homeland Security (now Department of Homeland Security) in November 2002 was soon followed by the establishment of the Department of Public Safety and Emergency Preparedness (now Public Safety Canada) in 2003. Furthermore, in 2002 the US introduced a new US military command for North America, US Northern Command (NORTHCOM). In 2005 Canada Command was established at least in part to create an institutional equivalent in Canada to interface with the new US command (Canada Command's responsibilities were subsequently rolled over into Canadian Joint Operations Command in 2012).

The major trilateral initiative addressing North American security was the Security and Prosperity Partnership (SPP) announced on 23 March 2005 at a summit meeting between Paul Martin, George Bush, and Vincente Fox. Described as a trialogue between the three countries, the SPP was aimed at creating common approaches to emergency preparedness and infrastructure protection, improving aviation, border, and maritime security, and exploring ways to enhance economic cooperation. The SPP reflected the divergent interests of the partners, with the security imperative driving US policy and the trade imperative driving Canada and Mexico.

The North American security agenda was not devoted entirely to the threat of terrorism. Motivated by growing concern over North Korea's long-range missile program, the Bush Administration withdrew from the 1972 ABM Treaty and began deployment of a national missile defence program in July 2004. The US was willing to place the program under the bi-national structure of NORAD, and in January 2004 the Martin government exchanged letters of intent indicating a willingness to participate. However, after an election the subsequent minority government was unable to finalize arrangements and in February 2005 the government announced it would not be joining the US missile defence program. The debate in Canada over the merits of participating in the system revolved around familiar themes, especially whether sovereignty was best secured through cooperation in missile defence or by remaining outside the system.

There was an effort to undertake a larger strategic assessment of North American security cooperation. In December 2002 the Canada-US Bi-national Planning Group (BPG) was established to study the future of Canada-US security cooperation. The final report of the group called for a combined vision statement by Canada and the US and the creation of a Comprehensive Defence and Security Agreement to provide policy guidance and direction to Canada-US security agencies. There was some expectation that the terrorist attacks of 9/11 would be the catalyst for the creation of new institutional security and defence arrangements in North America, and the creation of the BPG seemed to indicate momentum in this direction. However, the BPG concluded its work in 2006 and there was little follow up on its recommendations.

6 *Strong, Secure, Engaged* in North America

When it comes to the security of North America, *Strong, Secure, Engaged* is thus built on a long and extensive legacy of Canada-US security cooperation. In this context, it is not surprising that a commitment to Canada-US security cooperation remains in place. Along with NATO and the Five Eyes, NORAD is identified as one of Canada's three key global defence alliance and partnerships. In *Strong, Secure, Engaged* [8, p. 90] the Canadian government pledges to "...engage the United States to look broadly at emerging threats and perils to North America, across all domains, as part of NORAD's modernization." Specifically, the statement calls on Canada and the US to "jointly examine options to renew the North Warning System and modernize the Command, which is integral to fulfilling the NORAD mandate of aerospace warning and control, as well as maritime warning." While *Strong, Secure, Engaged* recognizes that "weapons technology, including ballistic and cruise missiles, has advanced tremendously" it does not commit Canada to participate in US ballistic missile defence programs.

While it is understandable for governments to be deliberately general when referring to possible future courses of action with defence arrangements, *Strong, Secure, Engaged* misses an opportunity to establish a larger vision for security cooperation in North America. Canada's NORAD-centric approach to North American security survives despite the statement's recognition of a changing threat environment and an explicit call for adaptation to changing security circumstances. While the defence statement does seek to break down the distinctions between domestic, continental, and international roles, there are no specific indications in the document about the implications of this development for the security and defence relationship between Canada, the US and Mexico. The threat environment to North America demands a much more holistic, less compartmentalized, and more coordinated approach to security cooperation.

The current threat environment to North America is characterized by old, resurgent, and emerging threats across the air, sea, land, space, cyber, and social environments. These threats require ongoing, improved, or new forms of cooperation between Canada, the US, and Mexico. Old threats include long-standing security issues that require continued cooperation on the security of air and maritime approaches, sovereignty enforcement, border management, search and rescue, and disaster and crisis response. Old threats also include security concerns that have appeared in recent decades but are now fixtures of North American security cooperation, such as domestic and international terrorism, organized crime, trafficking, and illicit financial activity. Resurgent threats that have returned to a position of heightened relevance include the North Korean ballistic missile threat to North America and increased Russian military activities around the northern periphery of the continent (including capability enhancements such as long range air-launched cruise missiles).

Emerging threats include cyberwar and cyber atacks, drone warfare, and the use of artificial intelligence and robotics systems capable of penetrating air and maritime surveillance or used from within North America. Significantly, most emerging threats represent a further blurring of the distinction between the external and the internal. Emerging threats will therefore require greater engagement and cooperation between institutions and agencies with mandates and practices traditionally defined in terms of foreign or domestic threats. At the same time, advances in technology, especially information systems, artificial intelligence, and robotics, are placing an increased premium on widening the circle of actors engaged in North American security and defence dialogues.

Ongoing Canada-US security and defence cooperation must prepare for the increased significance of information warfare designed to undermine social cohesion and sow suspicion and distrust for political purposes. This threat has manifested itself in many forms, including the use of hybrid war techniques by Russia in neighboring countries, Russian use of social media to interfere in electoral processes in the U.S. and France, the use of the internet by volent extremist groups for radicalization, recruitment, and incitement to violence, and the ongoing threat posed by hackers with varying motives operating individually or in groups. In the future more nuanced efforts could target security arrangements and institutions to create dissonance between their missions and the public. It is not difficult to envision such techniques being employed to undermine political support for North American security and defence cooperation. Responses must include robust measures to counter these efforts, while ensuring that domestic debate is free and informed.

The widening and deepening threat spectrum requires a comprehensive review of Canada-US security and defence cooperation. The increasingly diverse threat environment requires a holistic, integrated approach to continental defence. The threats are clearly not limited to military risks, thus a whole of government capacity is required at both the national and intergovernmental levels. Beyond that, a whole of society capacity will also have to be mobilized. This will require increased engagement between traditional defence, security, intelligence and law enforcement agencies on the one hand, and private sector, centers of research and development, universities, civil society actors, and media and information providers on the other. The vital importance of information and public perception demands the establishment of a communications, outreach and knowledge mobilization strategy that enhances public awareness and understanding of the political and military rationales for continental security cooperation across the information and social media landscape. This will strengthen the resilience of meaningful and informed debate and dissent on North American security cooperation.

7 The Next Steps: A New North American Security and Defence Architecture?

Strong, Secure, Engaged risks an overemphasis on continuity over change in the North American security and defence environment. After decades of incremental adaptations based on catalytic events or evolving circumstances, there is a need for a significant bottom-up review of the existing institutional architecture of Canada-US security and defence cooperation to meet emerging threats. This review would not necessarily imply the creation of any new institutional arrangements. It is something of an axiom that neither Canada nor the US have strong motivations for creating additional, or more in depth, institutional security arrangements. As described by Joel Sokolsky and Joseph Jockel,

> Both the United States and Canada have largely preferred a loose defence relationship. NORAD stands out as an exception. There has long been resistance on both sides of the border to integrative continental defence arrangements. Sometimes this resistance has been Canadian, sometimes American, sometimes both. Canadians have worried about the loss of 'sovereignty' to the Americans, while the Americans have worried that working too closely with Canadians would limit their freedom of action [9, p. 116].

Despite the ongoing formal existence of the PJBD and the MCC, no comprehensive, overarching Canada-US security institution or treaty arrangement exists to conduct the high-level strategic assessment and guidance functions required by the new threat environment. The possibility of such an arrangement should not be dismissed. It is sometimes forgotten that NORAD was regarded with some suspicion and even outright opposition within government and the military, and yet NORAD remains an essential and foundational arrangement in the North American security architecture. NORAD itself has evolved significantly from its early focus on air defence and ballistic missile early warning to include a large array of missions from space control through surveillance of domestic air space and maritime approaches to drug interdiction. While the future of security cooperation in North America must include NORAD, the broadening threat spectrum requires reform and renewal of the larger architecture and governance of continental security far beyond the NORAD mandate.

To this end, Canada and the US should create a North American security advisory council. This council would be intergovernmental and inter-agency, and composed of senior representatives from the executive and legislative branches of government, industry, academia, and the military. The council would be a permanent, standing body with the mandate to be a focal point for dialogue, discussion, analysis, and reporting on continental security. The council would provide strategic assessment on new and emerging threats, develop policy recommendations for responding to these treats, and develop proposals for enhancing consultation and communication across agencies. The council would play an important public outreach and knowledge mobilization function, providing support for the discussion and dissemination of information in the form of publications, conferences, videos, a social media presence, and a youth engagement strategy. The Council would convene a conference every two years, hosted in one of the three countries on a rotating basis.

Is a North American security and advisory council a politically attainable goal in the next few years? The current political climate is certainly not favourable, with the Trump administration generally suspicious of multilateralism and ill-disposed toward NAFTA, the keystone of continental cooperation across the three countries. A focus on "America first" approaches to security might divert political energy away from cooperation toward increased unilateralism on North American security matters. The Trump Administration's focus on peer competitors and traditional defence capabilities could compromise efforts to address the broader range of security threats facing the continent. In turn, the unpopularity of the Trump administration in both Canada and Mexico complicates the politics of support for cooperation with the US, as anti-American political backlash builds in both countries. There is a risk that substantive differences between the Trump Administration and the governments of Canada and Mexico, in particular over free trade, global governance, energy, and climate change, could compromise progress on security cooperation.

Wider uncertainties concerning the future of NAFTA are particularly significant. Doubts about the future of NAFTA suggest that political energy will be devoted to defending or dismantling the most significant cooperative arrangement in North America, rather than developing new cooperative ventures. Tensions over the future of NAFTA will test the linkage between economic and security cooperation on the continent. This is especially the case between the US and Mexico, where the creation of NAFTA facilitated increased security cooperation by raising confidence in the bilateral relationship. An ugly renegotiation process or unilateral American withdrawal could have a negative impact on security cooperation between the two countries, particularly on the high-profile issues of opioid drugs and immigration. On the northern border, ill-will over NAFTA or trade disputes would certainly complicate any efforts to enhance security cooperation in the near term. Increased political antagonism among the three North American countries does not mean there will be less security cooperation between them (though that is possible), but it almost certainly will mean little new security cooperation, and given the nature of emerging threats this alone represents a grave danger.

Care must be taken not to attribute the poor prospects for the immediate development of a North American security advisory council, or opposition to any other major North American security cooperation intitatives, entirely to the Trump Administration. A change in the current political environment in Washington does not mean that US support for an advisory council, or other major proposal, would automatically be forthcoming. Assuming the challenges facing such efforts will remain insurmountable in the next few years, what is to be done? In the absence of a larger mechanism for responding holistically to threats to North America, Canada and Mexico should advocate for increased consultation, coordination, and cooperation between existing security agencies and institutions at the national and intergovernmental level, building on the inter-agency relationships and the practical, day-to-day measures that have become part of the security landscape in North America. These business as usual measures will continue to lack the benefits of a larger governance framework, but are better than making no progress at all, especially in the face of emerging threats.

Unfortunately, there is a circumstance in which a North American security advisory council might be created even in the currently unfavourable climate. The stimulus would be a catalytic, impactful security event in North America that revealed serious shortcomings in coordination, information sharing, and interagency and intergovernmental cooperation. The political consequences of such an event would presumably create political momentum to addressing the failures and/or gaps in capacity that were exploited by the attackers. The idea of an advisory council is based on the precautionary principle, to reduce the prospects that such an event could occur or to mitigate its impact. However, as the 9/11 attacks demonstrated, awareness of vulnerability and increased security efforts to prevent future attacks often occurs only in the wake of a high impact event.

Whatever transpires, Canada needs to remind itself of its grand strategy roots now more than ever. While *Strong, Secure, Engaged* is an effective starting point for meeting the defence dimensions of Canada's strategic interests in world affairs, meeting Canada's security and defence needs in North America will require more attention and planning than is evident in the defence statement. The Canadian government must commit to the spending increases and procurement plan envisioned in *Strong, Secure, Engaged*. But it must also invest the political capital required to advance the kind of strategic coordination on continental security matters that is unaddressed in the defence statement and increasingly required in the face of old, resurgent, and emerging threats.

References

1. Hellyer P, Cardin L (1964) White paper on defence. Queen's Printer, Ottawa
2. Defence White Paper (1994) Minister of Supply and Services Canada, Ottawa
3. Whyte K (2011) In conversation: Stephen Harper. MacLean's. http://www.macleans.ca/general/how-he-sees-canadas-role-in-the-world-and-where-he-wants-to-take-the-country-2/. Accessed 12 Nov 2017
4. Fortmann M, Haglund HG (2002) Canada and the issue of homeland security: does the Kingston dispensation still hold? Can Mil J 3(1):18–22
5. Ørvik N (1973) Defence against help: a strategy for small states? Survival 15(5):228–231
6. Patterns of Global Terrorism 2002 (2003). United States Department of State. https://www.state.gov/documents/organization/20177.pdf. Accessed 25 Jan 2018
7. Nations Hospitable to Organized Crime and Terrorism. A Report Prepared by the Federal Research Division, Library of Congress under an Interagency Agreement with the United States Government. (2003). Library of Congress. https://www.loc.gov/rr/frd/pdf-files/Nats_Hospitable.pdf. Accessed 24 Jan 2018
8. *Strong, Secure, Engaged*: Canada's Defence Policy (2017) Department of National Defence, Ottawa
9. Sokolsky J, Jockel J (2012) Continental defence: 'Like farmers whose lands have a common concession line'. In: McDonough DS (ed) Canada's national security in the Post-9/11 World. University of Toronto Press, Toronto, pp 115–137

Future Uncertainty, Strategic Defense, and North American Defense Cooperation: Rational Institutionalist Arguments Pragmatically Suggest NORAD's Adaptation Over Replacement

Anessa L. Kimball[✉]

Department of Political Science, Université Laval, Quebec City, QC G1V 0A6, Canada
Anessa.Kimball@pol.ulaval.ca

Abstract. Uncertainty about the future strategic environment is a rational impetus for cooperation. Despite a joint reiteration, by the US and Canada, of cooperation's importance in managing and responding to future threats, interrogations about NORAD's potential for future contributions in the North American defense landscape are relevant as it marks six decades of operation in 2018. Is NORAD, in its present configuration, sufficient for managing future threats to North America as well as strategic defense? Should NORAD be adapted to meet expected defense challenges? Or, alternatively, should it be replaced with a different structure; and at what risks? This chapter examines those questions through a discussion the importance of cooperation for uncertainty management, the challenges to cooperation as well as the role and limits of NORAD. It continues with a presentation of the possibilities for adapting the command arrangement relative to replacement employing arguments drawn from rational institutionalism. Finally, an exploration of the centrality of NORAD for North American defense cooperation and strategic defense is provided based on a comparison of the risks of adaptation versus replacement. Should the partners decide to participate in strategic defense, a pragmatic adaptation of the NORAD command arrangement is recommended through a use of the institutional provisions denoting flexibility. The chances for a successful mandate adaptation of the existing command are increased if stakeholders manage information transparently and effectively to minimize the risks of politicization.

1 Introduction: The Demand for Defense Cooperation Under Uncertainty

1.1 North American Cooperation as Key to Continental Defense

Geographic constants (isolation, large maritime approaches, long border, shared navigable waterways etc.) have fundamentally affected North American defense relations. Over 200 cooperative defense and security arrangements link Canada and the US [1] including those managing continental air defense under the NORAD arrangement [2].

© Springer International Publishing AG, part of Springer Nature 2018
C. Leuprecht et al. (eds.), *North American Strategic Defense in the 21st Century:*,
Advanced Sciences and Technologies for Security Applications,
https://doi.org/10.1007/978-3-319-90978-3_10

At Kingston in 1938, there was a recognition of the inexorable link between the two states regarding territorial defense [3]. In 1940, the mandate of the Permanent Joint Board on Defense (PJBD) clarified "continental security was indivisible and could not be pursued by a single nation" [3, p. 144]. For the past 60 years, first air, then aerospace, defense has been coordinated through a uniquely designed binational command arrangement, NORAD. Though geography linked the states, for Canada the equilibrium between maintaining national defense policy autonomy while ensuring bilateral defense coordination in the context of securing the continent remains fragile. Pressures to centralize efforts at continental defense increase with rising uncertainty in the world. Rational institutionalists argue uncertainty about the future state of the world and future behavior are strategic problems to successfully manage with well-designed arrangements reshaping the negative externalities of uncertainty [4, 5]. Moreover, the demand for defense cooperation is substantial given the complex nature of threats facing the continent as well as their possibilities for occurrence and severity.

1.2 Strategic Defense, Uncertainty, and the Demand for Cooperation

ICBM proliferation to actors who might launch a limited strike of nuclearized missiles generates sufficient need for a strategic defense. A strategic defense system employs a number of fixed and mobile assets (radars and satellites) used in the integrated information collection, analysis and deployment of an interceptor response. However, due to both geometry and geography some locations for fixed assets could be preferred to others for obtaining information quickly which helps maximize counter-response effectiveness. An average launch-to-intercept window is minutes, so rapidly obtaining quality information provides precious time to decision makers. Due to the location of the probable missile threats to North America, some intercept paths for US targets occur outside territorial limits, thus there remains a need for cooperation to ensure consultation and information sharing among continental partners. With considerable maritime territory to defend, as well as an increasingly navigable Arctic, there are important strategic reasons to prefer transparency and coordination of defense policies and assets. While participating or not is the initial decision, other questions about relative contribution versus the delegation of control/command require discussion as part of the participation terms.[1]

As the US is the only country with interceptors in North America, the examination of by what means others could participate in strategic defense, either through adapting NORAD or replacing it is the goal herein. Drawing on rational institutionalist arguments and interviews with Canadian stakeholders completed in 2014,[2] this chapter argues NORAD's unique legal design and institutional structure enable adaptation without putting its survival at risk. Attempting replacement creates the temptation of

---

[1] They include: operational training and (interceptor/radar) assets acquired by or located in partners in exchange for the expected benefits from contract opportunities for the national defense industry.

[2] Université Laval's Ethics Committee approval (2012-245/07-12-2012). Interviewee names appear in capital letters to distinguish from references.

invoking the notice period to withdraw from NORAD as a bargaining chip, leading to a risk of a worse diplomatic and defense outcome; i.e. a dead NORAD without a replacement in force.

1.3 NORAD's Provision of Defense and Information Reduces Uncertainty

NORAD's current mission includes two domains and the Commander is the delegatory agent of both executives regarding aerospace defense (excluding strategic defense). The command's primary role is transferring information to national governments regarding aerospace and maritime threats. In performing its warning mandate in two domains using mobile and fixed radars as well as satellites, NORAD reduces uncertainty by providing information. Operationally, the NORAD Commander is directly linked to both governments. That link and information access cannot be understated in its importance for reducing the transaction costs of information transmission during crises. Since misperception and misunderstanding are considered key causes for disputes, the transparency of the NORAD link reduces uncertainty significantly between partners, facilitates communication and consultations.

Moreover, NORADCOM has operational responsibilities to defend the North American aerospace which require joint training and defense policy planning. The result is a high level of policy coordination and communication resulting in substantial trust among the stakeholders. For example, when it was agreed NORAD perform a BM warning role, in part, to prevent duplication, the arrangement's flexibility permitted the addition of an amendment [6]. PENNIE, DG of Strategic Planning at DND, [7] clarifies, "the amendment took away a lot of US angst because it meant they did not have to build another warning system just for MD or dismantle a core part of NORAD, and probably saved NORAD from irrelevance." That the US Commander has dual mandates from NORADCOM and US NORTHCOM facilitates decision making resulting in both political and economic efficiency. Moreover, NORAD reduces the transaction costs for Canada to interact with other US military services and agencies located at the Cheyenne Mountain headquarters.

Defense policy coordination and cooperation form the backbone of the US-Canadian bilateral relationship via various agreements differing in legalization [2], thus there is little risk of a complete cooperation breakdown. The main inquiry is into the nature and design of such cooperation and how it might manage the uncertainties associated with strategic problems. The US can deploy a strategic defense system sufficiently capable of detecting and reacting to territorial threats alone. However, cooperation may increase the quality and speed of information collection and transmission, thereby reducing uncertainty and transaction costs resulting in economic efficiencies and increased political capital (i.e. trust). Effectively designed cooperation improves the multilateral decision making efficiency so essential to effective command/control in crises.

2   Identifying Future Challenges to Defense Cooperation

2.1   In North America

Though rationalists identify factors affecting cooperation failure, space limitations herein prevent a lengthy treatment. Some suggest it results from issue indivisibilities and the credibility of commitments [8, 9]. Rationalists argue most issues/tasks are divisible in some manner to prevent contentions. Even securing the Arctic, which is perceived by Ottawa as being indivisible, could be delegated to trusted third-party actors under the correct institutional conditions or design. The challenge in the Arctic is overcoming a relative gains view of the expected positive benefits of economic development. An obsession with a relative gains conception of cooperation, similar to realists [10], by the current US administration is evidenced by an insistence cooperation being a 'good (economic) deal' instead of a focus on mutual gains poses a challenge to cooperation. Though rationalists contend repeated interactions create a long shadow of the future facilitating cooperation [11] and reciprocity [12] building the trust required to overcome the commitment problem. The current US administration discourse relies on signaling defection from cooperation as a bargaining strategy. The result is increased uncertainty about the credibility of US defense commitments [13]. Finally, defense stakeholders must consider the implications of market imperfections and how limited numbers of sellers affects offer bids on procurement contracts. The international defense cooperation and procurement market is oligarchic with a key supplier, the US [14, 15]. Kinsella shows, despite decentralisation in the arms market since the 1950s, the US maintains a central non-negligible role in a network analysis of seller-buyer links [16]. The US's role in the provision of strategic defense assets will provide it considerable negotiating power concerning what states offer in exchange for acquiring assets to participate.

2.2   Concerning Strategic Defense

For rationalists, the key issues for a strategic defense cooperation reduce to interrogations about (1) the (policy) autonomy versus security trade-off under uncertainty [17–19] and (2) the nature of the delegation relationships [5] in the command/control of a continental strategic defense. The autonomy-security trade-off strikes to the base of domestic cleavages concerned about the closeness of cooperation with powerful partners. In Canada, defense stakeholders (13/27 interviewees) almost uniformly preferred closeness, though there were skeptics among foreign affairs stakeholders. Those weary of "being too close to the elephant" as NORAD Regional Commander BOUCHARD opined, "it's the old (P.E.) Trudeau (quote) with the mouse in bed with the elephant, no matter how benevolent the elephant is...when it rolls over, it will crush you" [20]. Reflections about the command/control powers in a future continental strategic defense system are the essence of whether NORAD or some other configuration of power makes the decision to deploy assets or if the status quo continues.

Other strategic defense systems either limit interceptor range (e.g. Korean peninsula, Israel) or are under US command, Europe.[3]

2.3 Affecting NORAD

Defense cooperation managed through NORAD functions at a high level though it faces several challenges in the future. The first challenge is for Canada to fulfill its commitments concerning the provision of fighter jets to joint defense. Its defense procurement challenges stem from historical mismanagement, partisan politics, and systemic underfunding which it plans to rectify with long-term funding according to its 2017 defense paper [21]. Another challenge to defense cooperation is preventing possible spill-overs between defense procurement and frictions involving defense industry actors in other sectors, e.g. aviation trade. Canadian uncertainty about the F-35 acquisition despite paying 20 years of sunk costs of consortia membership affects both its NORAD and NATO commitments. In a trade dispute spill-over into defense procurement, Canada chose to purchase used F-18s from Australia in lieu of Boeing after import duties of nearly 220% were temporarily levied against Bombardier's CSeries importation by Delta Airlines [22].

To maintain the high level of defense cooperation between the US and Canada, each must avoid relative gains perceptions of continental security and focus on maintaining the functional and operational aspects of its indivisibility. In Canada, despite preferences for closeness with the Americans in defense circles, there exists a minority in both foreign affairs and the public questioning the wisdom of closeness to the US for increased defense benefits at the cost of autonomy [23]. Such tensions are logical given defense favors policy planning certainty to plan for the unknown while foreign affairs prefers flexibility. The need for territorial defense and the strategic uncertainty posed by missile threats provide substantial policy challenges under competing pressures. Reflections of how closely to align with, but not rely upon, the US are not new to Canadian defense analysts [3, 24]. Defense cooperation is the preferred strategy for a Canada with a struggling defense procurement strategy combined with US market dominance when faced with the plethora of future continental threat varieties and sources.

3 NORAD's Multi-faceted Role and Its Capacity to Meet Future Defense Needs

3.1 What Is NORAD?

NORAD is unique due to its bilateral command and, recently endowed, permanence. NORAD COM stood up before the legal agreement was completed. In 1957 the operational control center was taken over at Cheyenne Mountain though the notes legalizing it were not signed until 12 May 1958 [24, p. 3]. The arrangement, made

---

[3] NATO's Integrated Air and Missile Defense (NIAMD) falls under the control of SACEUR, an American who also commands the US European Command (US EUCOM).

through an "Exchange of diplomatic notes", was renewed multiple times with the 2006 renewal declared "in perpetuity" [25]. Though NORAD was at risk of obscurity at points, because it provides a tangible defense good, it endured. NORAD's designers kept it intentionally out of the public eye. Jockel discusses the logic for using an informal arrangement and placing the powers with an individual agent, the Commander instead of a new institution, as a "bi-national 'entity' that would have operational control over air defense forces of the two countries capable of operating within a minute of delay without actually having to call it a command... (that) to be sure... would need approval of their political masters" [24, p. 23], i.e. ratification. Using an informal arrangement permits a higher level of executive control due to a capacity to limit stakeholders, largely bypass the legislature, and create a flexible arrangement which can adapt to uncertainties.

3.2 NORAD: Provider of Defense Goods

NORAD's mandate includes aerospace/maritime warning and aerospace defense. As an informational agent, it transmits information collected from its assets to policymakers. It is also tasked with normal defense operational responsibilities. For example, NORAD planes escort unknown aircraft, those deviating from flight plans, or unauthorized in restricted zones several times monthly. It reduces the transaction costs of sharing information because both governments are represented in the command structure and receive information simultaneously. NORAD also tracks violent weather and helps in coordinating disaster and humanitarian relief, if necessary. It tracks (missile and satellite) launches worldwide providing added informational utility to both governments beyond direct threats. Finally, after 9/11 it developed defense plans for threats from civilian aviation sources, considered a natural adaptation of its mandate since some threat sources shifted to non-state actors [23].

3.3 NORAD: A Defense Investment

The positive externalities emerging from the efficiencies generated by cooperation [26] free resources, otherwise allocated to defense, for spending towards public goods that help re-election prospects [27]. The efficiencies created from defense cooperation permit governments to distribute resources elsewhere, notably towards social spending [19]. As a defensive investment, DELVOIE offers "NORAD has been a bargain for Canada from the beginning. It gives us access to a defense system which we could never think of affording ourselves in terms of detection and counter-action" [28]. MEYER, DG of International Security at foreign affairs continues, continues

> It has a specific function and it's still... a cost-effective way for the two countries to meet that function of control of their airspace and some capacity for assessing a threat to the continent... Those core tasks of NORAD have an enduring value and there is a both a strong tradition now and also a good cost-benefit case made for sustaining the cooperation represented by NORAD. [29]

NORAD pre-commits its partners to sustaining a certain level of defense capacity. And, in Canada, the maintenance NORAD and NATO commitments are invoked in the defense procurement discourse; the desire to prevent a "commitment-credibility gap" [30–32]. NORAD assets are also used for non-defense purposes such as violent weather tracking and domestic security, thus it provides other indirect positive informational externalities.

3.4   NORAD: A Diplomatic Symbol

NORAD is "foundational for our defense relationship" [33] and utilised as "an essential element of the definition of the relationship between Canada and the US" [34]. It provides "more than a seat at the table, it's the guy making the call. I mean there are Americans in the room, but the Canadian guy is in charge (when the US Commander is gone)" as stated by Ambassador CHRÉTIEN [35]. When it came to renegotiating NORAD, those inside such as WILLIAMS understood "there was a strong feeling within DND that being a player and a partner in NORAD gave us a seat at the table in a recognized senior position. And that was something we wanted to protect and preserve" [23]. The high value of NORAD to Canada meant it is protected from politicisation; as Clerk of the Privy Council CAPPE offered "NORAD is enormously valuable to us…it is differently valuable to us than the US. The US is a huge beneficiary having the Canadian landmass between them and a bunch of bears, of all kinds" [36].

NORAD rarely escapes discussions of US-Canadian defense relations, defense reviews and security strategy papers as noted in this volume. It is institutionally unique, provides defense goods and fulfills an operational function at a reasonable economic cost. The partners have diligently modernized both its assets and the command structure over the years through renewals and other mechanisms identified below. It is also a symbol of proximity, the essence of the link is the American Commander with the Canadian Deputy Commander in direct counsel linked to both executives.

4   Agreement Adaptation Versus Agreement Replacement Under Uncertainty: A Rational Institutionalist View

4.1   Rational Agreement Design Under Uncertainty

Informal arrangements create a vast substructure of legalized interactions between states. Lipson argues "the scale and the diversity of such accords indicate that they are an important feature of world politics, not rare and peripheral" [37]. Informal arrangements, in the US, are identified by an absence of legislative ratification distinguishing them from formal treaties. In parliamentary systems, the fusion of the executive and legislature complicates the categorization of such arrangements based on ratification. The salience of such arrangements in parliamentary systems is understood by whether parliamentary debates, public consultations, standing committee consultation/notification[4] took place regarding an agreement. Their form varies but includes Memoranda of Understanding (MOU), Agreements, Joint communiqués,

---

[4] The difference between consultation and notification being notification removes influence, whereas consultation implies, at minimum, a consideration of its position.

Exchanges of diplomatic notes or letters [2]. In parliamentary and presidential systems such arrangements generally require legislative notification. Lipson states the distinctions between such agreements are ignored by international law but "virtually all international commitments, whether oral or written, whether made by the head of state or a lower-level bureaucracy, are treated as 'binding international commitments'" [37, p. 498]. Indeed, "most Canadians view NORAD as a treaty" [34].

Non-treaty status allows informal agreements several advantages including *flexibility*, lack of a need for ratification making them less public permitting actors to *manage information* [37] with less risk. Flexibility in arrangements permits adaptation necessary for survival when uncertainty is high. It manifests in several ways. First, arrangements include provisions for a limited duration, renegotiation and renewal, and/or withdrawal [38]. Second, an amendment provision denotes flexibility. Finally, provisions for the management of disputes arising from the arrangement are also indicative of flexibility.

Flexibility is crucial in defense cooperation as there is "considerable uncertainty about the distribution of future benefits under a particular agreement" [37, p. 518]. Flexibility permits adaptation to changing contexts, i.e. end of the Cold War, 9/11, because stakeholders renegotiate, amend, or modify an arrangement reflecting the changed state of the world. Flexible arrangements are pragmatic insofar as their design meets practical needs. NORAD addresses the pragmatic problem of North American aerospace defense cooperation but is malleable to adapt itself. Koremenos states "renegotiation clauses allow adjustment in the face of international uncertainty without dismantling cooperation" [38, p. 92]. Renegotiation and renewal help actors deal with two rationalist cooperation problems: uncertainty about behavior and uncertainty about the state of the world [38]. Specifically, actors are concerned about the security, economic, and political consequences of an arrangement. Rational institutionalists posit flexibility increases with uncertainty [4]. Notice periods prevent incentives to defect from cooperation and eliminate the withdrawal advantage [38, p. 96] preventing enforcement problems (i.e. incentives actors have to cheat). Delegating power for dispute management/mediation is considered centralisation. Centralisation increases with uncertainty about the state of the world and the severity of enforcement problems [39]. Future uncertainty favors the centralization of efforts.

Precision, as one of the three aspects of legalization [39, 40] along with delegation and obligations, is key to conveying what conduct is authorized within the relationship. An arrangement with a limited scope is more precise, likewise with those containing clear mandates. The powers delegated in an arrangement may include rule-making and implementation as well as dispute mediation (adjudication). They may be delegated internally or externally though external delegation increases constraints. The existence of an adjudication process indicates the parties consider the arrangement has legal authority. Obligations are the provisions specifying the partner's responsibilities and commitments.

Lipson contends informal arrangements are less public so they permit actors to control information and such secrecy is an asset.

Because of their lower profile, they are also more tightly controlled by the government bureaucracies that negotiate and implement the agreements and less exposed to intrusion by other agencies. Agencies dealing with specific international issues, such as environmental pollution or foreign intelligence, can use informal agreements to seal quiet bargains with foreign counterparts, avoiding close scrutiny and active involvement by other government agencies with different agendas. [37, p. 500]

Informal agreements require legislative notification but not approval, a key distinction. "Informal agreements shift power toward the executive and away from the legislature" [37, p. 517]. Milner's study shows the elimination of legislative approval permits the executive to keep the agreement closer to its ideal point and increases the bargaining range facilitating agreement [41]. They permit executive management of information in bypassing the influence of others. Some informal arrangements are limited in scope, effectively reducing stakeholders. Moreover, executives vary in how much they permit the influence of others in decision making, their willingness to accept counsel and implement recommendations as well as their prioritization of defense issues on their personal agenda. Some executives may employ informal arrangements when seeking to centralise power or expedite matters. "Informal agreements are often chosen because they allow governments to act quickly and quietly" [37, p. 518]. Even if the claim that stakeholders manage information to keep NORAD uninteresting so it stays off the top of the US policy agenda is true, it argues rational actors use their power strategically to shape the decisional environment. Executives manage information by determining which actors sit at the negotiation table and to what extent information about the content of an agreement is revealed (i.e. to legislators and constituents). By managing information, stakeholders limit the risk of an agreement's politicization.

Agreement flexibility (via review and renewal, amendment, adjudication procedures, etc.) permits the adaptation to uncertainty required to meet a changing strategic environment. In addition, the successful management of stakeholders and information produces the speed and efficiency conducive to the adaptation necessary for future defense cooperation.

4.2 NORAD's Possibilities for Pragmatic Legal Adaptation to Meet Future Defense Needs

Informal arrangements contain various mechanisms indicative of the flexibility needed for adaptation. Table 1 identifies those mechanisms in the current NORAD arrangement. Moreover, recent modifications reveal an increased legalization of the arrangement [2]. For example, opening dispute management to PJBD consultations increases constraint (and, thus legalization) because it adds external players. Legalization is also increased due to its renewal "in perpetuity". Though Brister is less optimistic [42] concerning the concept of perpetuity. Sokolsky and Jockel's opinions are also mitigated [43].

A second aspect of informal arrangements is important; the consequences of the executive determining the actors involved. If stakeholders effectively manage information (centralisation), then an agreement is less likely to become politicised increasing its chances of successful adaptation. Limiting scope may also decrease actors (Table 2).

Table 1. NORAD arrangement provisions on flexibility

Provision	Present/Absent	Details	Notes
Withdrawal provision with notice period	Present	12 month notice period	
Amendment provision	Present		
Limited duration	Present	5 year period	2006: Renewed "in perpetuity"
Review and renewal provision	Present	5 year reviews	2006: Renewed "in perpetuity" with reviews at 4 years or by request
Dispute management	Absent until 1996		1996: Environmental dispute management undertaken in consultation with the PJBD

Table 2. NORAD arrangement characteristics regarding information management

Characteristic	Yes/No	Notes
Limited scope	Yes (scope limited to defense; specialised on air warning, control, and defense)	1996: specialisation enlarged to aerospace (air + space) 2004: BMD warning amendment 2006: scope opened to maritime warn
Formal consultation provision	No until 1996	1996: added
Number of actors	2 (DND/Air Force* and foreign affairs "co-lead")	Others present for CDA: PCO, PMO, legal affairs
Legislative debate required	No	Executive prerogative
Legislative notification required	Yes	By report to standing committee
Public consultation required	No	Executive prerogative

The arrangement's characteristics are consistent with aspects of information control facilitating its adaptation. The arrangement is limited and specialised in scope and its limitation to air defense reduces the number of bureaucratic stakeholders (i.e. DND/Air Force and FA). The executives control information as legislative debates and public consultations occur on their request. The only requirement is legislative notification accomplished by briefing the Standing Committee which may offer recommendations.

Based on a study of NORAD's institutional provisions, its potential adaptation is based on two principle factors. The first factor identified elements within the arrangement itself (i.e. its institutional design) contributing to its adaptive capacity, whereas the second factor identified the rational activities of (institutional) stakeholders regarding information management. First, the arrangement's flexibility, derived from its review and renewal process as well as its amendment provisions, permitted the partners to adapt it over time to differing strategic contexts ensuring its relevance. Second, the ability of key stakeholders to manage access to and the dissemination of information shapes the chances an agreement's adaptation is successful. Adaptation potential for the NORAD arrangement is high but ensuring actor mandates, military service roles and delegation chains are transparent requires attention to its institutional design and precision regarding delegation details.

4.3   Possibilities for a New Arrangement and Future Defense Needs

Some suggest NORAD's mandate be enlarged to add maritime options and, perhaps, the entire BMD mission, but others contend it is a command too far in the context of the arrangement and requires replacement with a new agreement. One of the key reasons why NORAD has endured is due to a limited number of stakeholders. The BPG's report suggested NORAD consider mandate enlargement to include maritime aspects [44, p. 55], specifically warning and control. The mandate was extended to include only maritime warning as adding control inserted two players on each side (Coast Guard and the Navy). FINDLEY, the NORAD Deputy Commander, concluded "we looked at control (for the 2006 renewal) but (it) never (caught on). It was a bridge too far. There was this sense of why do we need to do this bilaterally, this is a national vulnerability, it's a national thing to deal with, we have a great Navy and Coast Guard so why do we need a continental approach" [45]. Despite the logic of centralising efforts, Defense Minister GRAHAM points to inter-service coordination being the most important reason why the maritime mandate was limited, "there is a good reason to have that under control of NORAD but when you try to apply that and you got a US system where the Coast Guard has control of coastal waters out to 200 miles, then you got the Navy. So there was a kind of turf war between the Navy and Coast Guard" [46]. Concerns about bureaucratic politics due to increased actor number in the context of adapting an existing arrangement are magnified under the uncertainty of negotiating a new arrangement including all of NORAD's current responsibilities plus the full strategic defense mandate. The risk of negotiation failure in the current political environment favors the option of leaving the current NORAD arrangement intact until a successful replacement structure is 'in force'.

5   Is NORAD Central to North American Cooperation and Strategic Defense?

NORAD provides an important function and has kept itself relevant in different strategic contexts. Despite the key defense information it provides to partners, it equally signals an indivisible close strategic link which cannot be undervalued. Some aspects of continental strategic defense might be made more efficient through the addition of partners creating an opportunity for increased defense cooperation. However, whether future changes to its mandate or membership would prove too difficult to manage efficiently in the current command arrangement deserves additional study. That notwithstanding replacement has important risks as well.

5.1   Institutional Trade-Offs in North American Defense Cooperation

Uncertainty favors NORAD adaption over replacement based on a rational institutionalist analysis of the arrangement. NORAD's structure permits adaptation without risking cooperation failure so partners can patiently and, incrementally, adapt it. The focus of this chapter was whether it is feasible from a legal institutional perspective and desirable from both geostrategic and delegation perspectives to do so; this reflection excludes considerations of philosophical or operational concerns. The NORAD command could be adapted, but at risk to its own efficiency and insulation from outside influence. The command might function less efficiently with increased actor involvement or if the delegation chains and obligations lack sufficient precision [4, 38]. In contrast, negotiating a replacement creates a possibility of enlarging the mandate and, perhaps, the membership.

5.2   Understanding the Risks Associated with Replacement

If the partners were sufficiently capable of managing information and actor numbers, it is possible to replace NORAD with a new informal arrangement but they must avoid the incentives to give 'a notice to withdraw' from the current agreement in bargaining. Moreover, replacement negotiations today would attract significant media and public attention leading to calls for a formal agreement increasing the failure risk as the addition of the legislative ratification game complicates negotiations [41, 47]. Adding Mexico might also result in calls for a formal agreement. The addition of Mexico publicly into a new command would affect border security, trade, and other aspects of relations. A more effective option if NORAD wants to become continental is to enhance trilateral air force training and defense policy planning to lay the foundation for greater cooperation.[5] Replacement could be done, but the risk of failure is sufficiently large enough to recommend a more pragmatic strategy of a legal adaptation of the existing NORAD command.

5.3   Favoring Survival Through the Existing Mechanisms for Pragmatic Legal Adaptation

Adapting the NORAD command is facilitated by existing provisions within the arrangement largely making its replacement unnecessary. NORAD's permanent status also strongly facilitates adaptation. Renewals ended in 2006 when it was renewed "in perpetuity" seen by WILLIAMS and FINDLEY as an acknowledgement of its essential function and key role in defense [23, 45]. Should the command want to adopt the full strategic defense role under its current legal arrangement quickly, Canada would invoke the formal consultation provision added in 1996 renewal to review the

---

[5] The addition of Mexico does not require replacing the current arrangement based on comparative agreement data [2]. The issues are related to economic and military capacity combined with political will versus institutional/legal obstacles. Modifying about a half-dozen key agreements [2] would permit Mexico a sufficient role and the integration of their informational assets into a continental strategic defense.

arrangement. That provision prevents NORAD's BM mandate from being changed without formal consultations between the partners. Formal consultations could result in an amendment to the mandate and other aspects of the command. Alternatively, an amendment could be added at the quadrennial review or using the same mechanisms employed in 2004 when BM warning was added.[6]

6   Final Recommendation: The Benefits of Adaptation Over Replacement

The political capital, defense economic benefits, and information efficiencies derived from adapting the existing command to adopt a strategic defense role are sufficient reasons to favor adaptation over replacement, particularly as NORAD's future is certain unless one the partners decides to leave the command by invoking the 12 month notice period to withdrawal provision [39]. Relations between the partners must have deteriorated substantially or be in crisis for Ottawa to publicly engage itself to withdrawal from NORAD given the perspectives offered by over two dozen interviewees. Also, interviewees were adamant NORAD could not be replicated, as CALDER, a DND DG and ADM Policy, involved in the last three NORAD renewals, argues "it would be a daunting task. If NORAD did not exist, we could not create it today. It needed the right moment in time to be created" [48]. But as Regional Commander BOUCHARD asserts "the agreement is the framework, (and) when it comes to execution, it is put in the top drawer and forgot about. We do whatever feels right at the time. As long as you do not break the spirit of the agreement you can get away with a lot" [20]. If deterrence fails then, there may be medium-term threats to continental defense. In the presence of adequately motivated political will and the appropriate legal knowledge of the adaptive mechanisms of the arrangement and information management, the arrangement could be adapted in less than a year, PENNIE indicates in late 2003 the BMD warning amendment negotiations started [7] and the amendment was formally adopted on 4 August 2004.

The NORAD command provides both tangible and intangible defense goods and while its preservation is not under question, the defense demands of tomorrow as well as the need for strategic defense provides an opportunity for NORAD adaptation in anticipation. NORAD's rational institutional design provides the mechanisms for implementing changes [2, 4, 49]. The addition of strategic defense to its mandate requires Canadian consent per the terms of the 1996 provision but there rests room to maneuver. Canada could set distinct terms for its participation in strategic defense within NORAD in the context of the amending agreement. But Canada faces the policy and information challenge of demonstrating strategic defense is not inconsistent with its stated policy against weapons in space to a public already skeptical of the need for it.

---

[6] Exchange of letters between Defense ministers in January 2004, following an exchange of diplomatic notes between the Secretary of State and Canadian ambassador to the US confirming the new amendment in force.

Because NORAD is favorably viewed and its future is secured by not needing renewal, an alternative question is posed, can the partners manage information by providing sufficient transparency to the stakeholders to accomplish strategic defense by adapting the command's mandate as a consequence of agreement management similar to the "normal course of business" for NORAD. "But the challenge I think is to manage an entente like (NORAD) as a normal course of business...keep (it) from becoming an issue" as CAPPE points out [36]. Strategic defense is not weapons in space as defined by Canadian policy,[7] it fulfills a strategic need for the country given future threats, and the NORAD command provides an ideal space to manage strategic defense if the partners decide to give it the mandate. However, with the appropriate mix of political will, institutional precision [50], and information management adaptation of the existing command arrangement, even if slow [51, 52], is a lower risk option than attempting to negotiate a replacement with the strategic defense mandate given the uncertainties of domestic partisan politics and deterrence diplomacy.

References

1. Kavanagh J (2014) U.S. security related agreements in force since 1955: introducing a new database. RR763. RAND Corporation, Santa Monica, CA
2. Kimball A (2017) Examining informal defense and security arrangement's legalization: Canada-US agreements, 1955–2005. Int J 72(3):380–400
3. Brister B (2012) The same yet different: continuity and change in the post-9/11 Canada-US security relationship. Canadian Defence Academy Press, Kingston
4. Koremenos B, Lipson C, Snidal D (2001) The rational design of international institutions. Int Org 55(4):761–799
5. Hawkins D, Lake D, Nielson D, Tierney M (2001) Delegation and agency in international organizations. Cambridge University Press, New York
6. Embassy of Canada (2004) Exchange of diplomatic letters between Canada and the US concerning missile warning and constituting an agreement to amend the NORAD agreement. JLAB-0095. Dated 4 Aug 2004. Embassy of Canada, Washington, DC
7. Pennie K (2014) Interview on 5 Feb 2014. DG Strategic Planning, DND-Ottawa. 2000 NORAD renewal
8. Fearon J (1995) Rationalist explanations for war. Int Org 49(3):379–414
9. Gartzke E (1999) War is in the error term. Int Org 53(3):567–587
10. Grieco J, Powell R, Snidal D (1993) The relative gains problem for international cooperation. Am Polit Sci Rev 87(3):727–743
11. Powell R (1999) In the shadow of power: states and strategies in international politics. Princeton University Press, Princeton
12. Axelrod R (1984) The evolution of cooperation. Basic Books Inc, New York
13. Snyder S (2017) America first or US-South Korean alliance first in dealing with North Korea? Asia Unbound. Council on Foreign Relations, Washington, DC. https://www.cfr.org/blog/america-first-or-us-south-korea-alliance-first-dealing-north-korea. Accessed 22 Jan 2018

---

[7] Canada could explicitly state what NORAD "cannot do" in accomplishing its mandate in the context of that policy in the amending agreement.

14. Kimball A (2015) What Canada could learn from US defence procurement: issues, best practices and recommendations. University of Calgary SPP Research Papers 8(7), April 2015
15. Watts B, Harrison T (2011) Sustaining critical sectors of the US defense industrial base. Center for Strategic and Budgetary Assessments, Washington DC
16. Kinsella D (2013) Power transition theory and the global arms trade: exploring constructs from social network analysis. Political science faculty publications and presentations. Paper 15. https://pdxscholar.library.pdx.edu/polisci_fac/15. Accessed 22 Jan 2018
17. Morrow J (2000) Alliances: why write them down? Annu Rev Polit Sci 3(2000):63–83
18. Altfeld M (1984) The decision to ally: a theory and test. West Polit Q 37(4):523–544
19. Kimball A (2010) Political survival, the distributional dilemma, and alliance formation. J Peace Res 47(4):407–419
20. Bouchard C (2014) Interview on 5 Mar 2014. NORAD Regional Commander, 2006 NORAD renewal
21. Department of National Defence (2017) Strong, secure, engaged: Canada's defence policy. National Defence Department, Ottawa
22. Brewster M (2017) Boeing super hornet jet purchase likely to become 1st casualty in possible trade war: critics question Trudeau's tactic of linking super hornet purchase with bombardier trade dispute. CBC News. http://www.cbc.ca/news/politics/boeing-bombardier-trade-war-brewster-1.4308734. Accessed 18 Jan 2018
23. Williams R (2014) Interview on 3 Apr 2014. DG Western hemisphere policy, DND-Ottawa. 2006 & 2006 NORAD renewals
24. Jockel J (2007) Canada in NORAD, 1957–2007. McGill-Queen's University Press, Kingston
25. Canadian Treaty Series (2006) Agreement between the USA and Canada on the North American aerospace command. CTS 2006. Treaty Law Division, Department of Foreign Affairs and International Trade, Ottawa
26. Palmer G, Morgan TC (2006) A theory of foreign policy. Princeton University Press, Princeton
27. Bueno de Mesquita B, Morrow J, Siverson R, Smith A (2003) The logic of political survival. MIT Press, Cambridge
28. Delvoie L (2014) Interview on 20 Feb 2014. ADM Policy, FA-Ottawa, 1996 NORAD renewal
29. Meyer P (2014) Interview on 25 Feb 2014. Minister-Counsel Policy at CDN Embassy in Washington, DC; DG International Security, FA-Ottawa, 1996 & 2000 NORAD renewals
30. Milewski T (2016) Is Canada's credibility gap 'military' or 'political?': defence minister says Canada lacks the ships and planes, but there's no plan to fix the problem. CBC News. http://www.cbc.ca/news/politics/defence-procurement-jets-ships-1.3667326. Accessed 22 Jan 2018
31. Standing Senate Committee on National Security and Defence. (2017) Military underfunded: the walk must match the talk, Apr 2017. Senate of Canada, Ottawa
32. Harrison B (2016) Canada's greatest threat: how to mitigate the dangers of free riding. Canadian Global Affairs Institute, Calgary. http://www.cgai.ca/canada_s_greatest_threat_how_to_mitigate_dangers_of_free_riding. Accessed 22 Jan 2018
33. Macdonald G (2014) Interview on 16 Jan 2014, NORAD Deputy Commander, 2000 NORAD renewal
34. Fowler R (2014) Interview on 6 Mar 2014, DM Policy, DND-Ottawa, 1996 NORAD renewal
35. Chrétien R (2014) Interview on 11 Apr 2014, CDN Ambassador to the US, 1996 NORAD renewal

36. Cappe M (2014) Interview on 6 Mar 2014, Clerk of the Privy Council, 2000 NORAD renewal
37. Lipson C (1991) Why are some international agreements informal? Int Org 45(4):495–538
38. Koremenos B (2001) Loosening the ties that bind: a learning model of agreement flexibility. Int Org 55(2):289–325
39. Koremenos B, Nau A (2010) Exit, no exit. Duke J Comp Int Law 21(1):81–120
40. Abbott K, Snidal D (2000) Hard and soft law in international governance. Int Org 54 (3):421–456
41. Milner H (1997) Interests, institutions, and information. Princeton University Press, Princeton
42. Brister B (2007/8) When perpetuity doesn't mean forever. Policy Options, Dec 2007/Jan 2008, 78–83
43. Sokolsky J, Jockel J (2015) NORAD does not need saving. Int J 70(2):188–195
44. Binational Planning Group (2004) Interim report on enhanced Canada-US Cooperation. Peterson AFB, Colorado Springs
45. Findley R (2014) Interview on 14 Feb 2014. NORAD Deputy Commander, 2006 NORAD renewal
46. Graham W (2014) Interview on 28 Jan 2014. Minister of Defense-Ottawa, 2000 NORAD renewal
47. Martin L (2000) Democratic commitments: legislatures and international cooperation. Princeton University Press, Princeton
48. Calder K (2014) Interview on 4 Mar 2014. DG, ADM Policy, DND-Ottawa, 1996, 2000, & 2006 NORAD renewals
49. Koremenos B (2008) When, what, and why do states choose to delegate. Law Contemp Probl 71(1):151–192
50. Bélanger L, Fontaine-Skronski K (2012) Legalization in international relations: a conceptual analysis. Soc Sci Inf 51(2):238–262
51. Barkin J (2004) Time horizons and multilateral enforcement in international cooperation. Int Stud Quart 48(2):363–382
52. Langlois C, Langlois J-P (2001) Engineering cooperation: A game theoretic analysis of phased international agreements. Am J Polit Sci 45(3):599–619

The Future of North American Strategic Defense

Beyond Modernization

Andrea Charron$^{(\boxtimes)}$ and James Fergusson

University of Manitoba, Winnipeg, MB, Canada
{Andrea.Charron,James.Fergusson}@umanitoba.ca

Abstract. While most attention on NORAD and North American defense cooperation is focused on the modernization of the North Warning System (NWS), significant developments have occurred that suggest modernization will be accompanied by evolutionary changes to the Command. The new threat environment, centered upon Russian behaviour in Crimea, Ukraine and Syria, a new Russian strategic doctrine, and a new generation of advanced Russian long-range cruise missiles dictate not only layered, multi-sensor early warning systems, but also changes in NORAD command arrangements. In addition, the maritime component of the cruise missile threat, alongside continuing concerns of terrorists employing freighters as cruise missile platforms, raise the question whether or not NORAD should evolve into a binational air-maritime defense command. These considerations are central to the ongoing Evolution of North American Defense (EvoNAD) study, emanating from the Canada-United States' Permanent Joint Board on Defense (PJBD), under the lead of NORAD, in collaboration with the Canadian Joint Operations Command (CJOC) and United States Northern Command (USNORTHCOM) (the tri-command structure) to advise national authentics. The final result is difficult to predict. However, it is clear that both modernization and evolution will be driven by the engaged militaries, with some civilian authorities guiding the process, and the public and Canadian government paying less attention.

1 Introduction

Almost since its inception in 1957, little public attention is paid to the North American Aerospace Defense Command (NORAD) even though both the Canadian and American governments reflexively point to NORAD as the institutional centerpiece of a deep and broad Canada-United States' defense relationship. From its original air defense mission, NORAD has evolved through the acquisition of ballistic missile warning in the 1960s, the provision of support to drug interdiction in the 1990s, and, most recently, maritime warning in 2006. Today, NORAD is on the cusp of another major evolutionary step forward that goes beyond upgrading and modernizing aged infrastructure and equipment.

Current attention to NORAD, however, has almost exclusively focused upon the modernization need, centered upon the requirement to replace the aging, and outdated North Warning System (NWS). While this requirement is certainly pressing and likely to be very costly, it masks much more significant evolutionary changes to the

© Springer International Publishing AG, part of Springer Nature 2018
C. Leuprecht et al. (eds.), *North American Strategic Defense in the 21st Century:*,
Advanced Sciences and Technologies for Security Applications,
https://doi.org/10.1007/978-3-319-90978-3_11

Command. Indeed, the very factors driving NWS modernization are also driving the need for evolution. Moreover, NWS modernization can be neither truly understood, nor undertaken without an understanding of broader factors at play and the underlying requirements necessary to integrate NWS modernization into the Command.

2 The New Threat Environment

The post-Cold War/911 era is ending. In the future, observers are likely to identify the period between 2014 and 2016 as the defining moments shifting attention from intra-state conflict and 'the war on terror' back to state-on-state great power politics and deterrence. In 2014, Russia annexed Crimea, and then covertly supported rebels in Eastern Ukraine. In 2015, the Russia military engaged in the Syrian civil war in support of the Assad Regime. At about the same time, China expanded its military activities in the disputed South China Sea, and refused to recognize the Permanent Court of Arbitration's 2016 tribunal award on the South China Sea in favour of the Philippines [1]. Both Russia and China continue to develop advanced, technologically sophisticated military capabilities, clearly indicating an attempt to challenge American military superiority.

The most immediate and pressing concerns facing North American defense are from Russia, largely because China, for the time being, has adopted a regional access denial strategy, rather than an inter-continental one. Strategically, Russia has adopted the doctrine of 'escalation to de-escalate'.[1] In a regional crisis or conflict, likely around Russian borders as a function of the expansion of NATO into Eastern Europe, Russia may seek to escalate the crisis by threatening or striking at a target outside the region as a means to force NATO/United States to de-escalate the crisis or conflict. In effect, the threat or act of escalation is designed to indicate the credibility of the possibility that Russia will go up the escalation ladder to the ultimate use of strategic nuclear weapons.

Combined with this doctrine, a new generation of military capabilities, nuclear and conventional, have been developed by Russia, along with significant increases in overall defense spending.[2] Of major concern for North American defense is the new

---

[1] In some ways, Russian military doctrine is a reflection of NATO's Cold War doctrine. Whether in the context of massive retaliation of the 1950s, or flexible response of the 1960s and beyond, NATO's conventional military inferiority dictated a posture of first use of nuclear weapons, and domination of the escalation ladder to deter Soviet military aggression in Europe. Today, the situation has been reversed. Russia faces conventional military inferiority, and has responded by adopting a policy of first use of nuclear weapons, and a doctrine designed to provide Russia with escalation dominance.

[2] In 2011, the Putin government announced an RUR trillion-dollar state armament investment program for the next ten years [2]. The planned investments have slowed somewhat as a function of economic issues directly related to the decline in the price of oil. Nonetheless, Russia has emerged as the third largest defense spender in the world, but its level is still dwarfed by American defense spending ($US 596010 million in 2015 versus Russia's $US 66419 million in 2015—calculated in constant 2015 $US) [3].

generation of air (ALCMs) and surface/submarine launched cruise missiles (SLCMs).[3] These new long-range cruise missiles can be launched from their platforms at distances far outside of North American airspace in the Arctic, potentially from Russian maritime and airspace.[4]

The NWS, as currently configured, is inadequate to meet this threat and has been for some time. It is not in a physical position to be able to identify cruise missile launch platforms (bombers) at distances emanating from the Russian Arctic far before they reach North American airspace as is required currently for NORAD to mount a response. Nor is the NWS capable of identifying and tracking cruise missiles because of their low radar and flight path profiles. This also has direct implications for the final decision on the CF-18 replacement. In addition, the current location of NORAD forward operating locations (FOL) for jet fighters are likely too distant to be able to intercept and destroy the platforms prior to launch. There are no radar systems currently available, except for a limited supply of American Airborne Warning and Control (AWACS) platforms, to be able to detect ALCMs or SLCMs from a long distance off the east, west, and north coasts of North America. Finally, Canada, in particular, does not possess any ground-based air defense capacity to intercept the missiles.

In effect, there exists a significant gap in North American defense especially with respect to cruise missiles, which in turn, cedes escalation dominance to the Russians. In other words, it provides Russia with a valuable tool for coercive diplomacy, central to the doctrine of 'escalation to de-escalate' by undermining the credibility of western deterrence, which would then rest upon the threat of strategic nuclear retaliation with all its credibility concerns.

This gap extends into another area of concern. Following the 9/11 experience and the ongoing proliferation of cruise missile technologies, potentially to terrorist organizations, the threat of a maritime platform (freighter) approaching North America armed with cruise missiles has become a security concern. While significant improvements have been made in North American maritime domain awareness (MDA), partially as a function of NORAD's newest maritime warning mission, Canada and the United States still face the possibility of a cruise missile attack by an ambitious nonstate actor.[5] In this scenario, the maritime threat transitions into an air threat, and North American defense then faces the same problem as in the Russian case; the inability to defeat a cruise missile that crosses into North American airspace.

---

[3] In addition, Russia also recently deployed a new generation of ground-launched cruise missiles (GLCM) in violation of the 1987 Intermediate Nuclear Forces (INF) Treaty. In 2016, the United States convened a meeting of the special verification committee created by the Treaty to raise formally the violations. Of note, Russian leadership, in the past, has threatened to withdraw from INF in response to United States/NATO ballistic missile defense developments, and have also argued that the Treaty is obsolete as a function of the development and deployment of intermediate range ballistic missiles by others not party to the Treaty [4].

[4] The KH-101 cruise missile, first employed in Syria from a Blackjack bomber, is estimated to have a maximum operational range of 5500 km. at a cruising speed of 700 km, and capable of delivering either conventional ordinance or a 250 kt. nuclear warhead [5].

[5] For details on this mission and North American MDA, see [6].

3 NORAD Modernization and Evolution

The 'new' threat or strategic environment is the primary driver behind both modernization and evolution. There are major gaps related to NORAD's aerospace and maritime warning missions, and its air defense control mission. Essentially, the requirements to fill these gaps dictate a response beyond simply modernizing the NWS and replacing aged radars, jets and ships. Concomitant with the new threats is the need for evolved command and control arrangements as well as potentially expanded delegations of authorities, and the potential acquisition of new missions, especially maritime control, to NORAD. In effect, the NORAD of tomorrow may be appreciably different from the NORAD of today which also means that the defense of North America will be different, assuming, of course, both governments agree to taking the necessary steps forward.

This modernization/evolution debate is not new. In 2013, General Jacoby, the commander of NORAD and United States Northern Command (2011–2014), launched the NORAD Next study on the direction of the Canada-United States Permanent Joint Board on Defense (PJBD) [7]; an in-depth examination of future North American defense requirements. Subsequently, it was reduced in scope, largely because of resource constraints, especially on the Canadian side. In 2016, following a briefing on future requirements, the PJBD formally tasked NORAD, USNORTHCOM, CJOC, the NORAD regions and subordinates as well as the departments of defense on both sides of the border to examine future requirements. The PJBD requested that the study, now labeled the Evolution of North American Defense (EvoNAD), identify and establish priorities for modernization and evolution beyond just potential changes to NORAD. The first results of will be briefed to the PJBD sometime in 2018.

The modernization side of EvoNAD is focused naturally on the next generation of the North Warning System (NWS). However, modernization entails more than the simple replacement of the aging ground-based radars. The 'new' NWS will require the capability to identify and track air-breathing threats farther from North America and may well need to be able to identify maritime threats as well. This cannot be achieved simply using ground-based sensors so some mix of ground, air, space and sea-based sensors, are likely required. In addition the NWS will likely move farther north, and contribute to a layered system of sensors including potentially down the coastlines of North America.[6]

These requirements to modernize the NWS are also directly informed by strategic considerations. Rather than focusing on the threat projectile or 'arrows' (the missiles), the ideal strategy is to intercept the launch platforms or 'archers' as was the case during the final decade of the Cold War. Then, intercepting the 'archers' was not politically problematic, as such intercepts would take place near or in North American airspace in response to clear violations of international law and an armed attack against North

---

[6] The United States has faced numerous problems with trials of the Raytheon high altitude tethered aerostats for cruise missile defense [8].

America. However, this strategy now implies potential intercepts close to, or in Russian airspace or elsewhere far outside of North America. This, in turn, has significant political implications in times of crisis. It could entails a pre-emptive strategy and thus potentially shift NORAD's posture from pure defense *per se* to one of offensive-defense.

Two key issues thus arise which extend beyond modernization to the evolution of North American defense more generally. First, such a doctrine of detecting, deterring and defeating the archers far from North America would potentially require a delegation of new authorities to NORAD, or under the purview of the Tri-Command relationship between NORAD, Canada Joint Operations Command (CJOC) and USNORTHCOM. Such new delegations would then have implications for command and control (C^2) constructs between and within the tri-command structure. Second, the American and, in particular, Canadian governments must clearly understand the political implications of such doctrinal changes.

A pre-emptive posture has long been central to American strategic doctrine. However, Canada has traditionally eschewed pre-emption mainly because of political and resource constraints, as well as the much smaller size and reach of its military. As such, the Canadian government may prefer to leave the 'archers' to the United States, and adopt a counter-cruise missile defense function of intercepting the 'arrows'. This, however, has two related implications. It suggests that Canadian fighters dedicated to NORAD will not undertake the 'archer' mission, thereby potentially leaving a significant Northern gap that would likely be filled by the United States. If so, Canada could agree to allow fighters from the United States to deploy to the northern FOL in lieu of Canadian fighters for the 'archer' mission. Politically, it does not really matter *per se*, as Canada, by virtue of its Article 5 NATO commitment and the reality of the indivisibility of North American defense, would end up engaged regardless of who undertook the pre-emptive mission. The other option, however, is for Canada to disagree or not agree. This would then re-create the 'defense against help' situation of the late 1940s, which somewhat strained Canadian and United States' relations.

A preemptive United States posture, in which Canada stands aside, could potentially lead Canada to invest in cruise missile intercept capabilities, air, ground and sea-based, in the context of a binational military division of labour.[7] Currently, Canada possesses, at best, limited, if any such capabilities. Indicative of this missing capability, the last NORAD Vigilant Shield exercise in 2017 entailed the deployment of American Avenger short range surface-to-air missile systems to CFB North Bay with sixty members of the South Carolina Army National Guard's (SCNG's) 263rd Army Air and

---

[7] This is not necessarily new. There already exists a *de facto* division of labour. Canada is not engaged in ballistic missile defense, and the United States is not formally committed to defend Canada from a ballistic missile attack. This option was first raised in 1985 in the context of the invitation by the United States for the allies to participate in the Strategic Defense Initiative (SDI). Canada would take responsibility for modernizing the NWS and air control mission, and leave the missile defense mission to the United States. See, [9].

Missile Defense Command.[8] If Canada failed to invest as a function of costs, then arrangements would likely be required for Canada to accept more personnel from the United States and equipment in Canada. This, in turn, would have implications for current command and control arrangements in NORAD.

At the same time, the cruise missile threat extends into the maritime environment, in which a maritime threat, the platform, can quickly produce an air-breathing threat—a SLCM. This then raises the question of integrating maritime and air defense, and thus whether NORAD's mission suite should expand into maritime control. Currently, maritime defense cooperation is undertaken based on a longstanding relationship, underpinned by memorandums of understandings (MOUs), between the Royal Canadian Navy (RCN) and the United States Navy. It lacks, however, a formal integrated centralized Canada-United States command structure[9] which would, require linkages between North American command and control and the other United States combatant commands, especially European Command (EUCOM) and Pacific Command (PACOM), as well as NATO. Events in EUCOM's area of responsibility (AOR), for example, can have an impact in North America faster and more profoundly than was the case in the past as a function of the speed and technology of new weapon systems.[10] Deepening the connections to other combatant commands and regular strategic updates are essential to ensure that AOR's are not stove piped or situation-specific. The future of North American defense cooperation also extends beyond the aerospace and maritime sectors. One such sector is military outer space, which currently is managed bilaterally outside of NORAD, even though NORAD still tracks for inbound missiles and other objects in orbit. Here, of course, the thorny issue of ballistic missile defense (BMD) resides as a barrier somewhat.[11] As a result of the integrated nature of North America *writ large,* cyber defense is another area of concern. While the United States has stood up Cyber Command, Canada has no equivalent in terms of size and is, for now, behind the curve. In addition, cooperation in the land environment remains largely nationalized, notwithstanding existing MOUs related to consequence management (for example, mutual assistance after a natural disaster).

Of course, this does not necessarily mean that NORAD is the only solution to command and control requirements for the defense of North America. Moreover, there are distinct differences among the air, cyber, land, maritime and space defense

---

[8] Vigilant Shield is the annual NORAD air defense exercise.

[9] In the case of the United States, such a structure exists as a function of United States Fleet Forces/NAVNORTH under United States Northern Command (USNORTHCOM). In Canada CJOC & the joint force maritime component commander (JFMCC) execute the missions. More study needs to be made of the http://www.usnorthcom.com/navnorth/cjoc/jfmcc.

[10] Of note here, United States Northern Commands AOR extends 500 miles into the Atlantic, whereas Canada Maritime Atlantic Command (MARLANT) only extends to the limits of the Canadian exclusive economic zone of 200 nautical miles.

[11] Canada, although not a part of BMD-a USNORTHCOM mission, does cooperate in missile defence in that NORAD is mandated to provide warning & characterization of missile threats under NORAD's aerospace warning mission.

environments. Nor is it necessarily the case that all of the environments need to be integrated into a single binational command structure. Nonetheless, NORAD is an obvious solution to the demands generated by the new threat environment, especially in the air and maritime sectors, not least of all because of its highly successful track record as the centerpiece of North American defense cooperation. In addition, NORAD is no longer simply an aerospace command. As a function of its maritime warning mission acquired in 2006, NORAD has already become much more.

The more domains surveilled under the NORAD commander, the more information the commander has, in theory, to take decisions presumably farther out in time and space. In other words, an expanded range of missions sets allow NORAD to see and react farther away on the threat to "bang" continuum. If the addition of maritime warning to NORAD in 2006 is any guide, such decisions will be made with caution and then, if adopted, will be slowly accepted, with needed intervention at the highest levels before the militaries and federal agencies responsible for such domains are working seamlessly, if ever.

4 Conclusion

One might be quick to conclude that the primary driver behind EvoNAD is the military and NORAD itself, following a pattern of evolving military cooperation that led to the creation of an operational NORAD command in 1957, followed by its political formalization in 1958. However, it is evident that modernization and evolution is on the higher political agenda. In the joint statement concerning the first meeting of Prime Minister Trudeau and President Trump in February, the two agreed that: "North American Aerospace Defense Command (NORAD) illustrates the strength of our mutual commitment. United States and Canadian forces jointly conduct aerospace warning, aerospace control, and maritime warning in defense of North America. We will work to modernize and broaden our NORAD partnership in these key domains, as well as in cyber and space" [10].

Of course, how the President and Prime Minister, and their senior advisors understand and interpret the meaning of modernization and evolution, and whether they share a common interpretation, remains, for now, an open question. In addition, the priority attached to EVONAD is likely to differ between Washington and Ottawa. For Canada at least, trade and border issues remain, as always, the priorities.

NORAD will celebrate its 60th anniversary on 12 May 2018 and given the current geopolitical threat environment, both military and civilian authorities on both sides of the border are considering the future of NORAD and the evolution of North American defense. NORAD, however, is arguably the least understood of all the Canadian Armed Forces' (CAF) and United States' commitments. The PJBD has yet to announce its American co-chair and attention to its role and purpose by governments on both sides of the border waxes and wanes. NORAD is also quite literally out of sight and out of mind for both publics: NORAD is considered in the vaguest of terms peaking at Christmas and the arrival of Santa.

This can be argued as evidence of NORAD doing its job well; usually press coverage is for failures not successes. On the other hand, NORAD can be more easily marginalized if it is not fore in the minds of governments and the publics. From the perspective of Canada, if past reactions involving increased United States military cooperation with Canada outside of a foreign deployment is any guide, political resistance will be strong to changes to NORAD that involve a visible increase of United States presence in Canada especially now when many Canadians are very suspicious of the current United States administration. On the United States side, any suggestion that the United States is not clearly in control of its homeland defenses requiring the aid of its much weaker neighbour would be treated as conspiracy and nonsense, especially in today's political climate. In the end, the future of EVONAD and NORAD, and thus Canada-United States North American defense cooperation will emerge initially from the militaries, with civilian authority engagement guiding the process, and the government and public playing catch up not unlike the lag between the operational inception of NORAD in 1957, followed by its political inception in 1958.

References

1. Permanent Court of Arbitration (2016) PCA Case No. 2013–19: In the matter of the south China sea arbitration. Permanent court of arbitration, 12 July 2016. https://pca-cpa.org/wp-content/uploads/sites/175/2016/07/PH-CN-20160712-Award.pdf
2. Oxenstierna S, Westerlund F (2013) Arms procurement and the Russian defense industry. J Slav Mil Stud 26(1):1–24
3. SIPRI (2017) Military expenditure by country, in constant (2015) US$ m., 1988–2016. https://www.sipri.org/sites/default/files/SIPRI-Milex-data-1988-2015.xlsx
4. Gordon MR (2017) Russia deploys missile, violating treaty and challenging Trump. New York Times, 14 Feb 2017. https://www.nytimes.com/2017/02/14/world/europe/russia-cruise-missile-arms-control-treaty.html. Accessed 31 Jan 2018
5. Akulov A (2016) Russian Kh-101 Air-to-Surface cruise missile: unique and formidable. Strategic culture foundation, 19 Oct 2016. www.strategic-culture.org/news/2016/10/19/russian-kh-101-air-to-surface-cruise-missile-unique-and-formidable.html. Accessed 31 Jan 2018
6. Andrea C, James F, Nicolas A (2015) *Left of Bang: North American Domain Awareness and NORAD's Maritime Warning Mission.* Winnipeg: Centre for Defence and Security Studies. http://umanitoba.ca/centres/cdss/media/0_NORAD_Maritime_Warning_Mission_Final_Report_8_Oct_2015.pdf.
7. Miles D (2013) US Canada think ahead to NORAD next. Airforces Press Service, 7 Jan 2013. http://archive.defense.gov/news/newsarticle.aspx?id=118926. Accessed 31 Jan 2018
8. James F (2010). *Canada and Ballistic Missile Defence 1954–2009; Déjà vu all over again.* Vancouver: University of British Columbia Press.
9. Judson J (2016) After blimp's wild ride, JLENS program will fly again, NORAD say. Defense News, 11 Feb 2016. https://www.defensenews.com/breaking-news/2016/02/11/after-blimp-s-wild-ride-jlens-program-will-fly-again-norad-says/. Accessed 31 Jan 2018
10. PM.GC.CA (2017) Joint Statement from President Donald J. Trump and Prime Minister Justin Trudeau (Washington, D.C.), 13 Feb 2017. http://pm.gc.ca/eng/news/2017/02/13/joint-statement-president-donald-j-trump-and-prime-minister-justin-trudeau. Accessed 31 Jan 2018

NORAD'S Future: St-Amand's Revelation, Gortney's Complaint, and Vigilant Shield 17's Component Commander

Joseph T. Jockel[✉]

St. Lawrence University, Canton, NY 13617, USA
jockel@stlawu.edu

Abstract. The Trudeau government's 2017 defence white paper promised that, "Canada will work closely with the United States to ensure NORAD is fully prepared to confront rapidly evolving threats including exploring new roles for the command, taking into account the full range of threats." This chapter explores current trends in North American missile defence, maritime defence and air defence that could affect the future of the binational command in 2018, as the two governments observe the 60th anniversary of the NORAD accord, and in the years beyond. It suggests four possible models for the command's future: first, an enhanced multi-domain NORAD to which responsibility has been given, in addition to its current roles, for maritime defence, or missile defence, or both—a North American Defence Command in other words; second, a NORAD that has been reduced to its original role as an air defence head-quarters and moved out of Colorado Springs in the form of a combined joint task force; third, a variant of the second option in which the task force, i.e. NORAD would act as a stand-by entity; and finally, NORAD unchanged from what it is today.

1 Introduction

According to the Trudeau government's defence white paper, *Strong Secure Engaged,* "Canada will work closely with the United States to ensure NORAD is fully prepared to confront rapidly evolving threats including exploring new roles for the command, taking into account the full range of threats" [1, p. 61]. Later the white paper specifies that the "threats facing North America have evolved significantly in the air and maritime environment, as well as other emerging domains, and weapons technology, including ballistic and cruise missiles, has advanced tremendously" [1, p. 90].

Where might this lead? In September 2017, NORAD was 60 years old. With the 60th anniversary coming up in May 2018 of the exchange of notes constituting the NORAD agreement (which did not create the command but gave it a diplomatic framework eight months after it was up and running) Ottawa and Washington may well want to seize the occasion to unveil an updated agreement, as the white paper also indicates [1, p. 90]. While the defence white paper and NORAD's 60th anniversary provide the immediate focus for this chapter, the purpose here is also to examine the

© Springer International Publishing AG, part of Springer Nature 2018
C. Leuprecht et al. (eds.), *North American Strategic Defense in the 21st Century:*,
Advanced Sciences and Technologies for Security Applications,
https://doi.org/10.1007/978-3-319-90978-3_12

trends that might continue to affect NORAD beyond May 2018 and to point to some possible models for NORAD's evolution not just on, but also beyond that date.

We can turn to a recent revelation by NORAD's deputy commander, a complaint by its previous commander, and the designation in a recent air defence exercise of a component commander as three indicators of what some of the possibilities may be for NORAD future in respectively, missile defence, maritime defence and air defence, especially inasmuch as they have implications for the structure of NORAD. They in turn point to five possibilities: (1) an (upgraded) multi-domain NORAD, (2) a (downgraded) air defence NORAD, (3) a (downgraded) air defence NORAD when necessary, (4) and a no-change NORAD.

2 St-Amand's Revelation: Missile Defence

Inevitably, when thinking about NORAD's future new roles what first comes to mind to anyone who follows Canadian defence politics is missile defence. From the very moment of its creation in 1957, NORAD regularly has expected eventually to be given the missile defence mission, only to see the two missile defences that the U.S. has deployed, the Sentinel/Safeguard system in 1975–76 and the current missile defence system be given to the other major Colorado Springs command of the day, i.e. the all-U.S. one. In both cases it was Ottawa's decision that Canada would not become directly involved in the operation of missile defence that has led to the system being kept out of NORAD's hands. Between 1968 and 1981 the NORAD agreement even specified at Ottawa's behest that NORAD could not be given missile defence.

It is hard to tell if Ottawa's aversion to North American missile defence will soon come to an end. (Canada is in the odd position of supporting missile defence for its allies but not for itself.) To be sure, the Trudeau government's white paper also observes that "The number of countries with access to ballistic missile technology, including some with the potential to reach North America or target Canadian and allied deployed forces, has increased and is expected to grow and become more sophisticated. North Korea's frequent nuclear and missile tests underscore this point" [1, p. 54]. The document goes on to offer two carefully counterpoised sentences: "Canada's policy with respect to participating in missile defence has not changed. However, we intend to engage the U.S. to look broadly at emerging threats and perils to North America across all domains, as part of NORAD modernization" [1, p. 90]. One can only guess at how many seemingly endless hours Canadian diplomats, bureaucrats, military personnel, and politicians may have spent in negotiating that specific language. In the wake of the summer, 2017 North Korean nuclear and missiles tests, Prime Minister Trudeau stuck to that same double formulation, linking the specific to the vague. Canada's policy on missile defence has not changed, told a press conference in New York in September 2017, while "we continue to engage in thoughtful ways to ensure we are doing everything we can and must do to keep Canadians safe" [2].

It is worth underlining that the current state of binational affairs concerning missile defence is just fine with the U.S. It gives some Canadians a thrill to think that they are standing up to Washington, maybe even angering it, by staying out of missile defence. But unlike the case with air defence, the U.S. does not need Canadian territory, airspace or military forces, or political support—in short it does not need Canada—for the missile defence system. Washington has never pressured Canada to join in, nor was it upset when Canada did not, any tales about Paul Martin and George W. Bush notwithstanding. (This is not to say that U.S. and Canadian officials at NORAD have not tried from time to time to bring what suasion to bear that they could on Ottawa.)

NORAD and along with it, Canadians today are not entirely uninvolved in missile defence; as a result of the 2004 amendment to the NORAD agreement, the binational command provides USNORTHCOM, which has operational command of the missile defence, with missile warning information. The arrangement appears to be working well. If Canada had not agreed to the amendment it would not have been much of a problem for the U.S., for the sensors NORAD relies on for detecting and tracking ballistic are all-U.S. as well; none of them is located in Canada or operated by the Canadian military. Their information can be delivered and assessed though all-U.S. channels, instead of through the binational NORAD. But without the amendment NORAD would have had to be reduced to an air defence arrangement of some sort.

Prime Minister Trudeau's comments in New York were also made just after General St-Amand's noteworthy testimony to a parliamentary committee in Ottawa that when it comes to missile defence, "The extent of U.S. policy is not to defend Canada" [2]. If anything, his refreshingly straight talk had the remarkable effect of producing from U.S. Secretary of Defense James Mattis, a man who certainly does not have a reputation for being mealy-mouthed, the firm yet at the same time completely vague reaction, "We stand by Canada" [3]. That formulation does not seem to rule out standing by and doing nothing while tracking a missile heading for say, Calgary. The NORAD deputy commander deserves a round of applause for his comments; taking away the illusion that Canada is shielded by the U.S. they may help focus the debate in Canada over participation in missile defence where it really belongs: not on whether it would make the Americans happy (They don't care) or whether it would save NORAD (Right now at least, it doesn't need saving on this score) but rather on whether "doing everything we can and must do to keep Canadians safe" includes protecting them from North Korean missiles, and eventually missiles from other rogue states. This is not the place to get into that question, except to observe that it actually is a tough one, for it involves assessing just how important a target for North Korea Canadians should consider themselves and how much risk they want to take, especially since there are other defence needs that clearly are urgent and on which scarce Canadian defence dollars could be spent.

Let's suppose the Trudeau government decides that it does want into missile defence. This also is not the place to get deeply into what the specific contribution Canada might make to the missile defence, although as is usually the case in life, cash would undoubtedly be welcome. Alternatively, Canada might host an east coast radar site (there has been talk in the past of Goose Bay), or even conceivably an east coast interceptor site, although this would meet with objections in the U.S. Congress some of whose members are hoping to secure any new location for their districts. That includes my own representative, of the 21st congressional district of New York, where we are hoping that Fort Drum gets picked. It might be possible for Washington and Ottawa to identify a Canadian "asymmetrical contribution" to *another* aspect of North American aerospace defence, such as assuming a certain level of responsibility for the modernization of the North Warning System (which is part of the air defence), in lieu of a direct contribution to missile defence. That was the approach in the late 1990s and early 2000 when the Canadian military hoped to use an investment in space surveillance as the "asymmetrical contribution" to missile defence. As the then-deputy commander in chief of NORAD cabled Ottawa in 1998, "this non-contentious approach by Canada would make a major contribution to further the future of the binational area of BMD without risking potential negative Canadian political and public opinion" [4, p. 157].

Once Canada makes a mutually agreeable contribution in cash, real estate or whatever, the algorithm guiding the use of the missile defence can be adapted, along with the appropriate policy directives, to provide coverage for Canada. That would be the relatively easy part. The hard part for Washington would be to decide on whether missile defence should become a NORAD mission; that, is whether NORAD should be given operational control over the system, much like it operationally controls the air defences of the two countries. In practical terms, this would entail in the event of a missile attack, first, enabling Canadian officers on duty in the NORAD/USNORTHCOM operations center as command directors to advise the use of the missile defence, and second, enabling Canadian general officers, on duty in command at NORAD to order its release. Right now only Americans officers, acting under the aegis of USNORTHCOM may undertake both those responsibilities. Making missile defence a NORAD responsibility was also part of the plan for missile defence (as conceived in Colorado Spring) in the late 1990s. Ottawa should push for it if Canada makes a respectable contribution, directly or asymmetrically.

3 Gortney's Complaint: Maritime Defence

For the past several years, if you were to ask someone at NORAD/USNORTHCOM about what might need fixing at NORAD, you would not hear at first about missile defence, if at all. After all, the information flow through NORAD, as well as command and control of the missile defence system by USNORTHCOM appear to be working well.

Rather, you would hear about the problematic relationship between air defence and maritime defence. The previous NORAD/USNORTHCOM commander, Admiral William Gortney, was so vocal about this problem, that we might as well call it "Gortney's complaint." As he would put it (paraphrased from recollection), "Wearing my NORAD hat, I can use Canadian assets to shoot down a Russian cruise missile, but I can't sink the ship or submarine that launched it." NORAD is an aerospace defence command and has no maritime defence role. (Since the 2006 renewal, NORAD also has had a maritime warning role, but that is quite different from command and control of naval forces and so not relevant to this discussion.)

A NORAD discussion paper on "The Need to Evolve North American Defense," part of the recent "EVONAD" initiative, has formulated Gortney's complaint in these terms: "Consolidating authorities of U.S. and Canadian naval and air forces defending North America is needed in order to bring greater unity of action to this multi domain strategic scenario for which Russia is developing forces" [5]. Those forces are, in particular, sea-launched cruise missiles with longer ranges.

The Americans in Colorado Springs are all the more aware of the absence of a maritime defence role for NORAD because the problem does not exist on the U.S. side of the headquarters. Wearing her USNORTHCOM hat, the commander can use U.S. assets to attack both the cruise missile and the Russian vessel that launched it. Moreover, in an emergency a Canadian warship or Aurora CP-140 aircraft could be placed by the Chief of the Defence Staff, at the direction of the Canadian government, under the operational command of USNORTHCOM (or to its naval component NAVNORTH) and (depending upon the instructions at the time of assignment) used in sinking the Russian sub. But the Canadians at NORAD would not be directly involved in the command and control of the operation, NORAD having no maritime defence role. To be sure, in one sense things work about the same at USNORTHCOM's counterpart, Canadian Joint Operations Command, (CJOC); it can be given operational of U.S. forces. Nonetheless, CJOC is not the national command that is tightly linked to the binational aerospace defence command by a shared commander, headquarters, operations center, and some shared staff.

These anomalies date back to 2002 when USNORTHCOM was being stood up as a homeland defence command with responsibilities across several domains, whereupon the government of Prime Minister Jean Chrétien declined to enter into the discussions which Washington hoped to have with it about broadening at the same time NORAD's responsibilities. Such a broadening would have turned the binational command in effect, and perhaps in name, into the North American Defence Command.

The Trudeau government may want to revisit the question of expanding NORAD's responsibilities, specifically whether NORAD should have a maritime defence role. If the Canadian government does move in this direction, it will want to emphasize an important difference that would exist between NORAD's current air defence and any future maritime defence role. Unlike the air defence forces which have been placed under NORAD's operational control, and will remain so indefinitely, Canadian naval forces would only be assigned to NORAD for an operation upon the decision of the Canadian government, in the event of a real or anticipated crisis. That is the way it works with USNORTHCOM, and U.S. naval forces, too. It has no standing naval forces; these would have to be assigned to it in the event of a contingency by the Secretary of Defense.

The Canadian government should expect to meet two objections to giving NORAD a maritime defence role. The first is that such a step would limit Canadian sovereignty. The response, beyond emphasizing that the government would need to approve maritime forces being assigned to any NORAD maritime defence operation, would be to underline that the arrangements *already* exist to place Canadian assets under U.S. operational command (and U.S. under Canadian). Since this would create the possibility of placing naval Canadian assets under the binational NORAD, where Canadian officers would be involved in the command and control of the operation, it constitutes an improvement.

The other objection that can be anticipated is strategic, or better put, one about strategy. As the NORAD think piece observes "Just as it is preferable to engage Russian LRA [Long Range Aviation] prior to launch of their cruise missiles, it is preferable for U.S. and Canadian naval forces to engage Russian submarines prior to launch of their weapons" [5]. Just under what circumstances, it almost certainly will be asked in the public debate, will the Canadian government allow Canadian naval assets to be used in pre-emptive or preventive attacks on Russian submarines? The Canadian debate would play out within the broader one within NATO, especially in the U.S. over the extent to which the Russians truly have a doctrine of "de-escalation dominance" involving limited nuclear strikes, which could include sea-launched cruise missile strikes and if so, what the appropriate response by the alliance to it must be.

The U.S. government, in considering giving NORAD a maritime defence role, will undoubtedly consider the possibility that the Canadian government might, when asked to assign naval forces to a NORAD operation, place conditions on their use that would be unacceptable to the U.S. Yet this should not be reason enough not to go along with such NORAD enhancement, for the U.S. always would retain the option to conduct an operation entirely with its own forces under USNORTHCOM. The U.S. government might even agree to give NORAD a maritime defence role with the unspoken thought that it might just never be used.

4 Vigilant Shield 17's Component Commander

In October 2016, NORAD held, for 17th time, it annual Vigilant Shield air defence exercise. The exercise's major aim that year was "to deploy and conduct air sovereignty operations in the far north and high Arctic, thus demonstrating a combined ability to detect, identity and meet possible threats in some of the most remote regions of the world" [6]. One reason it is noteworthy is that F-15s from the U.S. Air National Guard deployed to Yellowknife in the Northwest Territories, one of NORADs Forward Operation Locations, where fighter aircraft are not permanently stationed. In a crisis with Russia the Yellowknife facility would be used to support air defence operations as far north as possible.

Another reason the exercise should be noteworthy is that during it, NORAD created for the first time a theatre Combined Joint Forces Air Component Commander (CJFACC), giving that designation to the commander of the Continental NORAD region (CONR), who is located at Tyndall Air Force Base, Florida. The two other NORAD regions, the Canadian (CANR) and the Alaskan (ANR) essentially became supporting commands and force suppliers. In other words, during the exercise NORAD maintained a subordinate headquarters, located outside of Colorado Spring, for North American air defence.

NORAD was itself created to be the sole headquarters for North American air defence, and at least for the moment is that again, the arrangements put in place during during Vigilant Shield 17 having only been temporary. That could change, as the exercise indicates.

For its first few years of its existence, air defence was NORAD's sole mission as well as the sole mission of the first U.S. command with which was linked, the Continental Air Defense Command (CONAD). "This mighty task of air defence," the command's first deputy commander-in-chief, Air Marshal Slemon, called it and to undertake it NORAD operationally controlled at its peak a force that included no fewer than 64 USAF regular fighter squadrons and nine RCAF regular fighter squadrons, surface-to-air missiles, many of which were equipped with nuclear warheads, as were many of the air-to-air missiles carried by the fighters, and three great detection systems spanning the continent, the Pinetree radars, the Mid-Canada Line and the Distant Early Warning Line [4, p. 1].

Just as NORAD was standing up, the Soviet Union began to test intercontinental ballistic missiles, heralding the shift in the threat away from manned bombers towards ballistic missiles, both intercontinental and submarine-launched, and potentially towards orbital (space-based) threats. The U.S. deployed ground-based missile detection radars in Alaska, Greenland, the U.K., and in the continental U.S.; and space-based sensors. It is worth noting once again that no such system was ever deployed in Canada. Other systems tracked objects in earth orbit; here Canada once made a contribution with ground-based tracking cameras. The air defence system was shrunk to but a mere shadow of itself, with upticks first as the Soviets deployed air-launched cruise missiles in the 1980s and then after the terrorist attacks on 9/11 led to the reconfiguration of the air defence system to be able to respond to threats arising from within the continent.

The headquarters structure at Colorado Springs was adapted to the new threats as they materialized, reflecting both military exigencies as the political realities of Canada-U.S. aerospace defence cooperation. NORAD moved beyond just air defence to acquire a missile detection and tracking role; these were eventually joined together to support what became NORAD's core function of integrated tactical warning and assessment of an aerospace attack on North America. The two new aerospace missions NORAD was kept out of, actively defending against missiles and actively defending against satellites (during the two periods the United State maintained an anti-satellite capability) went to the other Colorado Springs command. That command changed; CONAD was succeeded by a series of U.S. commands over the years that reflected the changing threat: the Aerospace Defence Command, (ADCOM), U.S. Space Command (USSPACECOM) and most recently, of course, USNORTHCOM.

Because USNORTHCOM is a multidomain theater combatant command, it is strikingly different from the earlier U.S. commands at Colorado Springs, whose responsibilities—first air defence, then aerospace defence and then space—were functionally much more limited in scope, and could all be said to fall within the domain of aerospace. On the other hand, the breadth of USNORTHCOM's multidomain responsibilities can be shown simply by plucking several phrases out of its self-description. It "partners to conduct homeland defense, civil support and security cooperation to defend and secure the U.S. and its interest." It has an area of operations "that includes, air land and sea approaches and encompasses the continental U.S., Alaska, Canada, Mexico and the surrounding water." And it "consolidates under a single unified command existing missions that were previously executed by other DOD organizations. This provides unity of command, which is critical to mission accomplishment" [7].

When the NORAD/USNORTHCOM commander looks at the full range of her several responsibilities wearing her two hats, air defence is but one of many. Yet it must stick out because it now has what can be called a disproportionate place in the Colorado Springs headquarters. There are three regional air defence headquarters in

North America whose relationships and demands have to be adjudicated in Colorado Springs, if need be by the commander. That can be explained historically by how NORAD evolved, and still might be justified by the special binational nature of the enterprise and by the fact that air defence forces, unlike those for say, disaster relief, have to be at the immediate ready.

Yet the NORAD structure today is at odds with how U.S. combatant commands often have tended in recent years to organize their headquarters and the command and control of their joint operations, which is to establish a task force for components, such as air defence. This allows the commander to concentrate on unity of command across domains and on cooperation with other combatant commander. It is specifically provided for in U.S. doctrine, too. As the Joint Chiefs of Staff publication, *Command and Control of Joint Air Operations* (2014) outlines, a Joint Force Commander (JFC) such as that of USNORTHCOM "establishes subordinate commands, assigns responsibilities, establishes or delegates appropriate command relationships, and establishes coordinating instructions for subordinate commanders. When organizing joint forces, simplicity and clarity are critical." It goes on to add, "If the scope or complexity of the operations is significant, the JFC should consider designating a JFACC. This will allow the JFC time to focus on the overall campaign vice spending it on directing air operations" [8].

So it should come as no surprise that NORAD, under the influence of evolving U.S. doctrine and preferences for command and control, tested a CJACC during Vigilant Shield '17. (The "C" for "combined" reflects the involvement of both the Canadian and U.S. militaries.) Informal discussions with NORAD/USNORTHCOM officials indicate that "some things worked and some things didn't." Given the importance of the CJACC to thinking about NORAD's future, it would be useful if NORAD released a study about the exercise and the state of the command's own thinking about any future use of a CJACC for North American air defence.

Although it almost certainly was not the intention of NORAD to do so, Vigilant Shield '17 raises what could be called some existential questions for the command: If, strikingly unlike 1957, North American air defence now can be headquartered outside of Colorado Springs, and given that the Canadian military's sole contribution to aerospace defence is air defence, (a contribution that consists of just some aging interceptors and radar stations) just why should the Canadians remain in Colorado Springs? In other words, just why should NORAD continue? Is a binational command at the four-star level really necessary? In fact, you could say that NORAD—again, probably unintentionally—rehearsed during Vigilant Shield '17 how its own demise could be arranged.

5   Four Potential Future NORADs

5.1   An (Upgraded) Multidomain NORAD

The picture changes dramatically if NORAD, and along with it, Canadians are involved in providing it with forces in other domains, and make thereby a claim on their command and control. The two possibilities are discussed above: missile defence and maritime defence. At the moment maritime defence seems more likely to be added, for two reasons. It appears to be higher on Colorado Springs' own set of priorities for how NORAD might be enhanced, unless the current commander sees the issue quite differently from her predecessors. Someone should try to ask her about this in a public forum. (The working assumption here is that the commander's preferences here will be approved in Washington, especially by those responsible for the Unified Command Plan. Maybe some researcher should try to ask someone in the Joint Staff, too about this.) Second, although maritime defence is fraught with the political difficulties discussed above, it does not carry the heavy historical freight that missile defence does in Canada and so might be easier for Canadian government to accept. In other words, Ottawa would not have to backtrack to on maritime defence the way it would with missile defence.

It is not inconceivable that NORAD might also be given responsibility for civil support/aid to the civil power, along the same lines as it would be given maritime defence: governments would need, in the event of a contingency, to assign forces to it to undertake a particular operation. This possibility has appeared in past discussions of NORAD's future. But there really is no need for this; cooperation in this area works more naturally through the relationship between USNORTHCOM and CJOC. Under standing arrangements, in the event of a contingency, such as a natural disaster, forces of the one country can be placed under the operational control of the other country's command; a task force can also be created reporting to one or both commands.

There also has been talk in the past of assigning to NORAD some form of responsibility for cyberdefence, parallel to whatever responsibilities for it USNORTHCOM might receive. The announcement in August 2017 that U.S. Cyber Command would be elevated to a unified combatant command indicates that Fort Meade, Maryland, and not Colorado Springs will be the locus for cyberdefence—for now, at least. This could change in the years ahead. Simply because space was so important, few would have expected at USSPACECOM's creation that it would be relatively short-lived; the same eventually could happen to USCYBERCOM.

If Ottawa and Washington agree to expanded NORAD's responsibilities to include either maritime defence, missile defence, or both, the stage would be set for an impressive public recommitment to NORAD in 2018, involving both the renegotiation of the agreement and, if maritime defence is in the deal, the renaming of the command to the North American Defence Command. If this occurs, it will be politically easy for NORAD—should the commander so desire—to re-create the CJACC at Tyndall on a standing basis, restructuring NORAD headquarters in Colorado Springs to concentrate exclusively on higher-level tasks of command and control.

5.2   A (Downgraded) Air Defence NORAD

But Ottawa might nix both missile defence and maritime defence as new NORAD tasks. What then? In the short run, as will be discussed below under the last option, probably little would happen. However, at some point either USNORTHCOM or the Pentagon may no longer want to accept the anomaly of, linked to a U.S. combatant command, a binational command to which one of the nations contributes little and whose role in which is very restricted. Perhaps NORAD's existence would come under threat as a result as a reshuffling of the Unified Command Plan in which the NORAD piece no longer fits. That might especially occur if James G. Fergusson was right in his standard work on Canada and missile defence that NORAD's missile detection and warning role will increasingly become redundant as the U.S. deploys new elements of the missile defence system [9, p. 263]. Or perhaps it would occur at the moment the American want to establish a JACC or CJACC and decide that the place for Canadians really is just Tyndall and not Colorado Springs. To be sure, Canada would formally have to agree to the dissolution of NORAD. But realistically, it could not insist on the continuation of the binational command over the objection of Washington.

The CJACC that was created during Vigilant Shield '17 was temporary and subordinate to NORAD. In order to continue Canada-U.S. air defence cooperation, such a component commander could be designated with an indefinite time frame; the designation would be standing or permanent, in other words. There would no longer be a NORAD in Colorado Springs under this scenario; the CJACC would report there solely to USNORTHCOM. Wouldn't that leave just the Americans in charge? Not necessarily. The answer to this question was provided over a decade ago by the Binational Planning Group, the entity created by the two governments in 2002 to see what could be done when the Chrétien government declined to consider an enhanced NORAD. Among the four options the Binational Planning Group recommended that Ottawa and Washington consider was one that would "give primacy to the two national commands," which today would be USNORTHCOM and CJOC, supported by what the planning group called a Standing Combined Joint Task Force, not unlike the CJACC, although broader in scope. The Standing Combined Joint Task Force would report to *both* national commands and "perform binational missions as assigned by them." "This concept", the Binational Planning Group went on to say, "relies upon the strengths of both national commands and the commitment of these commands towards a continental approach to defense and security" [10, pp. 38–39].

Moving the Canadians out of Colorado Springs would not necessarily entail bringing NORAD to an end, or at least the NORAD name. The CJACC at Tyndall could be named the North American Air Defence commander, his staff would continue to include Canadians, among them the deputy commander, as is already the case at CONR. NORAD would once again, as at its beginning, have the sole task of air defence. Given the symbolic importance both Washington and Ottawa attach to the NORAD name, this application of the name could be a politically attractive covering step to the dissolution of the binational command.

5.3 A NORAD When Necessary

But if we can rely "upon the strengths of both national commands and the commitment of these commands towards a continental approach to defense security" isn't that also the case for the three North American air defence regions, CONR, CANR, and ANR? Much of the command and control of air defence occurs within and between the three regional headquarters and not in Colorado Springs. This reflects in good part a desire on the part of both countries to counterbalance binational cooperation and unity of effort with national control in some aspects. NORAD's regional boundaries once crossed borders. Largely at Canada's behest they were redrawn along national lines.

The tendency towards national control has increased in one respect since the 9/11 attacks. NORAD arrangements long allowed (and presumably still allow) officers of either country within the command to order the destruction of hostile military aircraft (read: Soviet, Russian manned bombers or cruise missiles) within the air defence zones of either. After 9/11 it became evident that the authority to destroy highjacked civilian aircraft had been granted differently in each country. In the U.S., should the National Command Authority not be able to be reached in time, certain publicly unspecified U. S. officers in the air defence system could order the destruction of that aircraft, if necessary. In Canada, it had long appeared, the government had reserved that authority entirely to itself. Documents that the Department of National Defence inadvertently released to the CBC in 2017 in response to a request under the Access to Information Act request apparently revealed for the first time that Chief of the Defence Staff had been granted that authority, too [11]. In other words, within NORAD, no Canadians may order the destruction of civilian aircraft in the U.S. and no Americans may order their destruction in Canada.

It does not appear that a North American air defence headquarters is needed in peacetime today. Before 1957, the USAF and the RCAF air defence commands had in place arrangements that allowed for fighter interceptors from one country when necessary to cross the border, immediately fall under the operational control of the air defence command of the other, and even be directed to destroy an intruder while in the airspace of the other country. All this occurred without a single North American headquarters and at a time when there were vastly many more interceptors in the system. It is hard to believe that the RCAF and USAF, and the two homeland commands, USNORTHCOM and CJOC could not accomplish such coordination and cooperation today.

On the other hand, an exercise such as Vigilant Shield points to where unity in command and control can be essential in North American air defence, namely when the air defence has moved as far outward, including as far north as possible in order to engage attacking manned bombers as early as possible, preferably before release of air launched cruise missiles. At such times, a North American CJACC can be stood up. NORAD when necessary, that is.

5.4 A No-Change NORAD

It may be obvious by now that none of the pressures for change or the possibilities discussed above could be called particularly urgent. Canada still isn't needed for missile defence and the 2002 amendment to the agreement still seems to be working well. Canadians don't seem to feel the need to be protected from missile attack, or perhaps they just aren't yet paying attention to what General St-Amand said. Canadian naval forces are limited, and could be placed under the operational control of USNORTHCOM. The commander and her immediate successors may find the place of air defence and the Canadians at the headquarters anomalous, but the arrangement isn't dysfunctional. The Canadians and Americans at NORAD may get understandably irritated when NORAD is sometimes called "USNORTHCOM's air component," but there is a grain of truth in that otherwise formally inaccurate description. In some ways NORAD acts like air component headquarters for a larger command. To the extent that future commanders may want to think at the theater level, they may simply further empower the ND or other general officer at NORAD to act as if in that role, instead of designating a component commander outside of Colorado Springs. In a crisis, they will have the option of establishing a true CFACC at Tyndall, or at Winnipeg or Elmendorf, for that matter.

Since 2002 there has been plenty of discussions in Colorado Spring, such as the Bilateral Planning Group's report and the EVONAD study of possible changes to the structure of NORAD. But the commanders during this period have not thrown their weight behind any such changes. As far as can be seen from the outside, the current commander has thus far also approached NORAD issues very cautiously. However, in this light, General St-Amand's frank statement about the missile defence of Canada comes as a surprise.

Change may eventually come to NORAD if it shaken up from the outside. As suggested above, at some point the NORAD piece may no longer jive with the UCP. But that isn't in sight at the moment. Otherwise, if someone in power in Ottawa or Washington is truly hankering to change or get rid of NORAD, he or she has not made him or herself known publicly. The pledge in *Strong Secure Engaged* may just be nothing more than the sort of language that gets put into such policy document, because someone felt something had to be said about the matter, with the details to be worked out later or just forgotten about if necessary. No one should be surprised if, despite the white paper, and the opportunity provided by the anniversary of the agreement in 2018, NORAD is left by Ottawa and Washington for now pretty much as it is.

References

1. Canada, Department of National Defence (2017) *Strong Secure Engaged*: Canada's defence policy
2. Metro News Canada (2017) Trudeau weighs calls to join ballistic missile defence in face of North Korea. Report.ca, 19 Sept 2017. https://reportca.net/2017/09/trudeau-weighs-calls-to-join-ballistic-missile-defence-in-face-of-north-korea/. Accessed 20 Jan 2018
3. Shinkman PD (2017) Mattis says 'We Stand By' Canada amid concern about missile defense policy. USnews.com, 19 Sept 2017. https://www.usnews.com/news/national-news/articles/2017-09-19/mattis-says-we-stand-by-canada-despite-new-doubts-from-northerly-neighbor. Accessed 20 Jan 2018
4. Jockel JT (2007) Canada in NORAD, 1957–2007: a history. McGill-Queen's University Press, Montreal and Kingston
5. NORAD (2016) The need to evolve North American defense. North American aerospace defense command-unclassified concept paper
6. Strong M (2016) Exercise VIGILANT SHIELD 17 takes off in Yellowknife, Northwest Territories. NORAD.mil, 19 Oct 2016. http://www.norad.mil/Newsroom/Article/979834/exercise-vigilant-shield-17-takes-off-in-yellowknife-northwest-territories/. Accessed 20 Jan 2018
7. U.S. Northern Command (2013) About USNORTHCOM. northcom.mil. http://www.northcom.mil/About-USNORTHCOM/. Accessed 20 Jan 2018
8. U.S., Department of Defense (2014) Joint staff, joint publication JP-3-30: command and control of joint air operations, 10 Feb 2014

9. Fergusson James G (2010) Canada and Ballistic missile defence, 1954–2009: Déjà vu all over again. University of British Columbia Press, Vancouver
10. Bi-National Planning Group (2006) The final report on Canada and the United States (CANUS) enhanced military cooperation, 13 Mar 2006
11. Everson K (2017) Classified documents reveal Canada's planned response to 9/11 attack. CBC.ca, 1 Mar 2017. http://www.cbc.ca/news/politics/classified-military-operation-noble-eagle-1.4004551. Accessed 20 Jan 2018

NORAD, Tactical Fighter Modernization and the F-35: Operational Considerations, Process and Politics

Richard Shimooka[✉]

McDonald Laurier Institute, Ottawa, ON, Canada
richard.shimooka@macdonaldLaurier.ca

Abstract. Over its 60-year history, one of the most pronounced aspects of NORAD and its continental air defence mission has been the cutting edge technologies it has utilized. A key component of this area has been air defence fighters, which have been the most visible component of NORAD's mission. Over the past two decades, Canada and the U.S. have been undertaking a major modernization of said capabilities, which has revolved around the Joint Strike Fighter program. This effort has become mired in controversy, but for somewhat different reasons. For the U.S. this was largely in regards to the cost and delays of the program as well as questions over its capabilities. While concerns remain, the program has made significant progress over the past decade, and is on its way to replace a whole inventory of DoD aircraft. Despite being an early member of the Joint Strike Fighter program, Canada's modernization efforts have stalled since 2010. While cost and capability concerns were ostensibly the main focus of criticism, they were contextually different than those in the U.S. It illustrated a fundamental lack of understanding of military issues across a significant proportion of the population, as well as a willingness by political actors to interfere in the procurement process for their party's gain. The consequences of this perspective may have a dramatic impact on the future of NORAD and Canada-U.S. relations.

1 Introduction

Over its 60-year history, one of the most pronounced aspects of NORAD and its continental air defence mission has been the cutting edge technologies it has utilized. These systems pushed the boundaries of aerospace development: high-speed long-range bomber interceptors; ground-to-air and air-to-air missiles; powerful ground and air radar systems, advanced communication systems and groundbreaking computer developments. A key component of this area has been the development of tactical fighter aircraft for air defence, which arguably has been the most visible component of NORAD's mission.

For a number of years, Canada seemed to be in lock step with the U.S. From 1945 to 1959 it pursued an indigenous Canadian fighter development program, which produced the Avro CF-100 and designed the now infamous Avro CF-105 Arrow. However, in the 1960 and 70s disparities started to emerge. The end of the Arrow program in 1959 signalled Canada's withdrawal from domestic efforts to design and produce a

© Springer International Publishing AG, part of Springer Nature 2018
C. Leuprecht et al. (eds.), *North American Strategic Defense in the 21st Century:*,
Advanced Sciences and Technologies for Security Applications,
https://doi.org/10.1007/978-3-319-90978-3_13

military fighter aircraft. It then allowed its fighter aircraft capabilities to atrophy. Although this was somewhat rectified with the acquisition of the F/A-18A Hornet in 1980s, over the years, the technological gap has reemerged, and even widened.

Over that same timeframe, the U.S. continued to develop and field new aircraft and technologies. In the 1960s the U.S. Air Force (USAF) deployed the McDonnell Douglas F-4 Phantom, followed by the McDonnell Douglas F-15 in the mid 1970s and the General Dynamics F-16 in the early 1980s. These aircraft represented the cutting edge of aerospace technology during this period, including the supersonic, and agile supersonic revolutions [1, p. 4].

In August of 2007, Elmendorf Air Force Base in Alaska welcomed its first Lockheed Martin F-22 Raptor, a new generation of tactical fighter aircraft. Alongside its close relative, the Lockheed Martin F-35 Lightning II, these aircraft represent a new major technological and organizational innovation in the practice of war. As defined by Steven Rosen, a major military innovation involves a change in the concepts of operation of that combat arm, which is the ideas governing the ways it uses its forces to win a campaign [2, p. 7]. This has started to occur within the U.S. military, where we are now witnessing reorganization of its operations and organization in order to take advantage of the new capabilities offered by these aircraft. In particular, their mass data analysis systems and distributed network technologies are starting to revolutionize the conduct of war.

In the midst of this emerging innovation wave, Canada's own modernization program has become mired in controversy and delays. Despite being an early member of the Joint Strike Fighter program, the country's efforts to replace the CF-18s has stalled since 2010, in large part due to political interference in the procurement process. The Liberal government now expects the first aircraft to be delivered in 2025. The delay in acquiring a modern replacement for the CF-18, will have serious consequences for Canada's ability to provide an adequate qualitative contribution to NORAD and the northern defence mission.

The contrast between the Canadian and U.S. experiences is worth exploring: they can provide lessons for the future direction of defence innovation and acquisition in both countries. The first two sections of this chapter will offer a comparative analysis of the U.S. and Canadian acquisition systems in relation to the F-35. They will zero in on several aspects, with a key focus being the role political authorities play in the process, industry-government relations as well as some recent reforms to the system. The final section will compare the Canadian and U.S. experiences surrounding the Joint Strike Fighter, and the consequences for continental air defence.

2   U.S. Acquisition Process

The Joint Strike Fighter program's origins can be traced to the situation in which DoD found itself in the late 1980s. At the time, the U.S. Air Force, Navy and the Marine Corps, which had all recapitalized their fighter fleets during the so-called Carter-Reagan buildup of the late 1970s and 80s, foresaw the need to replace them staring in the late 1990s. This manifested itself in seven DoD programs intended to develop successor aircraft to the A-6 Intruder, F/A-18A/C, F-16 and A-10 [3]. Most of these programs only reached preliminary concept definition phase, but they were not all strictly focused on direct replacements. While some attempted to explore new technologies, all of them were affected by emerging trends in airpower.

One of the major innovations came as a result of the development of new low observable technologies. The F-117's development and entry into service in the 1980s and its successes during the Gulf War left an indelible impact on DoD's views on tactical aircraft survivability. For example, while the Multi-Role Fighter program was intended to be a low-cost replacement for the F-16, the industry concept design incorporated low observable features [4, p. 11]. The operational need for these technologies was based upon potent emerging threat capabilities. The USSR had developed a new generation of integrated ground and sea-based air defence systems, which threatened the viability of NATO air operations and NORAD operations. Consequently each of the major tactical fighter programs being pursued by DoD had similar design requirements.

In addition to the survivability offered by low observable technologies, developments in sensors, battlefield networking and data analysis offered potentially groundbreaking advances in aircraft lethality [5, p. 32-1]. Partially based on the experience of the F-22 development program, DoD realized that employing these technologies synergistically (colloquially known as sensor fusion) would allow aircraft to detect, identify and prosecute far more rapidly than existing systems.

The changing geostrategic environment and new fiscal realities of the post-Cold War period provided the greatest influence on the JSF's development. The immediate need for the replacement of existing aircraft evaporated with the collapse of the Soviet Union, as those currently in-service were likely to remain technologically relevant for longer and see less use than previously envisioned. A 1993 Bottom-Up Review undertaken at the behest of the then-Secretary of Defense Les Aspin showed that there was insufficient funding to cover all of the tactical fighter replacement programs [6]. Instead, they were amalgamated into a single program, which was hoped to incorporate these emerging innovations, while increasing commonality between versions, thereby reducing overall costs. This eventually became the Joint Strike Fighter (JSF) program.

Early on, the program confronted the question of the participation of foreign allies. Many had recapitalized their tactical fighter fleets during Carter-Reagan buildup with the same aircraft as the U.S. military, and therefore required replacement within the same timeframe. There was broad agreement within the U.S. Government that it would eventually export the JSF [7, p. 143]. Encouraging interoperability between allies was viewed as a key policy, which helped maintain the U.S.' geo-strategic position in the international system.

Where disagreement emerged was over the depth of foreign involvement. Some argued that the addition of more participants would prove disruptive to the program's development. At the same time, it was quickly acknowledged that simply selling an advanced aircraft was not sufficient. International arms sales between western states historically involved a reciprocal arrangement known as offsets, where the selling party agrees to invest some amount of the contract cost back into the purchasing country. However, in regards to JSF, an offset arrangement was viewed to be insufficient to generate sales, contrary to the situation during the Carter-Reagan era. Through the 1990s, European competitors were offering lucrative industrial investment enticements to select their aircraft.

In the end, the U.S. decided to pursue the deepest level of integration possible, which involved establishing unique industrial partnership schemes: a hitherto unprecedented level of international cooperation for a military program. It roughly emulated emerging practices in the civil aviation sector. Signatories' national industries would be given the opportunity to compete for subcontracts based on best value to the contract, which was a vastly more attractive approach for all parties [8, p. 48]. The JSF program would be able to employ foreign manufacturers that were often world leaders in specific areas. Furthermore, firms within participating nations would obtain work on a cutting edge technological program for over twenty years, which was much more desirable than typical offsets arrangements.

Industry played a strong hand in the initial definition phases. They helped guide DoD to understand what was the art of the possible. Throughout the late 1980s Lockheed Martin, in conjunction with the Defense Advanced Research Projects Agency, had undertaken significant development work into short take-off technologies. By 1994, the technologies were mature enough that a STOVL variant could be produced that would not compromise the other mission-specific variants, such as carrier take-off and conventional land-based take-off designs [9]. Initially, four competitors entered into the Concept Definition Phase, which DoD down-selected to two in 1996: Boeing's X-32 and Lockheed Martin's X-35. After a comprehensive evaluation, including a competitive fly-off of demonstration aircraft, the Lockheed Martin Team was selected in December 2001.

The program faced increasing challenges over the next few years. This included development program delays and performance issues. In 2004, the F-35B, the STOVL variant, was discovered to be well above weight specifications, which required a major redesign of all variants [10]. Other advanced systems, like the sensor fusion, introduced further delays and placed the development schedule in jeopardy. The cost estimates increased dramatically as well, calling into question DoD objectives for the fighter's affordability. By 2010, the program's total cost exceeded the 50% threshold of the original estimate, set out in the Nunn-McCurdy amendment. This led to several events, the first being the removal of the Program Executive Officer, Major General David Heinz, and the position elevated to a three star equivalent [11]. Heinz's replacement was Vice-Admiral David Venlet, a highly qualified naval executive officer with years of experience in the acquisition world. His experience, as well as the elevation of the PEO position to a higher rank, was an important signal of support by the political leadership. Venlet's main contribution was the "Replan," a major reform of the program that extended the program's development timetable by roughly five years, and slowing procurement while fixing the development costs.

The Nunn-McCurdy breach also triggered Congressional oversight, inviting political scrutiny the program had thus far largely avoided. Prior to the Replan, Congress had capped the near-term production rate of what were known as *Low Rate Initial Production* aircraft, which were being built while development was ongoing. The cut aircraft were re-added in later lots after the design had reached maturity. It should be noted, however, the relative level of interference was less than that which other programs in similar circumstances had experienced. Between 2003 and 2018, the total number of aircraft purchased in the program of record itself did not experience a cutback. Moreover it was shielded from the worst consequences of sequestration, an automatic cost reduction mechanism implemented as a result of Congress's inability to pass deficit reduction legislation.

Between 2012 and 2017 the program development stabilized, and moved forward roughly as planned. VAdm. Venlet retired in 2012, and was replaced by Air Force Lt. General Christopher Bogdan. His tenure would be characterized by slow, but steady progress, especially on realizing major cost savings. He employed a much more confrontational approach in public with Lockheed Martin, going as far as stating that the program's relationship with the manufacturer "was the worst he's ever seen" [12]. This continued behind the scenes, where DoD pursued a much harder tone with the company. This was evident in the over two-year long negotiation on the 9th production lot of 57 F-35s, which was ended with an unprecedented unilateral contract offer made by the government [13].

Efforts in this area benefited from broader reforms within the U.S. government to improve defence procurement. This included executive reforms undertaken by the Obama administration, known as the "better buying power" initiative, as well as incremental Congressional reforms implemented through successive *National Defense Authorization Acts* after 2012. They generally provided program managers like Lt General Bogdan with greater flexibility and more resources to undertake their roles. This can be observed in the contract negotiations, where the government was able to leverage highly detailed cost data from internal "should cost" efforts [14]. The program achieved significant successes during this period, including a rapidly declining production cost, and initial operating capacity for the USAF, USMC and the Israeli Air Force.

These achievements, however, were seemingly under threat almost overnight with the election of Donald Trump as President in November 2016. Early on, the candidate was a vocal critic of the JSF program, hinting that he might cancel the fighter, which he claimed was less capable than existing aircraft [15]. This carried on after his election, where he tweeted Boeing to price out a comparable Super Hornet to compete with the F-35 [16]. The latter statement and others like it made during this period were seen by many observers as an attempt to put pressure on Lockheed Martin, which was in negotiation with DoD for the 10th production lot of aircraft [17]. The two sides reached an agreement in February 2017, which was largely in line with projected cost estimates made by DoD earlier in the year. Still, the event gave the new President the opportunity to claim that his intervention had achieved massive cost savings [18].

It is unlikely that the approach to publicize program relations will stop. In late January 2018, both the Undersecretary of Defense for Acquisition and Sustainment, and her deputy for the air force acquisitions, claimed the sustainment costs for the aircraft were seen as unaffordable [19]. The statements come before a new round of negotiation over a two-year sustainment contract were to begin, that presage a five-year contract award in 2020 [20, p. 23].

3   Canadian Acquisition Process

Since the end of the Cold War, Canada's tactical fighter fleets have had to accomplish two missions. The first is to provide credible air defence for Canada's contribution to NORAD. This requires Canada to maintain a constant rotation of under a dozen aircraft to intercept threats [21, p. 4]. The second is contributions in coalitions. This includes the ability to deploy a detachment of aircraft for NATO operations, both air defence and ground attack. Since 2001, this usually consists of a "six-pack" of CF-18s, which Canada has deployed to Libya, Eastern Europe, and anti-ISIL operations [21, p. 4].

Unlike the U.S., which typically develops its capabilities domestically, Canada generally purchases its equipment off-the-shelf from other countries' industries. Its defence industrial base is heavily integrated with its southern neighbour, and develops and produces sub-systems for prime contractors in other nations' projects. Canada maintained a domestic fighter industry in the years after the Second World War. However, as the cost of developing and manufacturing tactical fighter aircraft increased substantially, the government halted developing designs in the early1960s, and dissolved the industry entirely a decade later.

Canada's first formal introduction to the JSF program occurred in 1997, when the Department of National Defence was invited to join the Concept Definition Phase for an investment of $10 million. This would allow Canada to gain access to the program to inform its own decision-making. At the time, however, senior members of the RCAF were more concerned with protecting their funding for an upcoming and very necessary upgrade of the CF-18 fleet. Canada joined as a System Development and Demonstration partner in 2002, which gave them more ability to influence the program.

In 2006, Canada signed *JSF Production Sustainment and Follow-On Development Memorandum of Understanding* (PFSD-MOU), designating Canada as a Tier III partner. It was a relatively uncontroversial decision at the time. Signing enabled Canadian firms to compete for subcontracts within the industrial partnership scheme. Joining the partnership also gave Canada the ability to influence the fighter's specification, especially on requirements related to northern operations such as cold weather start temperatures [22].

At the time of the MOU signing, it was understood within government that it did not commit Canada to purchase the aircraft, though it made it more likely. Over the next four years, DND sharpened its understanding of the capabilities required for Canada's follow-on to the CF-18, preparing for a final evaluation and selection. This would come in 2010. The political leadership was asked to make a gesture to signal their commitment to the program. While this did not require a final selection, the Conservative government decided to push ahead with it regardless.

The statement of requirements that had been developed over the past four years reflected the two mission sets Canadian fighters were intended to carry out in the predicted future threat environment. The most demanding ones revolved around operating in highly contested airspace as part of a coalition like NATO, including stealth capabilities, secure data link/data sharing, and long range sensor systems [23, p. 14]. Although many of these were also useful in a NORAD context, several requirements were added that addressed continental security. The most critical would

permit a "pilot to visually operate the aircraft in no-light conditions." This was insti-
tuted to allow safe operations in the arctic in winter, which was among the most
dangerous environments Canadian fighters could operate in.

According to DND and Public Works and Government Services Canada's analysis,
the F-35s was the only option that met all of Canada's requirements, at a significantly
lower life cycle cost and with the best industrial benefits [23, p. 16]. With the decision
made, the government unveiled it at a large ceremony in a hangar in Ottawa. The
announcement would be poorly timed, however, given the emerging cost and development troubles in the U.S. The first major blow came with the publication of the
Parliamentary Budget Officer's (PBO) report, which claimed the entire program cost
would be $12 billion more than stated by DND [24, p. 1]. An even more damaging
blow came a year later from the Office of the Auditor General. Their report claimed the
government had deliberately hidden the program's cost, which it pegged at $29 billion
over 30 years [25]. Although both analyses were based on faulty methodology, it added
to the public's perception of the aircraft's extreme cost.

The OAG report touched off a political controversy, with opposition parties crying
foul. Their particular target was the sole-sourcing of the F-35, which they argued
should have been selected in an open competition. In the OAG report's fallout, the
government set aside its original decision to select the F-35 and started a new process,
which was overseen by National Fighter Procurement Secretariat (NFPS). After two
years of analysis, it reached the same conclusion as the 2010 DND-led effort; the
previous SOR accurately reflected Canada's needs, and as a result, the F-35 was again
deemed to offer the best capability at the lowest cost with the most industrial benefits
[23, p. 28]. It also validated the earlier costing undertaken by DND, undermining the
PBO and OAG reports. The NFPS effort turned up an additional wrinkle; running a
competition was legally risky, given that the government already knew that under any
valid criteria the F-35 would likely win. Based on the findings, the Conservative
government moved ahead with acquiring the fighter. It negotiated with the Obama
administration to acquire four USAF F-35As, which would presage a much larger
purchase of aircraft. However, the plan was leaked to the public in September 2014,
renewing the controversy surrounding the program [26]. This led the entire plan to be
scrapped until after the next election, slated for September 2015.

During the subsequent campaign, the Liberal party explicitly promised to not purchase
the F-35, and hold a competition to select what it described as a more "affordable option"
[27, p. 3]. It highlighted, as an example, the Super Hornet, which it pegged the cost to be
$65 million dollars per unit compared to the $175 million F-35. The figures were completely erroneous, but it would guide Liberal government policy for the next two years,
including a campaign promise to exclude the JSF from competing in a competition.

Upon entering government, the Liberal party confronted the contradictions between
their campaign promises and reality. It could not legally bar the F-35 from competing,
nor would it be feasible to establish a framework that would ensure Canada obtained
the lowest cost option, when it was that option they had misguidedly committed to
eliminate. They were almost certainly advised of the NFPS findings on the F-35s
superiority over all other options in all categories.

Despite the information provided to them, the Liberal government pressed ahead.
They sought to tamp down internal criticism, by forcing staff working on the program

to sign a lifetime gag order on their work [28]. This also enabled the political leadership to marginalize the military from the policymaking process, despite their strenuous objections. Next, they worked to establish the foundations for their preferred policy, which they announced in early June 2016. The government discovered that Canada faced a fighter capability gap, where it could not simultaneously provide fighters for its NORAD and NATO requirements. They stated that they would move to address this quickly since, in their view, it was unacceptable to risk manage. This was a flimsy pretext. Such a scenario was exceedingly unlikely, while the military was forced to undertake risk management on a wide range of scenarios, which were far more likely than what the Liberals claimed was unacceptable for the tactical fighter fleet.

They unveiled their plan in November 2016, which involved the "interim" purchase of 18 Super Hornets. This would allow them to undertake a five-year competition for 88 aircraft to replace CF-18, 23 more than originally envisioned by DND. The shortcomings of this plan were severe and deleterious. Operating two distinctly different fleets of aircraft would place impossible strain on the personnel management system for pilots and maintainers, likely resulting in a situation where the RCAF would have less total combat capability and be unable to meet either NATO or NORAD requirements. Over the following months, the government worked to implement the decision, including requesting a contract price for the Super Hornets from U.S. Defense Security Cooperation Agency (DSCA). In late September 2017, the government received its reply; $5.7 Billion CAD for 18 Super Hornets and the associated support package [29]. This was far more than the government had anticipated, nearly as much as the Conservatives had planned for 65 F-35s.

However, the cost issue was overshadowed by a growing trade dispute between the Liberal government and Boeing and its efforts to press for anti-dumping duties against Bombardier. In late September, Prime Minister Trudeau warned Boeing that "We won't do business with a company that is busy trying to sue us and put our aerospace workers out of business" [30]. Reportedly, the government made several entreaties to Boeing, including a willingness to proceed with the Super Hornet procurement in return for the manufacturer dropping the trade complaint. On December 12th 2017 the government officially cancelled the purchase, instead announcing that it would acquire a number of F/A-18As from Australia as they are retired during the RAAF's transition to the F-35. The government stuck to its timeline for a permanent replacement to be introduced, which would see a selection by 2021, the first deliveries by 2025 and the full operating capability by 2032 [31].

4   Consequences and Concluding Thoughts

At their outset the U.S. and Canadian acquisition process to replace their tactical fighter fleets were determined by a careful assessment of their current needs and the future threat environment. The JSF program was an attempt to harness the various requirements from different services and distill them into a single aircraft in order to improve sustainability and affordability. Canada's initial process followed a slightly different path, but emphasized many of the same capabilities in the end.

Where the processes diverged is over politics. In the U.S., the executive branch has maintained a consistent position on the JSF program over three administrations and nearly twenty years. They have restated the need for the fighter, its capabilities and the number of aircraft to be purchased. Congress provided oversight, only intervening in their statutory capacity after the program underwent the Nunn-McCurdy Breach. However this was largely non-partisan and focused on improving the program. At the same time, major actors have increasingly publicized problems in order to gain an advantage in negotiations with industry partners.

Political intervention in the Canadian case by comparison led to highly negative outcomes. Little regard was given to military considerations or expert opinion by either the Conservative or Liberal governments; domestic political consequences trumped the orderly decision-making. This went as far as ignoring military advice about the consequences of their action.

The operational consequences are already significant, and will only grow over time. Unlike the quantitative capability gap suggested by the Liberal government, the qualitative gap between RCAF tactical fighter fleet and the threat environment is very real. Canadian CF-18s have already faced advanced Russian air defence systems in operations in Eastern Europe and Syria, which puts their survivability in severe doubt. Furthermore, observed technological and doctrinal innovations among irregular forces (like in Eastern Ukraine), and near-peer adversaries (like China) indicate an increasing level of sophistication in countering existing western tactics and strategies.

In order to counter these developments, the U.S. is exploring a radical new approach to operations, known as Multi-Domain battle. This organizing concept will rely heavily on resilient formations, which according to a draft circulated by the U.S. Army's Training and Doctrine Command, requires systems that;

...are cross-domain capable; avoid detection and survive contact with the enemy ... and train cognitively to execute mission command in degraded conditions with tools that allow commanders and staffs to converge capabilities across domains, environments, and functions [32, p. 24]

These requirements align with Canada's 2010 SOR, and the capabilities of the F-35. They include the ability to operate across domains, including cyber, while operating in degraded conditions. CF-18s by comparison possess none of these required capabilities, given their increasing obsolescence.

In addition, Canada's current fighter fleet is also less able to meet the new challenges facing NORAD. One example is the growing threat of Russian and Chinese submarine launched cruise missiles, which the former has displayed during recent operations in Syria [33]. Countering this threat will require many of the same capabilities as outlined in multi-domain battle, including advanced sensors, information processing systems and datalinks, which the CF-18 is largely bereft of.

The entire episode calls into question Canada's commitment to its continental defence. From NORAD's inception to the early phases of the JSF program, Canada was seen as a reliable and equal partner. In the last seven years, the Canadian government has approached the U.S. government with a decision on its fighter fleet three times, only to cancel: the 2010 F-35 selection, the 2014 agreement for four F-35s, and the 2016 purchase of F/A-18E/F. Now, at of the time of this writing, it is expected that the RCAF will not fully modernize its fleet of fighters until 2032. The practical effects of what appears to be a highly political yet not unprecedented, decision could mean that Canada's contribution to continental defence will diminish rapidly, placing a greater burden on the U.S. The USAF may have to devote additional assets, precisely when they could be needed elsewhere to check an increasingly unstable global order.

The long-term consequences of this situation hinges on the political response of U. S. As Leuprecht and Sokolsky point out, Canada has frequently pursued the "just enough" strategy, eschewing high-end capabilities to acquire less effective, more reasonably priced platforms [34]. While this approach has been successful in the past, the current situation is unprecedented in a number of ways. Continental air defence remains a high priority for the U.S. military and Canada plays a critical role in its planning, as Lindsay Rodman, a former Obama National Security Council official, made clear:

> We do depend on Canada's fighter capability in terms of how we've planned our North American defence, so making good on the promises that Canada has made is going to be more important than new promises that Canada could make in the future, which would be something like ballistic defence [35].

However the Canadian government's vacillation ensures that the RCAF's capabilities will fade into irrelevance. While this has not escaped the notice of U.S. policy- and law-makers, the question is whether they will apply punitive measures to correct the situation. This may cause a deep rupture in the NORAD relationship, a prospect that has never occurred in the organization's 60-year history.

References

1. Lorell M (2003) The U.S. combat aircraft industry-1909–2000: structure competition innovation. RAND, Santa Monica
2. Rosen S (1991) Winning the next war: innovation and the modern military. Cornell University Press, Ithaca
3. Pre-JAST History (2018) Joint strike fighter program http://www.jsf.mil/history/his_prejast. htm. Accessed 27 Jan 2018
4. Report of the Defense Science Board Task Force on Aircraft Assessment (1993) Office of the Undersecretary of Defense for Acquisition, Washington, DC. https://www.acq.osd.mil/dsb/reports/1990s/1993AircraftAssessment.pdf. Accessed: 3 Feb 2018
5. Brower R (2001) Lockheed F-22 raptor. In: Spitzer C (ed) The avionics handbook. CRC Press, London, pp 32-1–32-11
6. Aspin L (1993) Report of the bottom up review. Office of the Secretary of Defense, Washington, DC
7. Kapstein E (2002) Allies and armaments. Survival 44(2):141–155
8. Joint Strike Fighter Production (2007) Sustainment, and follow-on development memorandum of understanding. Joint Strike Fighter Program. http://www.jsf.mil/downloads/documents/JSF_PSFD_MOU_-_07_Feb_07.pdf. Accessed 4 Feb 2018
9. Renshaw K (2014) F-35B lightning II three-bearing swivel nozzle. Code One Mag. http://www.codeonemagazine.com/article.html?item_id=137. Accessed 21 Jan 2018
10. Pappalardo J (2006) Weight watchers. Air Space Mag. https://www.airspacemag.com/military-aviation/weight-watchers-13117183/. Accessed 24 Jan 2018

11. Whitlock C (2010) Defense secretary Gates fires general in charge of Joint Strike Fighter program. Washington Post, 2 Feb 2010. http://www.washingtonpost.com/wp-dyn/content/article/2010/02/01/AR2010020103712.html. Accessed 8 Mar 2018

12. Clark C (2012) F-35 program's relationship with lockheed 'Worst I've Ever Seen,' says Gen. Bogdan. Breaking Defense, 17 Sept 2012 https://breakingdefense.com/2012/09/f-35-programs-relationship-with-lockheed-worst-ive-ever-seen/. Accessed 24 Jan 2018

13. Giangreco L (2016) Unilateral negotiations still in play for F-35 contract. Flight Global, 19 Dec 2016. https://www.flightglobal.com/news/articles/unilateral-negotiations-still-in-play-for-f-35-cont-432564/. Accessed 24 Jan 2018

14. Shalal-Esa A (2013) Pentagon sees progress on cost of F-35, long way to go. Reuters, 23 Dec 2013. https://www.reuters.com/article/us-pentagon-weapons-costs/pentagon-sees-progress-on-cost-of-f-35-long-way-to-go-idUSBRE9BN01R20131224. Accessed 24 Jan 2018

15. Hewitt H (2016) Donald Trump on today's Benghazi hearing and state of the 2016 race. Hugh Hewitt show. http://www.hughhewitt.com/donald-trump-on-todays-benghazi-hearing-and-state-of-the-2016-race/. Accessed 25 Jan 2018

16. Trump D (2016) 22 Dec 2016. https://twitter.com/realdonaldtrump/status/812061677160202240?lang=en. Accessed 8 Mar 2018

17. Waldmeir P, Dye R (2016) Trump puts pressure on Lockheed Martin over cost of F-35. Financ Times, 22 Dec 2016. https://www.ft.com/content/1e059836-c89e-11e6-8f29-9445cac8966f. Accessed 8 Mar 2018

18. Cappacio T, Jonhsson A (2017) Lockheed wins $8.2 Billion F-35 contract after Trump intervenes. Bloomberg News, Feb 3 2017. https://www.bloomberg.com/news/articles/2017-02-03/u-s-said-to-plan-announcement-of-8-2-billion-f-35-contract. Accessed 25 Jan 2018

19. Metha A (2018) Pentagon can't afford the sustainment costs on F-35, Lord says. Defense News, 1 Feb 2018. https://www.defensenews.com/air/2018/02/01/pentagon-cant-afford-the-sustainment-costs-on-f-35-lord-says/. Accessed 1 Feb 2018

20. Government Accountability Office (2017) F-35 AIRCRAFT SUSTAINMENT-DOD needs to address challenges affecting readiness and cost transparency. https://www.gao.gov/assets/690/687982.pdf. Accessed 2 Feb 2018

21. Bourdon S, Hunter G (2014) A comparative analysis of minimum resource requirements for single and mixed fleets for the national fighter procurement evaluation of options. Defence Research and Development Canada, Ottawa

22. Confidential interview. Conducted 23 June 2014

23. Shimooka R (2016) The fourth dimension: the F-35 program, defence procurement, and the conservative government, 2006–2015. CDA Institute, Ottawa. https://cdainstitute.ca/wp-content/uploads/2016/07/Vimy_Paper_33.pdf. Accessed 2 Feb 2018

24. Yalkin T, Weltmann P (2011) An estimate of the Fiscal impact of Canada's proposed acquisition of the F-35 lightning II joint strike fighter. Parliamentary Budget Officer, Ottawa. http://www.parl.gc.ca/PBO-DPB/documents/F-35_Cost_Estimate_EN.pdf. Accessed 3 Feb 2018

25. Reed J (2012) Chap 2—Replacing Canada's fighter jets. 2012 Spring Report. Auditor General of Canada, Ottawa

26. Koring P (2014) Pentagon briefing suggests Canada about to buy at least four F-35 jets. The Globe and Mail, 7 November 2014. https://www.theglobeandmail.com/news/politics/pentagon-briefing-suggests-canada-about-to-buy-at-least-four-f-35-jets/article21496659/. Accessed 8 Mar 2018

27. Liberal Party of Canada (2016) Real change: real change: a new plan to strengthen the economy and create jobs with navy investment. https://www.liberal.ca/wp-content/uploads/2015/09/A-new-plan-to-strengthen-the-economy-and-create-jobs-with-navy-investment.pdf. Accessed 2 Feb 2018

28. Berthiaume L (2016) Liberals imposed gag order on officials over fighter jets. Macleans, 24 November 2016. http://www.macleans.ca/politics/liberals-gag-order-officials-fighter-jets/. Accessed 3 Feb 2018

29. Shimooka R, McDonough D (2017) Liberals need to end the farce over fighter jets. The Globe and Mail, 17 Sept 2017. https://www.theglobeandmail.com/opinion/liberals-need-to-end-the-farce-over-fighter-jets/article36281581/. Accessed 3 Feb 2018

30. CBC News (2017) Boeing lands direct hit in Bombardier fight, but battle is far from over. CBC News Online, 27 Sept 2017. http://www.cbc.ca/news/business/boeing-bombardier-1.4309000. Accessed 3 Feb 2018

31. Pugliese D (2018) Here is how Canada's fighter purchase will unfold. Defence Watch Blog, 2 Feb 2018. http://ottawacitizen.com/news/national/defence-watch/here-is-how-canadas-new-fighter-jet-purchase-will-unfold. Accessed 3 Feb 2018

32. Army Capabilities Integration Center (2017) Multi-domain battle: evolution of combined arms for the 21st century, 2025–2040. http://www.arcic.army.mil/App_Documents/Multi-Domain-Battle-Evolution-of-Combined-Arms.pdf. Accessed 4 Feb 2018

33. Janes (2017) Game changer: Russian sub-launched cruise missiles bring strategic effect. http://www.janes.com/images/assets/147/70147/Game_changer_Russian_sub-launched_cruise_missiles_bring_strategic_effect_edit.pdf. Accessed 4 Feb 2018

34. Leuprecht C, Sokolsky J (2015) Defense policy "Walmart Style": Canadian lessons in "not-so-grand" grand strategy. Armed Forces Soc 41(3):541–562

35. Rodman L, Perry D (2018) How the United States views Canadian defence policy. The Global Exchange–A Canadian Global Affairs Institute Podcast, Feb, 2018. https://soundcloud.com/user-609485369/how-the-united-states-views-canadian-defence-policy. Accessed 8 Mar 2018

The Arctic and the Strategic Defence of North America: Resumption of the "Long Polar Watch"

Rob Huebert[(✉)]

University of Calgary, Calgary, AB T2N 1N4, Canada
Rhuebert@ucalgary.ca

Abstract. Not since the early days of the Cold War when, as Melvin Conant wrote in 1962, the US and Canada had assumed the "long polar watch" against Soviet bombers has the arctic been of such importance to North American strategic defence. The relationship between Russia and the two North American allies is deteriorating, and the Russians have strengthened their military. At the same time, the North Korean nuclear threat has caused the United States to enhance their ABM capabilities in Alaska. The Russians perceive the ABM systems to be directed against them, leading to a redoubling of their efforts to build up strategic forces which will be predominantly based in their arctic region. Furthermore, the Chinese have begun to turn their attention to the arctic. Consequently, both Canada and the United States need to refocus their efforts to protect their shared northern flank. The core means will remain within NORAD but it requires modernization and expansion. Both states will need to ensure that the maritime mission is given greater attention. At the same time Canada will need to revisit its decision to opt out of the United States' ABM system. The 1990s and 2000s had created the false impression that great-power rivalry was a thing of the past. With its re-emergence, the arctic has regained its position as a major factor in the strategic defence of North America. After a thirty-year hiatus, it is time to resume "the long polar watch."

1 Introduction

Canadians and Americans do not like to think about the North American arctic in strategic terms. Canadians prefer to think of it in terms of part of their national psyche; of its stark beauty; of the experience of its northern indigenous peoples; and in terms of both its economic potential and its environmental fragility. American think of it as the last frontier and place of both beauty and opportunity. But most of the time Canadians and Americans simply do not think about this region. What they miss is that the arctic is a region of growing geopolitical complexity that challenges the need to think in terms of the strategic defence of the continent. In a book dedicated to understanding North American strategic defence and NORAD, understanding the role that the arctic plays is both necessary and challenging. The issues concerning northern arctic security are transforming, and at an increasingly rapid pace. Senior policy makers in both Canada and the United States have acted in the past to provide for the northern defence of the continent, but they prefer to place their attention elsewhere. Even among senior

Canadian military leaders today there has been a longstanding tendency to downplay the importance of the arctic in strategic terms. A "joke" repeated by some of the most senior of Canada's officers throughout the 2000s was that only "real" military challenge that Canada faced would be to "rescue" any invaders that might try to "invade" Canada's north. Of course this "joke" missed the point that any threat to the arctic would be either maritime or aerospace based.

It has only become "fashionable" to think of the North American arctic in geopolitical terms, let alone the need to understand and provide for the strategic defence of the region, in the last few years. Many will point to the aggressive actions of the Russian Government and, specifically, their military intervention in Ukraine in 2014. However, there has been a need to think of the defence of North America from its arctic region since the Second World War. What is happening today is that the combination of the greater geopolitical realities of the renewed and increased tensions between the United States and Russia and the growing strength of China is now forcing a rethink of many of the issues that developed a long time ago. The geography that both connects and separates these three states, along with the nature of modern weapon systems (notably nuclear weapons and their delivery systems) means that the arctic will remain central to any discussion regarding the strategic security of North America. Geography forces the inclusion of Canada.

The objective of this chapter is to consider what the arctic means in terms of North American strategic defence and the future of NORAD. Though many had hoped that the end of the Cold War would make such considerations irrelevant, current events show that this is not the case.

One of the challenges in coming to terms with the significance of the arctic to North American strategic defence are the impacts of climate change. The arctic is experiencing some of the highest rates of warming on the planet. This has resulted in significant changes in the arctic region. At the forefront of these is the melting of the permanent ice cap of the Arctic Ocean. As a result, the security requirements of the region have altered considerably. There is a need for all of the coastal arctic states that surround the Arctic Ocean to begin to develop the means and capabilities to provide for the constabulary protection of their respective maritime zones. This includes monitoring and responding to illegal activities in the region, being able to respond to environmental challenges and providing search and rescue capabilities—all the normal requirements of coastal states. As the arctic melts, the Arctic Ocean will increasingly provide both the opportunities and challenges that are common to other oceans, meaning an increase in a variety of activities. However, while this requires an increase of military and security capabilities, these will not be the driving feature of the new strategic reality for the strategic defence of North America. A melting arctic will facilitate, but will not determine, the core strategic requirements for its defence.

1.1 The History

There have been four main geopolitical eras of arctic security that have required attention in the context of the strategic defence of North America. The first occurred between 1947 and 1960. In this period the Second World War alliance between the USSR and the western powers broke down, and the two sides quickly transformed from allied to adversarial. The development of nuclear weapons and the delivery system of long-range bombers meant that as tensions increased between the two powers, the arctic became more important as a strategic transit location. In order to stop the Soviet bomber attack on the United States and Canada, it became clear that the strategic defence of North America would require joint action between the air forces of the two countries.

Between 1960 and 1989, tensions between the United States and the USSR remained high, but the strategic defence of North America was complicated by the development of long-range missile delivery systems that were either land based (ICBM) or submarine based (SLBM). This deployment had two core ramifications. First, if utilized, they would be fired with a trajectory that took them over the arctic. Second, and more importantly, there were no defences capable of stopping these missiles once they were launched. This changed the requirements from defending against a bomber attack to deterring the strike from occurring in the first place. As such, both the United States and the Soviet Union developed their nuclear arsenals with the understanding that if one was to launch an attack, the other had the capability to retaliate and there was nothing that either could do to defend themselves. Both sides therefore retained the capability of destroying the other, but in doing so would also be destroyed. It was assumed that this would result in deterring both sides from launching in the first place. It also meant that both sides needed to understand that the other side had the ability to know that they were being attacked and to be able to launch their weapons before they were destroyed. For the two North American countries, this required the building of surveillance systems necessary to provide the necessary alert of an incoming Soviet attack.

The need to coordinate both the surveillance and defence of North America required that Canada and United States agreed to a coordinated system. This resulted in the creation of NORAD, supported by the Distant Early Warning System (DEWline). Initially the system was designed to alert North American leaders to any incoming Soviet bombers, and to provide for a joint defence against them. As the delivery system changed to missiles, the focus of the agreement was to provide notification of a Soviet missile attack over the arctic region. This would allow the United States time to mount their retaliatory attack. There was also close coordination between the navies of the United States and Canada regarding the transit of the United States' nuclear powered attack submarines (SSNs) through the arctic region to defend against Soviet submarines. Canada twice considered buying its own nuclear powered submarines to assist in the defence against the Soviet submarines in the arctic region, but in both instances decided that the cost was prohibitive and left that task to the United States.

When the Cold War ended, the third era of North American arctic security (1989–2007) began with a general acceptance that the Soviet threat was over. As a result, much of the active efforts to protect against a Soviet attack were relaxed. NORAD continued to exist, but its importance in the maintenance of nuclear deterrence was seen as increasingly less relevant to the overall security and strategic defence of North America. Both the United States and Canada took active steps to assist the Soviet Union and then the Russian Federation in the safe decommissioning of their submarine fleet. Initially, the United States and Norway worked with Russia through the Arctic Military Environmental Cooperation Agreement (AMEC). Subsequently, the United

Kingdom also joined. The three western countries provided direct economic and technological assistance to allow the Soviet Union/Russia to begin the process of safely decommissioning their nuclear powered submarines. The economic collapse of the USSR had resulted in the bulk of the Soviet fleet being left to rust in harbours along the Kola Peninsula. In many instances there was a danger that the submarines could experience significant radioactive leaks or even meltdowns. Subsequent to AMEC, the G8 agreed to also provide assistance to Russia. In this manner Canada also joined the effort to eliminate these submarines and both the military and environmental threats posed by this fleet to the security of North America were peacefully and cooperatively eliminated.

There was also a move among all of the arctic nations to create and improve international cooperation in the arctic region by developing a system of cooperative organisations and institutions, to both build confidence and to build better relations between the USSR/Russia and the other arctic states, including Canada and the United States. In order to facilitate this cooperation, Finland, along with Canada, developed the Arctic Environmental Protection Strategy (AEPS) in 1991. It focused on providing a forum for discussing environmental challenges facing the arctic. However, it was very much intended to provide a confidence building mechanism between the former arctic adversaries. Canada supported Finland's idea that by embracing the new Soviet/Russian leadership in such cooperation, the strategic threat to North America could be reduced if not eliminated. In 1996 Canada proposed to build on the success of the AEPS and successfully negotiated the creation of the Arctic Council. It brought together all of the eight arctic states—the United States, Canada, Norway, Finland, Sweden, Iceland, Denmark, and Russia—into a cooperative body of discussion and action. While it also focused on environmental issues, the Canadian intent was to have this body expand into other issue areas beyond the environment. This body eventually did begin creating legal agreements amongst its members pertaining to search and rescue in the arctic as well as agreements on scientific studies. As such, the strategic defence of North America at this time was focused on eliminating the military threat posed by the USSR/Russia through political cooperative means.

2   The New Arctic Security Era: Challenges and North American Responses

Throughout the 1990s there was a growing school of thought that suggested the end of the Cold War and the growing arctic cooperation among all eight arctic states was resulting in the reduction, or even the elimination, of the need to maintain a significant effort for the strategic defence of North America. NORAD was seen as becoming irrelevant and many thought the Arctic would never face a strategic threat again. However, events from 2007 to the current period reversed such considerations. This is the fourth arctic geopolitical era for North America.

There are three core factors that have restored many of the concerns and requires a vigorous North American strategic defence capability with an arctic focus. The first factor is the evolving relationship between the arctic states and specifically the growing tensions between Russia and the North American countries. The second factor is the growing nuclear weapon capability of North Korea. The third factor is the growing strength of China and its concurrent and growing interest in the arctic region for both political and strategic reasons. These geopolitical factors combined with key developing military technologies means that the arctic is once again becoming a critical location for the strategic defence of North America.

The issue, however, that gave renewed consideration to the significance of strategic defence of North America was not arctic specific. It was the terrorist attacks of 9/11. There was a realization that there was still a need to maintain a joint approach to the strategic defence of North America and that NORAD was relevant. While the post 9/11 period re-focused attention on NORAD's roles, especially with regard to internal North American air space and maritime security, the arctic did not figure highly in continental homeland defence until the middle 2000s.

2.1   Russia and the Changing Security Environment

However, the fourth geopolitical era of arctic security highlighted the renewed importance of the arctic region to the strategic defence of North America. The most important element that defines this time period is the changing relationship between Canada and the United States and Russia, and the impact it had on the arctic. This is a direct result of the election of Vladimir Putin and the new direction that he taken Russia. Under Boris Yeltsin's Administration, Russia's economic and military capabilities continued to diminish. Yeltsin continued to maintain good relations with the western powers despite the problems facing the new state of Russia, but this created widespread resentment among many Russians. This then saw the rise of Vladimir Putin and his election in May 2000. Putin campaigned on restoring Russia to its previous position of strength. Once elected, Putin attempted to restore Russia's position in the international system.

Upon consolidating his position within Russia, Putin moved to rebuild Russian military strength. There were three core factors that drove much of the effort in their arctic region. First, the arctic was recognized by the Russians as one of the most important regions for the future economic development of their country [1]. Russia's economic strength is based on the production and export of energy. Much of its existing production has been based around the Caspian Sea, but most of these resources were understood to be quite mature and coming to the end of their economic life. It is in the arctic that the Russians anticipate building up their future resource base, and therefore this region becomes critically important to Russia.

The second factor driving Russian interest in the arctic was because this geopolitical location was (and remains) the major area of operation for its nuclear strategic forces. Most of its submarine based nuclear missiles were located with the northern fleet, and many of its bombers were also based in the north. Any effort to rebuild Russia as a great power requires a modernization of its nuclear force, which had been allowed to deteriorate under the administration of Yeltsin. In 2007 the Russian government introduced a new set of policies dedicated to the rebuilding of Russian military capabilities. Initially these efforts were seen as being meant to improve Putin's domestic political standing. However, it now clear that the Russian government is intent on improving the country's strategic weapons systems. While some of the weapon systems promised in 2007 have not been delivered, such as the proposed 5 to 6 aircraft carrier battle groups, Russia has persevered in the rebuilding of its submarine forces, including both new SSNs and nuclear powered nuclear missile carrying submarines (SSBNs). There has also been a sustained effort to modernize the existing SSBNs that were not decommissioned at the end of the Cold War.

During the Yeltsin administration, the collapse of the Soviet/Russian navy meant that there were very few deployments of Russian submarines into the arctic on deterrence patrols. In 2008, the Russians began to redeploy these patrols into arctic waters. In 2009 the Russians sent two of their older submarines (Delta-IV class) into the arctic to demonstrate a test launch of their missiles. Since then the Russian navy has increased its ability to resume its arctic patrols, to the point where it is now believed that the Russians maintain at least one submarine on patrol at all times.

At the same time that the Russian navy moved to rebuild its strategic patrol mission, the Russian air force has also moved to rebuild its ability to maintain long-range arctic patrols. In August 2007, the Russian air force resumed its patrols. Once again, many western analysts believed that the Putin administration was merely attempting to posture in front of the domestic Russian audience. However, these patrols have increased in both numbers and complexity and now often include fighter escorts. At a time when relations remained positive, senior Canadian military officials approached their Russian counterparts and asked them to provide prior notification of these patrols when they came near to Canadian airspace as a confidence building measure. This request was refused.

The Russian bombers used on these patrols are based on older designs. The Tupolev-95 (Bear) was designed in the 1950s though the variants that are now being flown were built in the 1980s and 1990s. The Tupolev-22 (Backfire) was developed in the 1960s and the Tupolev-160 (Blackjack) was designed and first built in the 1980s. But more importantly the Russian military has been improving its main armament, which now is the Kh-55 and Kh-101/102 cruise missile. Both types can carry both conventional and nuclear armed warheads. The newer Kh-101/102, which has been in development since the 1990s, has a reported range of over 5000 km and is also reported to have effective stealth and low-level capabilities. Combined with the ability of the Russian bombers to fly deep over the Arctic, this allows the Russians to strike into North America.

As the Russians improved both their bomber and their submarine capability for arctic operations, they have also strengthened their bases in the arctic region. They have either reopened or created over 15 bases along their northern coastline, including three high arctic bases at Nagurskoye, Sredny Ostrove and Zvyozdny on the islands that run along their northern coast. Officially stated to be developed for search and rescue purposes for the expected increase in arctic shipping due to the melting ice cap, most western analysts point out that they can service all of their most advanced fighter and bomber aircraft. At the same time, they have also strengthened their northern land force capabilities at Alakurtti and Pechenga, which border Finland and Norway respectively.

Overall, the Russians have significantly improved their strategic force capability in the arctic region. It could be suggested that this is the natural progression of a powerful state rebuilding its deterrent capability following a period of economic decline. There is no question that the Russian military rebuilding has focused on their deterrent capability. However, in doing so, they have emerged as a regional hegemon. None of the western states are currently matching the Russian increase in military capabilities in the region. The only sign that currently exists is the United States' ongoing deployment of their SSNs. Since 2009, the United States' navy has participated in a scientific expedition known as ICEX. Taking place every two years, this exercise is nominally to utilize the United States' nuclear powered submarines to engage in scientific research. However, these highly publicized events are also the means by which the United States' arctic submarine capabilities are showcased to the world. The United States has ensured that each of their classes of attack submarines have been utilized in these exercises to demonstrate that all are capable of operating under the ice and are therefore capable of responding to the increased Russian submarine activity. The British also at times deploy one of their attack submarines to demonstrate their capabilities in the Arctic. Most recently, in March 2018, two of the United States' submarines (one LA class and one Seawolf) and one British submarine (Trafalgar class) engaged in this exercise.

The Russians have begun to utilize their growing power in the arctic region for purposes beyond the arctic. Elements of the northern fleet had been deployed off the coast of Syria and had demonstrated their capabilities, in particular their cruise missiles. Other elements of their northern capabilities have also increasingly been utilized to demonstrate displeasure with the west, through the deployment of the air and maritime assets near and in the maritime and airspaces of countries such as Finland, Sweden, Norway, the UK and the Baltic states. These forces are now being utilized in a power projection role and it is this growing power to which Canada and the United States must now respond.

At the same time that the military capabilities of Russia have been strengthened in the arctic region, the political relationship between the United States/Canada and Russia has deteriorated. While relations between the three countries had remained relatively good immediately following the election of Putin, there had been some signs that the high point of cooperation had been reached with the Yeltsin Administration. The Putin Administration became more vocal in its opposition to NATO expansion, and in particular to the states that are closest to the Russian border. The 2008 Georgian-Russian war was partly as a result of Georgia's efforts to join NATO, and signalled Russia's willingness to use military force to prevent NATO expansion.

However, the main political break between the United States/Canada and Russia came in 2014 when the Ukrainian president, who favoured closer relations with Russia, fell from power. The new Ukrainian government's move to strengthen relations with the west led to Russian forces seizing the Crimean Peninsula. Fighting also broke out along the eastern border of Ukraine between Ukrainian military forces and unidentified pro-Russian forces that were suspected to be Russian forces in disguise. This action has significantly altered the relationship between the three countries. Canada and the United States both placed sanctions against targeted Russian individuals and companies, many of whom operate in the Russian arctic. Much of the cooperation that had developed between the three countries during the third geopolitical era of arctic security have been significantly damaged.

There is growing concern that, since 2014, the Russian government has been directly involved in clandestine efforts to destabilize both the Canadian and United

States government. Currently in the United States there are significant efforts to determine to what degree Russian involvement was directed at influencing the 2016 Presidential election. While it is too soon to know how extensive these efforts may have been, or how significant a direct involvement of the Russian government was, there is no doubt that there is now a growing sense of distrust and tension between the North American countries and Russia. But what this now means is that there is a growing political divide along with a growing Russian military capability in the arctic region. In effect, the arctic has once again become an important geostrategic area from which Russia can threaten the strategic security of North America. This means that as a political relationship continues to deteriorate there is a need to ensure that the North American ability to both deter and defend in the arctic region will need to be strengthened. Consequently, while NORAD had been seen as losing some of its importance in the immediate post-Cold War era, the combination of a more antagonistic Russia along with a greatly improved northern strategic capability requires a stronger defence of the region from the United States and Canada.

2.2   The North Korean Threat

At the same time that relations with Russia have deteriorated, there has been a growing concern within North America regarding the emerging nuclear weapon and ballistic weapon program of North Korea (Democratic People's Republic of Korea). It is believed that they successfully tested their first nuclear weapon in 2006 and developed a functioning intercontinental ballistic missile that could reach North America in 2017. As a result of the ongoing tensions between North Korea and the United States and Canada, the development of this North Korean capability has heightened concerns for the strategic defence of North America, and directly involves the arctic region.

One of the main elements of the response to the growing North Korean threat has been to expand the capability of the United States' main interceptor base. From a geographic perspective, the best location from which to intercept incoming ballistic missiles from North Korea is Alaska. As such, the United States' largest missile defence base is found at Fort Greeley Alaska (close to the Yukon border). While the base was originally a test site, as North Korea developed its nuclear armed ballistic missiles, successive administrations in the United States have increased the number and capability of missile interceptors. The Trump administration made the decision in 2017 to increase the number of missile interceptors from forty to sixty. Thus the Alaska base remains central to defending North America from a North Korean attack. So, as in the Cold War, some of North America's most important defensive capabilities are in the northern territory. This is not to fight a war over Arctic territory, but rather the northern location of Alaska represents, from a geographic perspective, the United States' most effective defensive position.

However, it is important to note that there is a growing recognition that while the Alaska-based system will attempt to defend the territory of the United States, it cannot be automatically assumed that it will defend Canadian territory. As the United States further strengthens their missile defences in Alaska, Canadian officials have also begun to reconsider their decision in 2005 not to participate in the American anti-ballistic missile (ABM) programme. In testimony before a standing parliamentary committee on

Canadian defence, senior Canadian military officials testified that without a formal agreement, the military officials of the United States are not necessarily required to shoot down a North Korean missile that is coming towards Canada. It is assumed that, given the close relationship between the two countries, as well as the formal partnership that exists through NORAD, that any such missile approach in North America would be intercepted regardless if it was aimed at a city in the United States *or* a Canadian city. However, the testimony of Lt. General Pierre St-Amand (then deputy commander of NORAD and the senior Canadian officer) in September 2017 was that "(w)e're being told in Colorado Springs that the extant U.S. policy is not to defend Canada" [2]. This has caused some suggestions among some Canadian officials that there is now a need to work out an agreement with the United States to officially include Canada in their system. However, it is not known if there is willingness in the United States to re-engage Canada on this issue, or what the costs would be. Even if the United States were inclined to agree and the costs were determined to be acceptable, it is not at all clear what would actually be involved.

The United States' development of its Alaskan ABM system is also having an effect on their strategic relationship with Russia. While it is understood that the United States' current system would not suffice against a Russian nuclear attack, the Putin administration has increasingly become concerned about the possibility of the development of the United States' capability being used against them in the future. In March 2018 President Putin gave a public speech in which he spoke at length about the United States' ABM systems, and suggested that these are a threat to the maintenance of nuclear deterrence [3]. He suggested that the United States were building a system to provide a first strike capability. He then pointed out that this is leading the Russians to develop more sophisticated ballistic and cruise missiles against which the United States' defensive systems would be ineffective. While many suggested that he was overstating the effectiveness of the new Russian capabilities, the fact that he felt compelled to make such a speech indicates the impact that the United States' systems are having on Russian attitudes.

2.3 Chinese Arctic Interest

The third factor that will affect North American strategic defence is the growing Chinese interest and capabilities in the arctic region. To the surprise of many observers, China began to express an interest in the arctic at the end of the 1990s. They have subsequently significantly built up their scientific capability in the region and are in the process of improving their shipping capabilities to go through northern waters. They have described themselves as a near-arctic state and even issued a policy document in 2018 explaining their interests in the region, including their desire to be included in all arctic international governance mechanisms. Neither their statements nor recent policies have mentioned security interests, but since 2015 the Chinese maritime forces have been developing experience in operating in northern waters. In the fall of 2015 a five ship task force of the Chinese navy (PLAN) sailed through the Aleutian island chain and into the Bering Sea. They were very careful to remain within international waters and outside of the United States' waters. However, they timed their voyage to coincide with an official presidential visit to Alaska by president Obama. This is also the farthest north that their naval vessels had ever preceded before. At the same time three other PLAN naval vessels made their first port visit to Finland, Sweden and Demark. In the fall of 2017, the Chinese icebreaker *Xue Long* made the first voyage through the Northwest Passage by a Chinese vessel. In the same year three other PLAN vessels sailed to the Baltic where they operated with Russian naval elements from the northern fleets and then sailed for a port visit to Latvia and Finland. It is clear that they are intent on developing the expertise that is needed to operate in far northern waters. These capabilities are currently limited, but it appears that the Chinese are engaging in further development.

It not known whether or not they intend to develop the ability to send their nuclear powered submarines under the ice. Currently there has been no evidence or indication that any of their existing fleet of submarines has ever been under the ice in the arctic, or even if they have the ability to do so. A submarine must have substantially more capabilities than just nuclear power to safety go under the ice, including design characteristics such as upward looking sonar and retractable fins. This means that the Chinese need to consider such requirements when building new submarines. They are currently embarking on a number of new classes as they move to become a major maritime power. Of special note are the Type 95 SSNs that are now entering service. Should the Chinese decide to give these submarines the capability to operate under the ice, the overall maritime geostrategic environment will be substantially altered. A situation where the three major maritime powers operate will significantly increase the complexity for all parties involved. Since the Type-95 s also have the ability to launch nuclear-armed cruise missiles, these vessels could act as a strategic asset for China. Any future tensions between China and the United States would mean that the United States would need to take steps to protect against this threat. This is further complicated by the Chinese development of sophisticated cruise missiles that combine long ranges with hypersonic speeds (travelling at several times the speed of sound) and manoeuvrability. The deployments of such weapons systems will significantly complicate the existing North American defensive systems.

3   Current North American Thinking

Thus the deteriorating relationship between Russia and the North America states; the growing North Korean nuclear weapon threat; and the growing Chinese interest in the arctic have all combined to transform the role of the arctic in North American security. Within this rapidly changing security environment, both Canada and the United States have released documents that indicate their current thinking on these new challenges. In each case there are significant ramifications for arctic security. The Canadian government released its latest defence policy in 2017—*Strong Secure Engaged* [4]. In it, the Canadian government recognized the re-emergence of major power competition and the continued importance of deterrence. As a result it was noted that Canada needed to ensure that it takes its responsibilities seriously "to deter aggression by potential adversaries in all domains" [4, p. 50]. The policy also acknowledges Russia's ability to project force from its arctic territory, and specifically the threat posed by "adversarial cruise missiles and ballistic missiles which have become more complex and increasingly difficult to detect" [4, p. 79].

In order to meet these threats, the new policy outlines a number of new initiatives for improving and modernizing Canada's northern security capabilities. These are focused on both NORAD and NATO. The Trudeau Government restated its commitment to carry on a number of initiatives that were started by the preceding Harper Government. These included the continued building of the Arctic Offshore Patrol Ships; continued development of the RADARSAT satellites Constellation Mission and polar satellite communication project; acquiring remotely piloted aerial systems; and completing the construction of the Nanisivik Naval facility. The Liberal Government also committed to expanding the size and range of the Air Defence Identification Zone (ADIZ) to cover the entire Canadian arctic archipelago. This is in response to the increased Russian flight activity and the increasing range of their cruise missiles.

The Liberal Government is also reversing the Harper Government's reluctance to allow NATO to increase its participation in the Arctic. While it was never explicitly stated why it had opposed a greater NATO role in the arctic, the Harper Government was responsible for blocking a Norwegian effort to increase both the official role as well as improving its situational awareness of the area. The Liberal Government now supports strengthening NATO's situational awareness and intelligence sharing, as well as increased alliance-based exercises.

NORAD is also acknowledged as playing a central role in the protection of North American security in this new security environment. To improve NORAD's ability to respond to the new military technological elements of the threats, a commitment was made to modernize the North Warning System (NWS) (the successor to the DEWLine). To this end, *Strong, Secure, Engaged* announced that Canada and the United States have begun a series of studies to determine what is needed. The Policy also makes it clear that the modernization of the NWS is only one element of improving NORAD's surveillance capabilities. The Policy was explicit that both the air and maritime approaches are to be included in any effort to modernize the overall system, thus acknowledging the growing bomber/cruise missile and submarine threat.

The United States under the Obama Administration released a series of documents pertaining to the security of the Arctic, including publications from the Navy, the Department of Defence and the White House. Most acknowledged the importance of protecting the United States' interests in the region, but they were largely written before the events of the Ukrainian crisis had soured relations between the United States and Russia. As such, most were focused on the need to improve cooperation in the arctic region to allow for the better protection of the environment and its inhabitants.

The Trump Administration has not released an arctic-specific strategy. What it has released is a *National Security Strategy (NSS)* in 2017 [5] and a *Nuclear Posture Review (NPR)* in 2018 [6]. Neither document mentions NORAD and only the *NSS* mentions Canada—and even then only once [5, p. 51]. This suggests that the new administration does not recognise the specific role that the arctic plays in the security of the United States to the same extent as its predecessors. Nevertheless, there are some important elements that will have a direct impact on how the two states will focus on the modernization of the strategic defence of North America and how that will impact the arctic.

The two documents make it clear that the United States, as with Canada, recognize that a new geopolitical reality has emerged and that there has been a return to great power rivalry between the United States and its allies and friends, and Russia and China. Furthermore, both of the United States' documents also outline the manner in which the new technologies such as hypersonic and highly manoeuvrable cruise missiles are changing the context in which the deterrence system exists. To meet these new realities the *NPR* makes three important announcements. First, it affirms that the United States will be modernizing all three of the core elements of its strategic deterrent —new SSBNs; new ICBMs; and new bombers [6, pp. 44–50]. Second, the United States will be modernizing and expanding its nuclear command, control and communications (NC3) systems. Third, in order to meet a wider range of threats, the Americans will also be providing a greater range of weapon yields among their strategic forces. For example, some of their current SSBNs will be given a number of missiles that carry lower yield.

The ramifications of all three factors are significant for the strategic defence of North America. First, by acknowledging the need for modernizing their strategic deterrent and their NC3 systems, they will be entering into a period in which NORAD must be modernized. While the infrastructure of the system may be changed to one that is more satellite-based than ground-based, there will be an absolute need to ensure that the northern dimension of the United States' NC3 includes NORAD. Thus, the Canadian recognition in *Strong, Secure, Engaged* demonstrates that both states are on the same page on this need.

The ramifications of the United States' decision to include lower yield weapons in their strategic armoury is harder to determine. *NSS* makes it clear that this decision is about being in a better position to use nuclear weapons for war-fighting and making deterrence more flexible [5, pp. 54–55]. But as analysts argued during the Cold War, moves towards developing lower yield nuclear weapons raise the possibility of their use. Deterrence has always been understood as being based on weapons that were too terrible to use, so they were not used. If the weapons are ever seen as being "useable" then they may in fact be used and that then raises the possibility of a war in which nuclear weapons are used. If this is true, it raises the possibility that the new geopolitical reality may be moving back into an environment where nuclear war becomes "thinkable" [7]. This of course goes significantly past arctic issues and pertains to the entire strategic balance of the great powers, but obviously it will have a major impact on all elements of the defence of North America, including the arctic.

4   Conclusion

The arctic security environment is in a state of fundamental change. The relationship between Russia with the two North American allies is deteriorating and doing so very rapidly. As the political relationship has soured, the Russians have moved to strengthen their military capabilities in the region. Thus North America now faces an increasingly powerful Russia in the region that has moved away from the good relations of the 1990s and early 2000s. At the same time, the growing North Korean nuclear threat has caused the United States to enhance their ABM capabilities in Alaska. This in turn has caused the Russians to increasingly see the ABM systems as being directed against them, which is causing them to redouble their efforts to build up their strategic forces which will be predominantly based in their arctic region. As if this was not complicated enough, the Chinese have begun to turn their attention to the arctic as they continue to emerge as a great power.

The reappearance of great power competition at the top of the United States' national security agenda, along with the emergence of an intercontinental threat from North Korea, leaves both Canada and the United States with the need to refocus their efforts to protect their shared northern flank. As in the Cold War, they need to ensure that their surveillance capabilities are able to meet the threats that are now emerging/remerging. The core means will remain within NORAD but it will need to be modernized and expanded to ensure that the new weapon capabilities of the Russians and possibly the Chinese are countered in the arctic. There is also a need to go beyond the current configurations. Both states will need to ensure that the new maritime mission adopted in May 2006 is given greater attention as the submarines of Russia re-enter the region, and the submarines of China may also do so in the near future. At the same time Canada will need to revisit its decision to opt out of the United States' ABM system. Unless the North Koreans actually get rid of their nuclear weapons in the near future, Canadian officials will need to find a better strategy than simply hoping that North Korea does not notice Canada. The 1990s and 2000s had created the false impression that great-power rivalry was a thing of the past. With its re-emergence, the Arctic has regained its position as a major factor in the strategic defence of North America. After a thirty-year hiatus, it is time to resume the "long polar watch" [8].

References

1. Russia, Security council of Russia (2008) Principles of states policy in the arctic to 2020, 18 Sept 2008
2. Berthiaume L (2017) Policy says U.S. won't defend Canada from missile attack: Norad general. Globe Mail 14 Sept 2018. https://www.theglobeandmail.com/news/politics/policy-says-us-wont-defend-canada-from-missile-attack-norad-general/article36258719/. Accessed 16 Mar 2018
3. The Guardian (March 1, 2018) Putin threatens US Arms Race with new Missile Declaration. https://www.theguardian.com/world/2018/mar/01/vladimir-putin-threatens-arms-race-with-new-missiles-announcement
4. Canada, Minister of National Defence (2017) Strong, secure, engaged: Canada's defence policy
5. United States, President of the United States (2017) National security strategy of the United States, December
6. United States, Office of the Secretary of Defense (2018) Nuclear Posture Review, February
7. Kahn H (1960) On thermonuclear war. Princeton University Press, Princeton
8. Conant M (1962) The long polar watch: Canada and the defense of North America. Harper & Brothers, New York

Conclusion

The Strategic Defense of North America in the 21st Century

Christian Leuprecht[1,2(✉)], Joel J. Sokolsky[3], and Thomas Hughes[4]

[1] Royal Military College of Canada, Kingston, ON K7K 7B4, Canada
christian.leuprecht@rmc-cmr.ca
[2] Flinders University of South Australia, Adelaide, SA 5042, Australia
[3] Royal Military College of Canada, Kingston, ON K7K 7B4, Canada
sokolsky-j@rmc.ca
[4] Queen's University, Kingston, ON K7L 3N6, Canada
a.t.hughes@queensu.ca

Abstract. As we approach the end of the second decade of the 21st century, the uncertainty of the threat environment highlights the continuing importance of security and sovereignty in general, and the future of North American strategic defense in particular. Advances in Inter-Continental Ballistic Missile and nuclear arms technologies by countries such as North Korea and, eventually, Iran; advances in cruise missile, submarine-launched, and hypersonic warhead delivery capabilities by Russia as well as China; and the proliferation of a wide range of non-traditional threats to democracy, social harmony, and prosperity in North America and beyond have fundamentally altered the continental security environment. Thus, on the occasion of the 60th anniversary of NORAD, implications for force posture, command structures, binational defense cooperation between Canada and the U.S., and the prospect of greater security collaboration with Mexico are anything but clear, especially under volatile domestic and international political conditions.

As we approach the end of the second decade of the 21st century, the uncertainty of the threat environment highlights the continuing importance of security and sovereignty in general, and the future of North American strategic defense in particular. Advances in Inter-Continental Ballistic Missile and nuclear arms technologies by countries such as North Korea and, eventually, Iran; advances in cruise missile, submarine-launched, and hypersonic warhead delivery capabilities by Russia as well as China; and the proliferation of a wide range of non-traditional threats to democracy, social harmony, and prosperity in North America and beyond have fundamentally altered the continental security environment. Thus, on the occasion of the 60th anniversary of NORAD, implications for force posture, command structures, binational defense cooperation between Canada and the U.S., and the prospect of greater security collaboration with Mexico are anything but clear, especially under volatile domestic and international political conditions.

The chapters in this volume have offered some insights into the changes that are driving this uncertainty, the domestic constraints on which the U.S. and Canada's responses are contingent, and draw attention to mission sets that are marginal in public

© Springer International Publishing AG, part of Springer Nature 2018
C. Leuprecht et al. (eds.), *North American Strategic Defense in the 21st Century:*,
Advanced Sciences and Technologies for Security Applications,
https://doi.org/10.1007/978-3-319-90978-3_15

discourse, but core to mission success in the strategic defense of North America, including the continent's northern and southern flanks. That, in turn, may open up the spectre of new defense partnerships. Disruptions and discontinuities notwithstanding, there are also patterns that endure. As U.S. Secretary of Defense James Mattis observed: "great power competition, not terrorism, is now the primary focus of U.S. national security" [1].

Given U.S. global dominance and the fact that North American strategic defense encompasses the defense of the U.S. homeland, U.S. influence will remain pervasive. Still, Canada has an appreciable bearing on the past, present, and future development of the balance and shape of the bilateral relationship with the U.S., of which NORAD is the prime example and manifestation. NORAD is "the most important symbol of the Canada-US relationship" [2, p. 159], and its role and form is indicative of regional strategic defense. Rhetoric notwithstanding, both countries have long privileged the 'away game' over the 'home game'. After all, since the creation of the Permanent Joint Board on Defense in 1940—which has proven so useful to both the U.S. and Canada that it endures to this day—through the Cold War and throughout the post 9/11 era, the continental security posture has been about keeping the troubles of the world away from North American shores. As a result, a forward-leaning defensive posture in the form of proactive engagement in other parts of the globe has long been the core of North American strategic defense. However, the U.S. might adopt some version of 'offshore balancing'. That could entail the U.S. reducing its global strategic footprint and being more selective about where and when to apply its power. If the strategic defense of the U.S. homeland assumed greater importance as a base from which to surge forces, perforce the bilateral continental relationship will probably receive greater scrutiny. Such attention from Washington can be a double-edged sword. The political radar of the U.S. tends to be preoccupied with problems; so, showing up on that radar tends to be a liability. At the same time, with political bandwidth in Washington highly constrained, Canada has made a virtue of necessity, proving adept at capitalizing on rare yet short attention spans in Washington to move the goalposts of the bilateral relationship as far as it possibly can as windows of opportunity arise.

Canada's approach to its superpower neighbor(hood) is a delicate balancing act: maintaining its sovereignty and independence of thought and action by being the U.S.'s most reliable and valuable security partner. No contribution of Canada's is more instrumental to North American strategic defense than NORAD. Paradoxically, this functional defense arrangement has long benefitted from 'flying under the radar' in Washington by providing an essential service in the interest of the continent that the U.S. is better off with it than without, but sufficiently peripheral to U.S. defense policy to steer clear of close scrutiny. To this end, efforts to drive the evolution of NORAD have, at times, originated in Canada, and with the military in particular, rather than the White House, the Office of the Secretary of Defense or the Joint Chiefs of Staff. The inaugural national security and defense strategies released by the Trump administration call attention to the importance of homeland defense, but contain no indications that Washington is contemplating major changes to military collaboration with Canada, let alone to NORAD. Indeed, presidential administrations have consistently lauded the uniqueness of the bilateral security relationship.

Should the U.S. security agenda change, however, the structure of NORAD, the Canadian involvement in the organisation and, perforce, the bilateral defense relationship, could end up under greater scrutiny, or even questioned altogether. Agenda-setting may, therefore, be integral to the future of North American strategic defense. The U.S. has the capacity to replace the Canadian contribution of personnel and materiél—with the possible exception of monitoring systems that enables early warning of aircraft approaching the continent from the north. Regardless, Canada would hardly allow aircraft to transit through Canadian airspace to strike the U.S. Should Russia indeed deploy new nuclear-armed missiles, the value of Canadian territory may once again appreciate, along with the need for new air defense systems. And while the U.S. strategy appears to give lower priority to terrorist threats, it is unlikely that the extensive Canada-U.S. bilateral collaboration on a range of security issues and through a variety of means within the USNORTHCOM/NORAD/CJOC framework will be dispensed with entirely.

Whatever direction it takes, the Canada-U.S. defense and security relationship will be a major factor in shaping the character of North American strategic defense. Canadians may worry periodically about being too close to the U.S. with regard to the strategic defense of North America, but they are equally concerned about becoming estranged from the U.S. The future position of Mexico in continental relations and the development of a truly trilateral regional approach to security complicates matters further. Canada's relationship with Mexico in the North American context is complex [3], and defense is no different: on the one hand, Mexico helps to mitigate Canada's power imbalance with the U.S. but, as NAFTA shows, that menage-à-trois can quickly turn into a liability with Canada as collateral damage; on the other hand, Canada jealously guards its special relationship with the U.S. Although upgrading Mexico's contribution would likely be a net gain for North American defense, the benefits would accrue more to the U.S. than to Canada [4, p. 280]. Moreover, were the U.S. to take a truly trilateral approach, then its northern and southern borders may end up being characterised "as a single security problem, requiring a single set of border security policies" [5, p. 16]. Given the challenges of the U.S.-Mexico border, the result could be very much to Canada's detriment, especially if it culminated in changes to the NORAD arrangements.

Changes in the U.S. approach to defense and security relations with Canada will be the result of alterations in how the U.S. views its broader global relations: the U.S. "tends to look at the US-Canadian relationship through the lens of global politics, whereas Canada tends to look at global politics through the lens of its relations with the US" [6, p. 139]. Having borne witness to the late eighteenth century conflagration in Europe and the founding of the U.S., in his inaugural speech U.S. President Thomas Jefferson indicated that the U.S. would strive for "peace, commerce, and honest friendship with all nations—entangling alliances with none" [7]. For better or worse, this advice has not been universally heeded. Although Canada, by virtue of its status as a middle power is, perhaps, more invested in bilateral or multilateral institutions and agreements than the U.S., the U.S. is nevertheless at the heart of alliance networks across the Atlantic and the Pacific. Vibrations across the threads of this spider's web of alliances signal and drive how the U.S. will approach its defense. In the case of NATO and Russia, this is likely to be particularly consequential for Canada. The defense of North America is, as a result, truly strategic, requiring and relying on engagement across a broad array of actors. The geographic proximity of these partners to the "great powers" to which Secretary of Defense James Mattis refers brings any confrontation of interests into sharp relief. Confrontation need not lead to conflict or war, but the pattern of engagement over the past decades suggests that, at the very least, it will cause the U.S. to re-assess the strategic defense of North America.

In its practical and symbolic significance, NORAD bears testimony to the world's closest and most enduring defense relationship. In fact, NORAD epitomizes the broader strategic defense and security relationship between Canada and the U.S. Yet a rapidly changing external threat environment is making the future of North American strategic defense, including NORAD's structure and salience to the defense relationship, more uncertain than at any time over the previous six decades. Tempering this uncertainty is the weight and wisdom of a familiar and workable security binationalism, helping to make sure that, however uncertain the future may be, the relationship is shaped by a high level of momentum and continuity. But the comfortable patterns of North American strategic defense are challenged for both the U.S. and Canada because the border that the U.S. shares with Mexico necessarily makes North American strategic defense a regional matter. In this trilateral context, Canada and Mexico will both strive to assert their independence and sovereignty, but they may differ as how far these concerns need to be compromised for the sake of preserving U.S. confidence in the commitment of each country to the security of a continent that happens to encompass the U.S. homeland.

In this trilateral, multi-dimensional, approach to North American regional security, NORAD may well find itself with an enhanced role in the maritime and land domains but one still necessarily dependent upon any changes to the roles, missions and structures of U.S. Northern and Southern Commands and perhaps other Combatant Commands. To be sure, the specific trajectory for the evolution of NORAD is ultimately at Washington's behest. At the same time, the apparent willingness of the U.S. to continue to work with Canada and—although with markedly lower intensity and intimacy—with Mexico, on broad and deep matters related to North American strategic defense, suggests that even when it comes to the direct protection of the homeland, the U.S. is cognizant of the benefits that accrue to multilateralism.

The chapters in this volume remind us that the international security environment that shapes North America's strategic defense posture can itself be shaped by how North America, as a region, responds to global security trends and challenges. The most profound change owing to the nature of present threats could see North American strategic defense become less 'defensive'; through old and new bilateral and trilateral arrangements the U.S., joined by Canada and increasingly also by Mexico, may well adopt more active measures in deterring adversaries and potential aggressors across a rapidly evolving spectrum of threats.

References

1. Ali I (2018) U.S. military puts 'great power competition' at heart of strategy: Mattis. Reuters.com., 19 Jan 2018. https://www.reuters.com/article/us-usa-military-china-russia/u-s-military-puts-great-power-competition-at-heart-of-strategy-mattis-idUSKBN1F81TR. Accessed 1 Mar 2018
2. Jockel JT, Sokolsky JJ (2012) Special but not especially important: Canada-U.S. defense relations through the doran lenses. In: Anderson G, Christopher Sands (eds), Forgotten partnership redux: Canada-U.S. relations in the 21st century. Cambria Press, Amherst, pp 149–168
3. Hale G (2012) So near yet so far: the public and hidden worlds of Canada-US relations. UBC Press, Vancouver
4. Haglund D (2010) Pensando lo imposible: why mexico should be the next new member of the North Atlantic treaty organization. Latin Am Policy 1(2):264–283
5. Sokolsky JJ, Lagassé P (2006) Suspenders and a belt: perimeter and border security in U.S. Canada relations. Can Foreign Policy 12(3):15–29
6. Doran CF (1984) Forgotten partnership: U.S.-Canada relations today. Johns Hopkins University Press, Baltimore, MD
7. Fromkin D (1970) Entangling alliances. Foreign Aff 48:688–700. https://www.foreignaffairs.com/articles/1970-07-01/entangling-alliances